Pedagogical Theory
of the Hebrew Bible

Pedagogical Theory of the Hebrew Bible

An Application of Educational Theory to Biblical Texts

ADRIAN E. HINKLE
Foreword by Martin O'Kane

WIPF & STOCK · Eugene, Oregon

PEDAGOGICAL THEORY OF THE HEBREW BIBLE
An Application of Educational Theory to Biblical Texts

Copyright © 2016 Adrian E. Hinkle. All rights reserved. Except for brief quotations in critical publications or reviews, no part of this book may be reproduced in any manner without prior written permission from the publisher. Write: Permissions, Wipf and Stock Publishers, 199 W. 8th Ave., Suite 3, Eugene, OR 97401.

Wipf & Stock
An Imprint of Wipf and Stock Publishers
199 W. 8th Ave., Suite 3
Eugene, OR 97401

www.wipfandstock.com

PAPERBACK ISBN 13: 978-1-4982-2861-9
HARDCOVER ISBN 13: 978-1-4982-2863-3

Manufactured in the U.S.A.   02/09/2016

"Scripture quotations taken from the New American Standard Bible®, Copyright © 1960, 1962, 1963, 1968, 1971, 1972, 1973, 1975, 1977, 1995 by The Lockman Foundation Used by permission." (www.Lockman.org)

I dedicate this book to my husband, Leland, and three children, Elaina, Grant, and Lauren. Thank you for supporting me through this process and your sacrifice of lost time together during the long hours of research and writing.

I love you deeply.

Contents

Foreword by Martin O'Kane | ix
Preface | xi
Acknowledgement | xiii
Abbreviations | xiv

Introduction | 1

Part One: Background

Chapter 1
Learning Theory and Active Learning | 13

Chapter 2
A Literary Approach to Biblical Literature | 29

Part Two: Pedagogy of the Pentateuch | 55

Chapter 3
Deuteronomy | 57

Chapter 4
Genesis | 80

Chapter 5
Exodus | 88

Chapter 6
Leviticus | 105

Chapter 7
Numbers | 111

Chapter 8
Part Two Summary | 117

Part Three: Pedagogy of the Deuteronomistic History | 121

Chapter 9
Joshua | 126

Chapter 10
Judges | 140

Chapter 11
1–2 Samuel | 150

Chapter 12
1–2 Kings | 158

Chapter 13
Part Three Summary | 165

Part Four: Conclusion | 167

Bibliography | 181

Foreword

It is both an honor and delight to write a brief foreword in acknowledgement of Adrian Hinkle's considerable contribution to scholarship with her volume, *Pedagogical Theory of the Hebrew Bible: An Application of Educational Theory to Biblical Texts*. For too long now, amidst all the widely different contexts to which the Hebrew Bible has been applied, remarkably little has been written about the place of education, pedagogy, and the position of children in relation to biblical thought. This lamentable lacuna in biblical scholarship has now been filled with the publication of this volume.

Starting from a review of past and current educational theories, and moving on to their relevance and application to a wide range of seminal biblical texts, the author argues persuasively for the presence of key themes in the Hebrew Bible that lend themselves admirably to contemporary pedagogical approaches. The magisterial sweep of the texts she surveys is indeed awesome: beginning with texts from the Pentateuch where she deals with pedagogy in legal contexts, she moves on to discuss with remarkable focus and clarity how historical narratives in the Deuteronomistic History can also be seen as didactic and pedagogical.

The eclectic methodology adopted by the author, which includes a combination of historical-critical and literary approaches, ensures that all angles of the topic are covered and allows the author to apply contemporary pedagogical theory with impressive results. Her approach also ensures that the reader whose primary area of expertise is education will feel just as much at home with this volume as will the biblical critic and commentator.

This present volume is the first of a series of three by the same author and I look forward with great anticipation to Volume 2, which deals with pedagogy in Wisdom Literature, and Volume 3, which deals with pedagogy in the Psalms. Collectively, all three volumes will fill a gap that has existed in Biblical Studies for far too long. The author is to be commended by all for her rigor, scholarship, and creativity in her completion of this challenging and comprehensive project.

Professor Martin O'Kane
Biblical Studies,
University of Wales Trinity Saint David

September 2015

Preface

Religious literacy is only maintained when one generation accepts the responsibility of training the next. The ethos that defines a community of believers permeates daily behaviors and purposeful activity for presenting and passing on one's core religious insight to other fellow believers. Additionally, religious communities find it incumbent to record their religious ideals in order to maintain their traditions and values.

This is likewise true of modern Christian churches. Because of their deeply rooted beliefs and traditions, parents and church leaders adamantly assume the responsibility to teach and train other faith adherents about their understanding and experiences with their God. Yet, is there a biblical model for religious training?

Within modern churches, the most popular teaching style is audible instruction to passive listeners. However, as presented in this book, this is one of the weakest teaching techniques for achieve long-term retention of the content presented. Learners who sit and passively listen without active involvement are consistently shown to fall behind those who are encouraged to actively seek information for themselves. Experiential learning is a more effective teaching technique than passive listening.

This book is the first of its kind to combine the disciplines of active learning theory and biblical exegesis. An examination of the Penteteuch and Deuteronomistic History supports the purposeful inclusion of how to train other adherents the religious ethos and mythos of the faith community through active learning.

While Wisdom Literature is valued for its illustrations of training on the social decorum of the faith tradition, other genres from the Hebrew Bible also incorporate examples of pedagogy for religious education. The contribution of this research is the investigation of pedagogical features within the Pentateuch and Deuteronomistic History with reference to the conceptual framework for active learning and learning styles introduced by Howard Gardner and Neil Fleming.

Biblical passages were selected based on their description of pedagogical features. These were analyzed in relation to the visual, aural, and kinesthetic learning styles to determine their categorization. The final analysis included the utilization of previous studies related to textual criticism to determine if the texts discussed in this thesis are regarded as later editorial revisions. Based on these three factors, it is concluded that later editors reworked biblical texts to either insert or emphasize the pedagogical features within the final form of the Pentateuch and Deuteronomistic History. The dominant pedagogical examples recorded in the Hebrew Bible surveyed are visual and kinesthetic. These two active learning features are utilized prior to or along with oral instructions and/or narrative. Therefore the active, experiential learning theory of modern studies within education are modeled and described within the Hebrew Bible. The conclusion is that the editor(s) purposefully bring the readers' attention to these pedagogical features so that later audiences would likewise model this pedagogy for religious training.

Acknowledgement

"If you see a turtle on a fence, you know that he had some help."[1] I am grateful for the many mentors in my life who have contributed to the strength I needed to reach this phase of my life. Thank you to my family's support throughout this process. Thank you, Dr. Martin O'Kane, for your many hours of reading and comments on the drafts of this project. I am grateful for your honest thoughts during each phase. Thank you, Dr. Reggies Wenyika, for your encouragement and enthusiasm. Most importantly, thank you for allowing me the time to commit to this. Thank you to my pastors who encourage me to dig and seek God's image within me when I do not see it myself. More than anyone, I am thankful for my mother. She alone has been such a source of strength and determination. By watching her life, she has been a silent example of perseverance despite disheartening circumstances. She never offers excuses, asks for pity, and most importantly, never quits. It is the many voices and influences from others that have shaped me. Thank you for helping me reach this milestone.

---

1. Haley, *US World Report*, quoted in Schaefer, *Building Great Working Relationships*, i.

Abbreviations

D	Deuteronomistic Source of Documentary Hypothesis Theory
4QJosha	Dead Sea Scrolls, Joshua, Chapters 5–10
DH	Deuteronomistic Historian
Dtr1	A conceptual theory that proposes a seventh century historian who revises the narratives of the DH during the reformation of King Josiah.[1]
Dtr2	A conceptual theory suggesting a sixth century exilic historian who edits the DH in light of the theological shifts occurring during his period.[2]
E	Elohim Source of Documentary Hypothesis Theory
J	Yahwist Source of Documentary Hypothesis Theory
IOSR	*IOSR Journal of Research and Method in Education*
JBL	*Journal of Biblical Literature*
JEDP	*Documentary Hypothesis Theory*
JHS	*Journal of Hebrew Scriptures*
JSOT	*Journal for the Study of the Old Testament*
JSOTSS	*Theological Word Book of the Old Testament Supplemental Series*
LXX	Septuagint
MT	Masoretic Text
P	Priestly Source of Documentary Hypothesis Theory
TWOT	*Theological Word Book of the Old Testament*

---

1. Niditch, *Judges: A Commentary*, 10.
2. Richard Nelson, *Double Redaction*, 127.

Introduction

The didactic nature of sacred writings is rarely contested. The sacred writings pertaining to Jewish faith adherents and revered as Holy Scripture are likewise admired for the insight and information that can be gleaned regarding the worldview and perspectives of the various writers and editors who contributed to this compilation. When pertaining to this literature, a reader's attention may center around two specific areas, Pentateuchal narratives and Wisdom Literature, particularly when investigating how religious values can be passed to a succeeding generation of religious adherents. The instructions within the Hebrew Bible are often highlighted as a means by which this group progresses their religious faith.

The rationale for this study is the existing research gap between studies completed on formal education systems of Israel,[1] didactic nature of the Hebrew Bible, and educational theory. Prior to the research for this book, biblical scholars have focused on two areas. The first area includes the didactic use of oral tradition and written narratives. The second area of focus relates to the formal education system. Henry Marrou and James Crenshaw have contributed excellent research toward the formal education system of Israel. Though Crenshaw acknowledges the religious education that transpired within the home, it is not the focus of his work. He mentions that it occurred but does not address the means by which this religious training occurred. As a whole, his focus has centered on the formal education system, or scribal schools, rather than specific details of pedagogy. This remains true for both informal religious education as well as the formal education he identifies. The distinction made between formal education and pedagogy is the research on the former is clearly in documenting the validity of its historical existence. The focus in this book is distinct in that it will document and support *how* religious training took place. This discussion will focus

---

1. This term is briefly defined within the glossary and expounded upon later within this chapter under, "Delimitations of Scope and Key Assumptions."

on the tools used within education rather than debating the existence of formal educational systems. Like Crenshaw, Marrou is also concerned with the formal education system and does not address pedagogy. Furthermore, the majority of his research concentrates on groups who occur later than those described within the Pentateuch and Deuteronomistic History.

Similarly to Crenshaw and Marrou, Christopher Rollston offers more recent research regarding the likelihood of developed, formalized scribal education. Like Crenshaw, Rollston notes the previous publications of Dürr (1932), Hermisson (1968), Lang (1979), Lemaire (1981), Puech (1988), Heaton (1994), and Davies (1995), who affirm the presence of formal schools in Israel. Rollston also notes the publications of those who argue for the inconsistent data regarding the existence of these schools including: Whybray (1974), Crenshaw (1985), Haran (1988), Puech (1988), Jamieson-Drake (1991), Golka (1993), and Weeks (1994). While Rollston does agree with Lemaire's critics that his assessment of data is largely based on "tenuous interpretations of the evidence,"[2] he goes on to approach this subject from a different perspective. Rollston collects and discusses evidence concerning paleography, orthography, and hieratic numerals before concluding, "There must have been a mechanism present that accounts for the orthographic consistency: namely, formal standardized education."[3] Unfortunately, like his predecessors, Rollston leaves the subject pertaining to the pedagogy of these schools unaddressed in his published work.

Yairah Amit is among the biblical scholars who focus on the literary properties of the biblical narratives and highlights their didactic nature. Like many others, Amit correctly addresses the use of narratives to guide and instill moral value and theological insight in its readers. However, this focus of the didactic purpose of narratives falls short of explaining the pedagogy described within these narratives. Didactic is distinct from pedagogy since its focus is the intention to teach while pedagogy is the method of instruction.

Walter Brueggemann is the only writer who addresses pedagogy within the narratives contained in the Pentateuch and Deuteronomistic History. Yet the focus of his study encompassed the use of canon as a model for modern Christian education. His brief study in this area does not adequately investigate the specific record of pedagogy or its development within the Pentateuch and Deuteronomistic History. His research is far too broad and brief to convincingly support his claims. Additionally, he excludes many of the significant passages that specifically explain the means of how religious

---

2. Rollston, "Scribal Education," 47.
3. Ibid., 68.

education should be done. Moreover, he does not address whether these examples were part of the original sources or the later supplementation of an editor. Without this latter perspective, the question remains whether this inclusion of pedagogy was coincidental or purposefully included to validate the means by which religious education was expected to occur.

Prior research is available that discusses editorial activity within the Hebrew Bible. There are also multiple studies that document educational theories. However, these two areas have not been brought together into a single study that addresses educational theory as it relates to examples of pedagogy within the Hebrew Bible. The research within this study will address this research gap by using published literature relating to educational theory, pedagogy, and literary criticism in order to determine if the Pentateuch and Deuteronomistic History include an observable pedagogy that is identified by the editors of the Hebrew Bible.

The research within this book addresses two questions. First, in addition to storytelling, what types of informal instructional methods can be observed in the Pentateuch and Deuteronomistic History in their current final form? Second, is there textual evidence that later editors either inserted or emphasized pedagogical features for religious instruction within the Pentateuch and Deuteronomistic History?

This research traces how religious adherents of Yahweh were taught the basics of their beliefs and historical religious heritage as it is observed within the current final form of the Pentateuch and Deuteronomistic History. This book presents evidence for an instructional method that was used to teach children, adults, and foreigners the principles of religious standards regarding the worship of Yahweh. The main objective of this research is to show that the Pentateuch and Deuteronomistic History include specific pedagogical examples used in religious education. The examples selected for this book demonstrate that a preceding event, object, or location prompts the storyteller. The evidence of this research will support that events, monuments, and specially named locations were used to evoke questions that led to the account of their purpose or to evoke the elder to initiate an account for the religious purpose for the object or location. Adults within the Israelite faith community used visual cues (such as monuments) and active role play (such as the feast of booths) as means of communicating and instructing children as well as other adults. These are pedagogical tools that were used in addition to but prior to oral instruction. This will be extensively discussed and supported through the research presented in chapters three and four. The faith community is defined as those who actively support and promote the worship of Yahweh through engaging in the religious festivals and laws recorded in the Pentateuch. This system of instruction will present a model illustrating the pedagogy. The research presented in this book will prove that the Pentateuch and Deuteronomistic History demonstrate a particular method for teaching the basic principles of faith to both Israelite children and adult adherents.

Biblical oral storytelling and formal education have been previously studied and expounded upon by scholars. Jan Fokkelmann posits that storytelling was used for retaining historical accounts and cultic beliefs.[4] The ethos of the narratives and their value for understanding the developing relationship between Yahweh and humanity is well documented, while authors, such as James Crenshaw, have surveyed the formation and development of formal education of Israel. However, each of these three areas leaves the question of how education occurred unaddressed. In other words, what was the pedagogy of Israel? Storytelling may appear as an obvious first choice, however, where were the characters when the story is told? What prompted the need to tell the story?

Observation and analysis of the Pentateuch and Deuteronomistic History, in their current final form, demonstrates a biblical paradigm for religious instruction through patterns and practices used by Israel as recorded in these narratives. Verifiable evidence exists illustrating pedagogy within these texts. The examination of specific examples of pedagogy practiced as it developed through the Pentateuch and Deuteronomistic history shows a larger cohesive structure of pedagogy.

This research will validate that the Pentateuch and Deuteronomistic History contain descriptions for pedagogy that promote a particular method for teaching the basics of the religious beliefs recorded in these texts. This research will conclude that the pedagogy of the Pentateuch and Deuteronomistic History was well formulated and articulated. This section of the Hebrew Bible has a consistent model for instructing both children and adults.

This study addresses the lack of published research pertaining to how Israel assumed the responsibility of religious education. Since Walter Brueggemann's study *The Creative Word: Canon as a Model for Biblical Education* is the only previous publication examining this topic, his work is used as a starting point in considering how biblical texts include examples of pedagogy. As the research develops through deductive[5] study of the Hebrew Bible, examples of instruction against Fleming's VARK Learning Styles are compared for determining patterns of teaching styles. Deductive reasoning

---

4. Fokkelman, *Reading Biblical Narrative*, 57–58.

5. Deductive research looks at the data and formulates a theory based on collected information. It is distinct from inductive research that begins with a theory and looks for data to support and confirm the theory.

seeks to collect the relevant facts and details of a situation from a wide body of biblical texts and observes patterns that repeatedly occur, leading to either the proof or disproof of the original hypothesis. The advantage of this method is the control of the scope of literature required for study. Early in this research, a clearly established pattern of visual and kinesthetic illustrations is confirmed and discussed to support oral stories and instruction as a formalized pedagogy for religious education in the Pentateuch and Deuteronomistic History.

The intention is to investigate whether or not the specific means for educating adults, foreigners, and children was purposefully included in the narratives contained within the Pentateuch and Deuteronomistic History in their current final form. Strong arguments for a Josianic DH and later editors have already been made by Frank Moore Cross and Richard Nelson and do not need to be repeated within this research except to emphasize a few of their key points, where relevant. Arguing for specific dates of editorial revisions is beyond the scope of this book. Instead, support is discussed related to the editors of the Pentateuch and Deuteronomistic History that purposefully included or brought attention to instructions and examples of how pedagogy for religious education should take place.

Biblical passages included in this study are examined to determine the pedagogical approach observed in each scene as well as the underlying principles behind the human behaviors encountered in the learning situations recorded in the Pentateuch and Deuteronomistic History. These situations will include accounts located in the Pentateuch and Deuteronomistic History texts that pertain to the participation and teaching during religious celebrations, such as Passover. These accounts also include the use of altars as instructional aids and commands for the instruction of children. Finally, accounts concerning the instruction of adults are addressed and examined for recorded similarities and differences between the pedagogical tools for training adults versus the pedagogy for training children. Examples of pedagogy within the Pentateuch and Deuteronomistic History describe situations provoking learners to inquisition. This was followed by the articulation of creed and highly stylized testimonies of faith from a teacher.

Two approaches were used when determining the selection of biblical passages for use in this study. First, passages that include specific descriptions of pedagogy were selected for further investigation. Second, the selected texts were then compared to those discussed by Campbell and Friedman as examples of editorial activity. Texts determined to include both descriptions of pedagogy and evidence of editorial activity were selected as the criteria for use in this study. The research within this book will focus on the examples of pedagogical activity in the texts selected based on this criteria. Again, the purpose of this investigation is to prove the intentional inclusion of pedagogy for religious education within the present final forms of the Pentateuch and Deuteronomistic History.

Several previous studies were used for the collective support for areas related to this book. A review of the literature revealed four specific areas. (1) Formal and informal education for groups similar to those described in the Pentateuch and Deuteronomistic History, (2) learning theories, (3) pedagogy of the Hebrew Bible, and (4) literary criticism. From these four areas conclusions are drawn regarding their interrelatedness as it corresponds to pedagogical theory within the Pentateuch and Deuteronomistic History.

Several studies are available in relationship to educational theory. Studies that address educational systems during historical periods similar to those described in the Pentateuch and Deuteronomistic History. They typically focus on formal education and endeavor to offer historical evidence of schools; they do not address pedagogy. Editorial activity within the Pentateuch and Deuteronomistic History are also readily available. Prior to the research completed in this book, educational theory has not been substantially applied to the Hebrew Bible.

Walter Brueggemann states, "Every community that wants to last beyond a single generation must concern itself with education."[6] As witnessed through the biblical narratives, the Israelite faith community adamantly assumes the responsibility of educating itself with the intentions of lasting for many generations to come. As Israel made observations and identified weaknesses, the writers incorporated corrections for these into their teaching praxis. The nation also observed chief, pivotal actions taking place and recorded them in such a way that these events would instruct future generations about their inheritance as a race and religion.

Perhaps the question could be raised as to whether or not the DH was an educator and thus made it a priority to include pedagogical references within the sacred texts. However, if this were true, it would be far more likely that this editor would have specifically addressed education and offered an unambiguous text that addresses education. At minimum, it would have been included in the Deuteronomistic law. As the research will show, much of the material used to describe the pedagogy demonstrated in this research is deduced by observation of religious events. Rather than specifically describing the instructional method, or pedagogy, it is observed through the description of religious events. This process thus became recorded in the Pentateuch and Deuteronomistic history. Though not always explicit, it is nonetheless present and serves as a frame to build further pedagogy upon.

---

6. Brueggemann, *Creative Word*, 1.

The Pentateuch and Deuteronomistic History, on the other hand, utilize tangible experiences, objects, and kinesthetic learning situations. Prior to a narrative instruction that examines the historical contributions of their faith community, something that was seen or touched provoked the audience member (or student) to inquire of its significance. This consists of much of the symbolism that is included in religious festivals and religious attire. Though the teaching itself is dialogical, as stated by biblical scholars such as Walter Brueggemann, Antony Campbell, and Brevard Childs, it occurs in a context that was set up to provoke curiosity. This natural curiosity of the observer thus provided a teachable moment in which the narrative story was told. This specific pedagogy of provoked curiosity through kinesthetic environments is also rigorously examined and expanded upon in part two.

Chapter 1 offers an introductory definition of active learning theory as well as a brief survey of two learning theories: Howard Gardner's theory of Multiple Intelligences and Neil Fleming's model of the VARK learning theory. The active learning theory discussed in chapter 2 will then be repeatedly integrated within chapters 4 and 5 as the biblical texts are discussed and compared to the learning theory model.

Chapter 2 will address how the literary approach to the Bible more adequately demonstrates the recorded pedagogy than a historical approach would allow. This chapter will also summarize some of the scholarly work that addresses the compilation of the Pentateuch and Deuteronomistic History. Chapter 2 will also address the process of canon as it communicates the discretion of the editors and their suppositions toward subjects relating to ethos that is normative, reliable, and enduring. This directly relates to the second guiding research question earlier stated. Beyond the analysis of single narratives, the purpose of this chapter is to validate the literary approach of examining these texts instead of attempting to validate the authenticity of their historical accuracy. This approach is justified by the lack of scholarly consensus regarding the historical reliability of the biblical narratives. Debating the historicity of the narratives is beyond the scope of this research and does not relate to whether or not pedagogical features are present within the biblical texts. Therefore, a literary approach is more conducive to validating the presence of teaching paradigms and determining whether editors purposefully inserted or emphasized their presence in the biblical texts discussed herein.

Part two of this book begins the examination of the recorded pedagogy in the final form of the Pentateuch as it now occurs. All five books of the Pentateuch are discussed as three areas specifically examined: instruction to children, instruction to adults, and instruction to foreigners. One of the primary texts examined is the command of parents to instruct children.[7] Much of the remaining research will demonstrate instances of this instruction taking place between the father and his children.

One example of how instruction is carried out between the father and the child will be from Exod 13:8, 14. In this particular passage, the father is told that the experiences of Passover will provoke the child to some type of questioning, at which point the father is then obligated to respond and begin teaching about the identity of Yahweh and His relationship with the Hebrew people. A second specific example of using the Passover as an event that precedes the use of oral narrative is observed in Exod 12:24–25. This same paradigm is consistently observed in other comparable festivals and celebrations such as the Feast of Booths and Purim, bringing about similar results of the children provoked to question their parents. Another form of this recorded pedagogy occurs in Deut 6:20, which states the son will ask about testimonies, statutes, and judgments. In response, again the father is required to teach his son about God's history with the Hebrew people.

Another subtle form of teaching took place by means of Mosaic legislation of resident aliens.[8] Resident Aliens (גֵּר, ger) were equally obligated to the law[9] and were instructed just as a Jewish child might receive at the hand of his parents.[10] While assimilated into Jewish society, the resident alien would repeatedly hear the recitation of God's deeds at the annual festivals (Deut 16:11, 14). Again, it is noted that the use of festivals is in place and is the given occasion for the instruction. This instruction is then compared to that of other adults and children to determine how they are related to one another.

Also within Part two, the use of symbolism in festivals, dress attire, and other situations that created learning environments for instruction are explored and discussed. Research indicates occasions were practiced in such a way that observers were brought to a point of disequilibrium and were therefore caused to ask questions. This then presented a teaching opportunity in which the teacher was able to give instruction. As the symbolism was discussed, instruction was also offered on the identity of Yahweh, His relationship with the Israelites, and events recorded in their literature. Evidence verifies that the Pentateuch utilizes tangible experiences and kinesthetic learning situations for various ages and groups to examine the historical contributions of their faith community. Further investigation will

---

7. Deut 4:8–10; 6:4; 31:11–13.
8. Exod 12:48; Num 9:14.
9. Deut 1:16; 12:12; 14:2; 26:12; Num 15:15–16.
10. Deut 31:11–12.

determine if this is the case in all examples or if there are instances when truth is taught in story without prior instigation from the person receiving the instruction.

Part three focuses on the literature of the Deuteronomistic History. Several narratives exist within the Deuteronomistic History that reinforce the pedagogy formulated in the Pentateuch, namely the use of visual reminders for religiously significant events. This literature attests to the use monuments (Josh 8:29), celebrations (Judg 2:4), verbal instruction (1 Sam 12:23), and instruction through song (2 Sam 1:18) as appropriate pedagogy for religious training. The research within this chapter reinforces the indications from the Pentateuch, that either a kinesthetic experience or visual object precedes the use of an oral story for educating faith adherents the ethos of the religious community.

Part three will also account for the editorial inclusion of the repeated phrase, "until this day," as evidence of a later editor drawing the readers' attention to pedagogical features within the narratives. An example of this occurs in Joshua 4 where a representative from each of the twelve tribes selects a stone from the bottom of the Jordan River as a reminder of Yahweh's actions that caused the miraculous crossing of this river. They were then to erect a monument with these stones to remind and reassure the Israelites of their religious ethos regarding Yahweh's involvement and covenants with them. This feature then becomes a tool for active learning through the kinesthetic learning for those who build the monument, but also the ability of those who did not witness the event to tangibly touch the monument and learn of its significance through the oral story that would follow their inquiry. Visual learning is also represented through this monument as passersby may look upon it and reflect on its significance. Therefore, it offers both a visual and kinesthetic teaching tool. A later editor then draws attention to the significance of this feature by inserting the phrase, "and they are there to this day," in verse 9. The insertion of this phrase indicates to later readers or audiences that the monument remains significant and continues to validate the mythos of the Israelite faith community. Additionally, attention is drawn to the pedagogical feature where those familiar with this narrative may go and visually see and physically touch this monument therefore further validating the authenticity of this story. This example along with several others from the Deuteronomistic History are explored and discussed within chapter 5 of this book.

These discussions will make no attempt to argue the various editorial revisions, dates, or rationale for later editors of the Pentateuch and Deuteronomistic History. Instead, previously established research is used to demonstrate how these textual revisions were used to draw the readers' attention to pedagogical features within the text. Literary criticism is used to document and support the editorial activity related to emphasizing pedagogy in the Pentateuch and Deuteronomistic History. The extent of freedom editors exercised in reworking inherited text remains undetermined, though it seems evident that phrases or perhaps even entire stories were reimagined to create the interconnections of structure, motif, and theology pertinent to the editor.[11] This is supported in the distinct retelling of events witnessed in Samuel and Chronicles.

The final conclusion summarizes the data collected and articulated in parts 1 through 3. It will then briefly synthesize these results into a formal conclusion for review as well as indicate how this topic can extend for future research endeavors. In summary, active learning theory and the literary approach for textual criticism is used in this research during the deductive study of the Pentateuch and Deuteronomistic History. This will begin to support the claim of the editor's intentional inclusion of an articulated pedagogy within these biblical texts.

---

11. Alter, *Art of Biblical Narrative*, 25.

Part One

Background

Chapter 1

Learning Theory and Active Learning

FORMAL AND INFORMAL EDUCATION

ARGUMENTS FOR AND AGAINST formal education systems are available for groups similar to those portrayed in the Pentateuch, Deuteronomistic History, and Wisdom Literature. James Crenshaw is one of the leading modern researchers on the formal education system for what he calls "ancient Israel." Crenshaw examines the beginnings of literacy and how Israel was transformed from an oral to a literate culture. According to his research, after the invention of cuneiform writing, scribal schools emerged in Sumer to teach this form of writing for employment purposes within palaces, temples, and administrative offices. "The School system flourished . . . and the variety of positions held by the scribes suggests that the schools were numerous and sizeable."[1] Numerous terra-cotta tablets containing written texts have survived through their modern discovery, providing abundant documentation of Mesopotamian culture.[2] Crenshaw further notes students were trained to become priests, engineers, administrators, or soldiers. Since priests were responsible for recording the lives of the dead and burying it with them, it is believed they may have been the first to use writing. Students attending both the Sumer and Egyptian schools were male children from wealthy families. Their education in cuneiform afforded them social positions in various vocations.[3]

1. Bromiley, "Education."
2. Crenshaw, "Education in Ancient Israel," 601–15.
3. Bromiley, "Education."

Similar characteristics of the "scribal" culture are found in the Wisdom Literature of the Hebrew Bible. This is particularly evident in Proverbs, where the son is, more or less, provided a handbook of moral instruction for training in civic obligations and traditional wisdom of the cultural milieu in which Israelite scribes lived between the tenth and seventh centuries BC.[4] These scribes were essentially responsible for mastering the technique of writing. Large amounts of vocabulary tested their memory skills and the complexity of form resulted in practical difficulty. Added complications of different Egyptian writing types (hieroglyphic, hieratic, and demotic) and Mesopotamian use of different languages (Sumerian, Acadian, and later Aramaic)[5] made education difficult to attain, seldom exceeding 1 percent of the population.[6]

The scribe was a civil servant whose primary obligation was recording legislative decrees for the monarchy. The initial vocational concerns of scribes were to oversee archives, accounting, and legal mandates. This fundamental importance was primal, before its developed use for recording theological dogma and philosophy. Therefore, because of their importance, scribes were elevated above the working classes. This elevation in social prestige gave room to exercise patronage resulting in an attached value of formal education to one's success. For children in early Israelite culture, education was the point of entry to the rankings of the socially elite.[7] However, as Marrou and Crenshaw both bring out in their studies, education within a formal setting was focused upon children's scribal literacy not religious education. As evidenced in the following pages, the primary medium for conveying the spiritual ethos of Israel remains critically connected to the family unit.

Crenshaw's mention of formal education raises several questions. At its center is the lack of evidence for its existence. Much of the current information remains inferential. "This deficiency of hard evidence exists despite many attempts to uncover the actual learning situation prior to the first explicit reference to a school, Ben Sira's reference invitation to acquire an education at his house of study (*bêt hammidraš*, 51:23)."[8] Using the analogy of schools existing in Egypt and Mesopotamia, it is logical to infer similar institutions existed for Israel. In addition to Crenshaw, this is noted and expounded on by several biblical scholars such as Leo Perdue and Philip

---

4. Marrou, *History of Education*, xiv.
5. Ibid., xv.
6. Crenshaw, *Education in Ancient Israel*, 40.
7. Marrou, *History of Education*, xv.
8. Crenshaw, "Education in Ancient Israel," 601.

King. Since the validity of these schools is beyond the scope of this book, they will only be briefly mentioned. A more thorough discussion is located in the writings of Crenshaw and Perdue. These same writers also contend that some type of formalized training must have existed during the early monarchy to support the bureaucratic government system and the role of Hezekiah's men mentioned in Prov 25:1, which suggests some type of court school. The lack of firsthand information regarding schools in Israel leads scholars to conclude that either they were so prevalent, writers did not deem it necessary to record information regarding them, or they did not exist.[9]

While these studies offer substantial argument and support, their conclusions still lack enough concrete evidence to acceptably validate their claims. Therefore, their conclusions regarding formal educational systems remain anecdotal. There are ongoing disputes over the viability of these schools and the nature of instruction that transpired before Ben Sira's invitation in the second century BC. Commentators, such as Crenshaw[10] and Walter Brueggemann,[11] insist that religious education was primarily practiced orally in the home. Other critics contend that a complex educational system existed before Solomon's era while others suggest it began during Hezekiah's reign in the eighth century.[12]

From the patriarchal narratives in Genesis through the early monarchy in 1–2 Samuel, families are depicted as carrying the core responsibility for educating their children. This education included vocational trade, social expectations, and religious beliefs. It is conceivable that schools within Israel may have imitated Egypt and Mesopotamia as models for education. However, the extent of this influence remains speculative.[13] Conclusive proof and consensus among specialists is lacking. Crenshaw argues that only a miniscule portion of the population is able to receive formal literary training, and that formal education was available only to the socially elite.[14] The majority of the population then, continues their education within the family setting. This training included vocational training, and social and religious expectations. As this trajectory continued, the importance of scribal abilities grew to document historical accounts, decrees, and prominent oral traditions.[15] By the early monarchy, formal specialized schools for training

---

9. Murphy, *Tree of Life*, 5.
10. Crenshaw, "Education in Ancient Israel," 614.
11. Brueggemann, "Passion and Perspective," 172.
12. Crenshaw, *Education in Ancient Israel*, 86–87.
13. Crenshaw, "Education in Ancient Israel," 609.
14. Crenshaw, *Education in Ancient Israel*, 16.
15. The argument for formal institutional education versus the role of education

in scribal literacy began to develop which later developed into the documented schools of Greek culture.

Little evidence exists that conclusively validates the use of formal education. Furthermore, whether or not these schools existed, religious education remained taught in the informal setting. The scope of instruction ranged from basic oral transmission of information between two people to formal scribal schools for education. On the formal side, instruction took place in a systematic manner with deliberate effort by elders to engage the younger members to engage them in training and the impartation. Informal education, on the other hand, focused on religious ideas and experiences, which were conveyed through modeling behaviors in a mutual process of example and imitation. Geoffrey Bromiley suggests principles from the preceding generation are amended to reflect the particular economic and industrial conditions pertinent to the modern culture. Stories are told and retold so that their fundamental truths become a part of the heritage of the younger generation. Storytellers allow for modest transmission modifications to occur to clarify archaic expressions so that the younger generation could understand the concepts contained therein.[16]

Though formal education is eventually developed, one would be mistaken to assume that all religious ideas transferred intergenerationally took place in this manner. The Pentateuch and Deuteronomistic History portray the informal instruction of children within their homes or communities by their parents, rather than in formal classrooms with instructors. The responsibility for parents to teach is expressed in Deut 11:19 as well as various other passages.

Birger Gerhardsson is among the many Hebrew Bible scholars who believe stories were widely used for the moral and religious education of children. In his book *Memory and Manuscript*, he contends that once Judaic texts became relatively fixed, either in oral or written transmission, the religious authorities emphasized the importance of memorizing the Pentateuch as well as other scriptures.[17] According to Gerhardsson, "to describe the way

---

within the home continues to be an open topic of debate with relatively little consensus. James Crenshaw offers a significant account of these ongoing discussions beginning with the 1908 publication from August Klostermann who emphasized the father's role in education based on Isa 1:2 and Proverbs 1–9. Crenshaw goes on to list and discuss publications that deny the existence of formal schools such as R. Norman Whybray, *The Intellectual Tradition in the Old Testament* (1974) and Stuart Weeks, *Early Israelite Wisdom* (1994), as well as those who argue in favor of them such as E. W. Heaton, *The School Tradition of the Old Testament* (1994). Crenshaw's account of this discussion may be located in *Education in Ancient Israel*, n. 6.

16. Bromiley, "Education."
17. Gerhardsson, *Memory and Manuscript*, 62–78.

in which oral Torah is transmitted is to describe a complicated interplay between basic solidity and complementary flexibility."[18] By this, Gerhardsson addresses both the fixed elements as well as the adaptations of the Torah. He further reports that the oral transmitters of the Torah were "traditionalists, *par excellence*."[19] Pupils were required to memorize substantial portions of the text for the purpose of reciting on demand. According to Gerhardsson, these students then became the "living library," some even becoming famous for their precision.[20]

Though Gerhardsson's work is interesting in its exceptional delivery of relating the concept of manuscript transmission, it has two shortfalls. First, Gerhardsson admits that the phenomena of physically recording the oral narratives of the Pentateuch, as a whole, has not been the subject of thorough research in a major monograph from either the point of view of history or religion, literature, or culture. Because of this, he chooses to focus the bulk his research on later figures within rabbinic education. Second, though he does address the use of stories for the training of children, like many other scholars, he does not address *how* these stories were used or the means by which teachers taught.

Currently, studies pertaining to the "education of Israel" focus on validating the historicity of formal education centers or schools. They do not address how religious education of children or adults occurred. As a result, a deficiency remains for publications relevant to instructional theory within the Hebrew Bible. Henry Marrou and James Crenshaw have progressed the studies of formal education. However, their arguments center on the historicity of formal education. They inadequately address informal education and do not address pedagogy in any way. In contrast, Birger Gerhardsson somewhat addresses pedagogy through his discussion on the memorization of the Pentateuch. However, his research focus is the transmission of sacred texts. As a result, pedagogy itself is superficially addressed and the training of religious ethos is not effectively discussed.

DEFINITION OF TERMS

Education

A primary distinction is made between education and pedagogy. These two areas are like rhetoric and eloquence; they share similar features but are not,

18. Ibid., 93.
19. Ibid.
20. Ibid., 95.

in themselves, synonyms for each other. Though education has certainly developed and adapted throughout history and different cultures, its fundamental premise has remained the same.

Education is understood as the entire process by which society transmits the accumulated "social, intellectual, and religious experience and heritage"[21] that is passed on from one generation to the next. Education is the product or what proceeds from the direct action of teachers. A distinction is also made between formal and informal education. Formal education is defined as "conventional, given in an orderly, logical, planned, and systematic manner."[22] On the other hand, informal education occurs through shared experience and distinctiveness. This type of education occurs through the daily interactions that provide circumstances in which learning can take place.[23] Within this process, informal participation in social activities exists on their own accounts that influence the arising generation and educates it in the interest of continuing this heritage and religious practices.[24] Robert Pazmiño defines education with a similar standard of integration.[25]

Israel is frequently engaged in diverse approaches of communication to assorted audiences with varied intended outcomes. Though modern education frequently utilizes stringent verbal communication observable in lectures worldwide, Israel often employed more than this now traditional method. This group recognized their need to preserve the educational value of the older generation and therefore began a process in which young children, new alien converts to the Israelite faith tradition, and Israelite adults could learn from the wise understanding of truth conveyed by elders within the faith community. This concept of education encompasses all aspects of speech that facilitate and support the definitive objective of knowledge of Yahweh and submission to his authority. It is the entirety of the processes in which a community passes on its accumulated social, intellectual, and religious heritage from one generation to the next. At its core, education is the transmission of knowledge, morals, and worldview from person to person, or commonly generation to generation. Education is the product of pedagogy.

> The degree to which religion continues preeminent in the educational system of a progressive nation depends upon the vitality of its religion and upon the measure of efficiency and success

21. Bromiley, "Education."
22. Good, *Dictionary of Education*, 175.
23. Pazmiño, *Foundational Issues*, 84.
24. Bromiley, "Education."
25. Pazmiño, *Foundational Issues*, 13.

with which from the first that religion is instilled into the very bone and sinew of each succeeding generation.[26]

Pedagogy

Pedagogy is a broad term that remains debated by scholars in the field of education. Within this book, pedagogy is the specific act or method of teaching. Peter Mortimore's definition of this term is accepted when he asserts that pedagogy is, "any conscious activity by one person designed to enhance learning in another."[27] It is not concerned with what the student learns, but how the student learns. Pedagogy is the practical method used to convey information from one individual to another. Pedagogy exists within the scope of education. Pedagogy is the strategy of teaching or instructional method; it is the process of setting forth doctrines and the methods utilized by educators. Specifically, pedagogy refers to the adult instruction to children. It is associated with the manner in which children learn from adults. It is distinct from andragogy, which addresses the learning characteristics of adults. Both pedagogy and andragogy will be examined through this research. This research will demonstrate and defend that the Pentateuch and Deuteronomistic History hold an articulated format for teaching children as well as adult religious adherents to the Israelite faith. These observations include the integration from various disciplines in the practice of education. The adult religious adherents referred to include both Israelite and non-Israelite people who support the worship of Yahweh.

The term andragogy is relatively new. It was introduced by the German educator Alexander Kapp in 1833, and later popularized by Malcom Knowles.[28] Based on the research of Kapp and Knowles, distinctions can be drawn between pedagogy and andragogy. Modern scholars in educational fields continue to highlight the distinct needs of child and adult learners.[29] However, pedagogy continues to refer to the entire context of instruction or method of instruction. Therefore, in this writing, the term pedagogy is used universally for both child and adult learners. Instruction or instructional method is also used as synonyms for pedagogy. The term pedagogy has a long history in educational discourse.

---

26. Bromiley, "Education."
27. Mortimore, *Understanding Pedagogy*, 17.
28. Knowles, *Modern Practice of Adult Education.*
29. Knowles et al., *Adult Learner*, 116.

> In the first place, the history of pedagogy possesses great interest from the fact that it is closely connected with the general history of thought and also with the philosophic explication of human actions. Certainly, pedagogical doctrines are neither fortuitous opinions nor events without significance. On the one hand, they have their causes and their principles in moral, religious, and political beliefs, of which they are the faithful image; on the other, they are instrumental in the training of mind and the formation of manners. [30]

Pedagogy considers the method of instruction. It focuses upon the environment or location for instruction, the relationship between the instructor and student, and learning format. These formats are typically classified as learning styles. A learning style is "the composite of characteristic cognitive, affective, and physiological factors that serve as relatively stable indicators of how a learner perceives, interacts with, and responds to the learning environment."[31] Learning models and their efficiency are highly debated and criticized between scholars in Education and Psychology. Two popular theories are directly related to the research in this book.

Ethos

An ethos is a philosophy or culture that defines an individual or community group. Ethos is often observable through the content and communication style expressed between individuals. It encompasses the reputation and integrity of a person or group as well as the expertise in a subject or vocation. Ethos is the system of presuppositions and cherished values held by either an individual or community of people.

LEARNING THEORIES

Central to the first research question is reviewing the prominent learning theories. Learning theories are represented under the larger conceptual framework of active learning. Active learning is a term that began in the 1980s and became popularized by Charles Bonwell and Jim Eison in 1991.[32] The active learning philosophy is a participatory form of education

---

30. Compayré, *History of Pedagogy*, xvii.
31. Furnham, *Psychology of Behaviour*, 189.
32. Bonwell and Eison, *Active Learning*.

that advocates learning through sensory experiences and emphasizes the learner's exploration of values.[33]

> Learning is situated in physical, social, and interactive contexts, and is best achieved when learners have varied and multiple opportunities to engage in inquiry at many different levels (Henderson & Antencio, 2007). It is a process involving children's perceptions, related encoding, and subsequent retrieval of information leading to modifications in future behaviors and attitudes. Since learning is social, it is oftentimes generated through dialogue with others and in reflection with others. In young children, learning is facilitated through their observations of others' actions and the subsequent replication of the behaviors observed into their own schemata.[34]

Studies related to active learning support that learning is maximized when the learner takes an active approach in the learning process. Furthermore, both children and adult learners benefit from an increased ability to retain information when participating in the learning process. For the purpose of this study, learning and remembering are used interchangeably since the terms "learning" and "remembering" overlap in their range of meanings. For example, if a student learns the attributes of Yahweh or remembers the attributes of Yahweh, the same end goal is reached. Learning is a broad term referring to many methods and mental processes that allow people to remember information, skills, and gain competency.[35] Active learning is achieved when the learner participates in the learning environment through touch, activity, or inquiry. It is different from passive learning where students merely receive information through audible instruction.

Howard Gardner

The first learning theory model discussed is Howard Gardner's theory of Multiple Intelligences. Gardner is considered by scholars to be one of the leading modern experts in learning styles. Gardner's theory of "Multiple Intelligences," first introduced in 1983, described the six main ways in which people learn. In 1999, he added two additional intelligences, naturalistic and spiritual. While Gardner identifies the plausibility of an existential

---

33. Farrell, "Active Learning."
34. Ibid.
35. Howe, *Principles of Abilities*, 9.

intelligence, it does not fully meet his criteria and thus he does not formally include it.[36] Gardner defines an intelligence as:

> A set of skills of problem solving—enabling the individual to *resolve genuine problems of difficulties* that he or she encounters and, when appropriate, to create an effective product—and must also entail the potential for *finding or creating problems*—thereby laying the groundwork for the acquisition of new knowledge.[37]

An intelligence is the main intrinsic means by which one prefers to obtain new information. It is the foremost mode by which one learns. Gardner's intelligences continue to be the most widely accepted list as described by Robert Slavin in *Educational Psychology*.[38]

The eight intelligences accepted by Gardner include: linguistic, musical, logical-mathematical, spatial, bodily-kinesthetic, personal, naturalistic, and spiritual. In his 2011 article, "Multiple Intelligences: The First Thirty Years," Gardner reports, "The theory has remained relatively constant in the last decade."[39] While he goes on to briefly mention other suggested intelligences, he maintains that no other intelligences are officially accepted due to lack of systematic review through his rigorous algorithm.[40]

Gardner describes spatial intelligence as referring to individuals who prefer to learn through the visual example or representation of the information necessary for memorization.[41] Linguistic learners are those to retain information the easiest through words, either written or spoken. This learning style has a high memory recall from verbal instructions.[42] Logical-mathematical intelligence pertains to those who readily obtain information through logic, abstraction, and scientific reasoning. The bodily-kinesthetic intelligence involves bodily action. It pertains to the physical, muscular movement as learning occurs. People who prefer this learning style desire to learn by "doing" the learning rather than simply hearing instructions or watching someone else model it.[43] People included in musical intelligence are often sensitive to tones and rhythms. Since languages are based in rhythms, people with this intelligence often also prefer to learn from audible lectures

---

36. Gardner, *Intelligence Reframed*, 66.
37. Gardner, *Frames of Mind*, 160–61.
38. Slavin, *Educational Psychology*, 117.
39. Gardner, "Multiple Intelligences," 8.
40. Ibid., 9.
41. Slavin, *Educational Psychology*, 170–204.
42. Ibid., 73–98.
43. Ibid., 205–36.

or instructions, though they may resort to a mnemonic device to assist in memorization.[44] Interpersonal intelligence involves those who prefer to learn within a group setting. Learning typically occurs as these individuals engage in discussion and debate over the pertinent information necessary for retention.[45] In contrast, intrapersonal intelligence involves individuals who prefer intrinsic reflection or meditation. They often focus on deciphering feelings and motivations.[46] Finally, naturalistic intelligence relates to those who nurture and relate their knowledge to nature or agriculture. These learners often categorize information based on the environment.[47]

Howard Gardner's theory of Multiple Intelligences has attracted criticism from other learning theory specialists. Thomas Armstrong, a specialist in educational theories, synthesizes some of the popular criticisms against Howard Gardner's theory of multiple intelligences in his book, *Multiple Intelligences in the Classroom*. Here, he notes that some critics relate the lack of solid research for this theory within the classroom setting. Instead, the most comprehensive study of this theory was documented from data collected from forty-one schools and was conducted by Mindy Kornhaber, who is a known advocate of Gardner's theory. It is further contended that the analysis of the collected data does not adequately explain the variables within the study and thus the results are convoluted. Respondents to this critique report that the "No Child Left Behind" law, within the United States, greatly hinders the objectives of valid research. "The demand for quantitative precision in education is an unfortunate nod toward *positivism*—the idea that ultimate truth can be expressed only through numbers or similarly precise scientific formulations."[48] The affects of this law do not allow for the variables represented within Gardner's Multiple Intelligence theory.

Many of the other criticisms related to Howard Gardner's theory of multiple intelligences do not deny the theory itself but center around semantic differences or the outcomes of testing using his categories of "intelligences." The strongest criticism against Gardner's theory focuses on the implementation of cognitive assessment based on his suggested intelligence categories. Harold Pashler, a distinguished professor in psychology at the University of California, San Diego led a study pertaining to learning styles. The conclusion of their review of literature disclosed ample evidence for the basis of both adults and children expressing preference for how information

44. Ibid., 99–127.
45. Ibid., 237–76.
46. Ibid.
47. Gardner, *Intelligence Reframed*, 48.
48. Armstrong, "Multiple Intelligences in the Classroom"

is presented, thereby suggesting that people do differ in regard to what mode of instruction is most effective for them. However, Pashler goes on to report that few studies have "used an experimental methodology capable of testing the validity of learning styles applied to education ... [or] justify incorporating learning styles assessment."[49]

Following the survey of reviews and critiques of Howard Gardner's theory of multiple intelligences, it is concluded that scholars within this field largely agree and support his theory. It has maintained respect among scholars in the disciplines of both education and psychology. This study relies on reviews similar to the above mentioned article by Harold Pashler. Though it appears that additional studies are necessary before cognitive assessment based on multiple intelligences is integrated into the classroom, this does not hinder the widely accepted recognition of diverse learning styles and necessity of diverse teaching styles.

Neil Fleming

The second popular learning theory relating to this book is Neil Fleming's theory of VARK Learning Styles. Fleming and co-author Coleen Mills introduced this theory in 1987. VARK is an acronym that stands for visual, aural, reading/writing, and kinesthetic. This theory was formulated to depict the various means by which learners assimilate information. This theory reports that learning typically occurs in a single or combination of four areas: visual, aural, reading-writing, and kinesthetic learning. Visual learning occurs when the student is given some type of object that can be visibly seen by the eyes. Information is taken in through observation of this visible object. Aural or audio learning occurs through audible instruction. This typically occurs when one person verbally communicates through a shared language. Those who learn through reading and writing prefer textual materials and independent study. Finally, kinesthetic learning occurs when the student is physically involved as he or she internalizes the information offered.[50] Rather than hearing a story or watching a demonstration, kinesthetic learning occurs by the student carrying out a physical activity.[51]

The theories for Multiple Intelligences and VARK Learning Styles share several characteristics. For example, Gardner's spatial intelligence and Fleming's visual learning style are strikingly similar. Though there are subtle variations, the linguistic intelligence most closely resembles the aural

---

49. Pashler et al., "Learning Styles Concepts," 105.
50. Dobson, "Comparison between Learning," 197.
51. *K12 Academics*, "Kinesthetic learning."

learning style. Gardner's bodily-kinesthetic intelligence and Fleming's kinesthetic learning style are nearly identical.

Fleming has also received criticism for his theory. Dr. Marilla Svinicki, Chair of Department of Educational Psychology and Professor of Learning, Cognition, and Instruction at the University of Texas reports that VARK is hard to statistically validate. However, she goes on to state that the strength of this theory is its value to educational models, giving [educators] and students something they may not have previously considered.[52] Like Howard Gardner, Neil Fleming continues to maintain the respect among the scholarly community of his field. Research completed by the Department of Educational Psychology and Instructional Technology at the University of Georgia, reinforces Fleming by stating four most popular learning styles include: visual, aural, reading/writing, and kinesthetic/tactile.[53]

Gardner's Theory of Multiple Intelligences and Fleming's VARK Learning Styles were used during the research of this book as a means to determine relevant examples of pedagogy that would prompt learning through one of the styles addressed by Gardner and Fleming. Because of its simplicity and maintained popularity with educators, the VARK Learning Styles was selected for use in order to offer common terminology for the modes of learning discussed herein. Therefore, student learning and pedagogy will be addressed using the terms proposed by Fleming. Since Fleming's "reading" category is obviously addressed through the written record of the Hebrew Bible, the scope of this study is limited to visual, audio, and kinesthetic learning styles. These learning styles will be discussed within the larger conceptual framework of active learning. This research will support the consistent use of active learning paradigms within the narratives of the Pentateuch and Deuteronomistic History, as well as Wisdom Literature. This will be examined in features such as monuments (visual), pneumonic devices such as songs (audio), and religious festivals (kinesthetic).

PEDAGOGY OF THE HEBREW BIBLE

In addition to learning theories, the first research question also addresses instructional methods observed in the Pentateuch and Deuteronomistic History. In general, the narrative genre within the Hebrew Bible is emphasized for its intention to communicate, teach, and bear witness to Yahweh as the supreme God. Scholars, such as Robert Alter, demonstrate that biblical writers were intent to convey Yahweh's religious stipulations and

---

52. Fleming and Baume, "Learning Styles Again," 3.
53. Giles et al., "Multiple Intelligences and Learning Styles."

ethical requirements for humanity through narrative stories.[54] Like Alter, Walter Brueggemann confirms this intentional didactic characteristic of the biblical narratives. Other scholars, such as Gerald Sheppard, confirm the common witness to religious ideals in Wisdom Literature.[55] More recently, Glenn Pemberton has discussed the use of the writings genre as a means for describing instruction in Israel.[56]

Children in the biblical world is a growing field of interest among biblical scholars. Studies such as Naomi Steinberg's *The World of the Child in the Hebrew Bible*[57] continue to advance the scope of awareness by discussing the social and developmental contributions that shaped and defined childhood as depicted in biblical literature. The construction of childhood remains a difficult subject due to the inconsistent use of terms for children within the Hebrew Bible and limited scholarly research that directly relates to this subject. The importance of the construction of childhood is acknowledged. However, this book remains focused on pedagogy and religious instruction. While the instruction of children is incorporated into this book, arguing the stages and transition from child to adult moves beyond the scope of its research.

Analogous to this, attention has also been given to the development of formal education in Israel. The term Israel is used in this research as a referent to the group described in the Pentateuch as descending from Abraham through his grandson Jacob. Henry Marrou offers an extensive survey as he traces the development of education. However, his focus on religious education does not begin until a time frame much later than the research described in this book, which are the periods described in the Pentateuch and Deuteronomistic History. He does trace Greek and Hellenistic schools back to the fifth century BC, though he is clearly referring to philosophy, literature, and the arts as the nucleus of the educational routine.[58] James Crenshaw has taken this research further as he specifically examines the development of education and schools in Israel. In his book *Education in Ancient Israel*, he traces this process from the earliest known Mesopotamian accounts of formal education in 2500 BC.[59] He then follows it through to the Nation of Israel, focusing on the eighth century BC onward. Though this work is monumental in the ability to see a panoramic view of educational

---

54. Alter and Kermode, *Literary Guide to the Bible*, 15.
55. Sheppard, *Wisdom as a Hermeneutical Construct*, 114.
56. Pemberton, "Rhetoric of the Father," 63–82.
57. Steinberg, *World of the Child*.
58. Marrou, *History of Education*, 46.
59. Crenshaw, *Education in Ancient Israel*, 15.

development, Crenshaw still stops short of answering one crucial question; *how* were religious precepts taught?

Walter Brueggemann discusses the Hebrew Bible's examples of how religious education was taught. He begins with the thesis that the Hebrew Bible was concerned with education and that this concern is explicit within the biblical text.[60] Using the designations of the Jewish TaNaK, Brueggemann considers three main areas during his discussions, the Torah, the Prophets, and the Writings. Though some references from the historical books are included, they are minimal.

Brueggemann's discussion of pedagogy from the Torah mirrors what many other scholars have argued, the primal means for the transference of knowledge was dialogical[61] through oral story. However, he asserts that care was taken to create rituals as a context in which these stories were told, such as the Passover described in Exodus 12–13.[62] He next moves on to discuss the articulation of the prophets as they refer to the narratives contained in the Pentateuch to challenge and critically engage old and/or irrelevant truth.[63] As Brueggemann argues, the writings that eventually comprised the written Pentateuch were not debatable for the followers of Yahweh. For those followers, the Pentateuch contained premeditated and consensual truth. The prophets, however, spoke of the religious laws in fresh ways. The instructions from the prophets revolved around suffering and hope, endings and beginnings, lament and celebration.[64] These teachings of the prophets created "a hard epistemological situation in the abrasion of old truth coming to terms with new truth."[65] The third and final area that Brueggemann explores is the Writings. Here, he asserts that educators used metaphors, hyperbole, numerical sayings, and other literary effects that invite the listener to classify and enumerate the boundaries of acceptable and unacceptable conduct.[66]

While Brueggemann accurately emphasizes the importance of education and its pedagogical inclusion in biblical literature, he does not offer exhaustive evidence for his claims. His objective to relate the value of these texts to Christian education has obscured his systematic approach to

---

60. Brueggemann, *Creative Word*, 1.

61. Dialogical is used here as the oral communication between two or more characters.

62. Brueggemann, *Creative Word*, 16.

63. Ibid., 45.

64. Ibid., 60–61.

65. Ibid., 63.

66. Ibid., 77–78.

critically evaluate the examples of pedagogy in biblical texts. Rather than an in depth approach, he merely acknowledges many of the references before moving into his discussion of their contribution to the pedagogy of modern Christian education. More importantly, he has regrettably ignored several significant texts that further develop the pedagogy recorded within the Pentateuch and Deuteronomistic History.

From this broad overview, it is necessary to refer back to the primary mode of family based education. It is already asserted that the Hebrew Bible does not document any type of formal school. It is articulated, by other scholars, that Israel employs oral narrative stories to recount their history and religious beliefs. An example of this scholarship is found in Gerhardsson's *Memory and Manuscript*, where he defends the usage of early oral tradition of the Pentateuch and the techniques used to preserve the accuracy of the stories therein. Within this oral tradition, the Pentateuch includes several vital narratives that demonstrate a particular pedagogy that is utilized prior to the use of the written narrative.

These studies on educational theory and literary criticism will be utilized throughout this research as these two areas are brought together and confirm textual evidence that support examples of pedagogy purposefully included or highlighted within the Pentateuch and Deuteronomistic History.

Chapter 2

A Literary Approach to Biblical Literature

INTRODUCTION

THE DISCRETION OF BIBLICAL editors dictates the inclusion or exclusion of details and story content. Acceptance of inerrancy, historical validity, or hermeneutical methodology establishes the protocol of interpretation. This chapter seeks to demonstrate the Hebrew Bible as an intentional and complex act of communication.[1] Authors and editors deliberately record and shape stories to become an agent through which they record their religious ethos and mythos. Along with this, they also intentionally include their pedagogical paradigms for the later training of learners. This chapter will cover two areas: First, the literary approach to the Bible is discussed as a viable advance of this study that more adequately demonstrates the recorded pedagogy than a historical approach will allow. Second, the role of editors in relation to the Pentateuch and Deuteronomistic History is described. This will become the foundation for the arguments presented in later chapters where the purposeful inclusion of instructions and examples of pedagogy by editors is defended. In these latter chapters, it is asserted that textual evidence indicates one of the roles of editors, in relation to the Pentateuch and Deuteronomistic History, was to draw the readers' attention to pedagogical feature by rearranging texts or inserting key phrases to emphasize important pedagogical features.

1. Vanhoozer et al., *Theological Interpretation of the OT,* 324.

Nation of Israel

It is reiterated that the methodology of research includes a literary approach to biblical texts rather than a focused debate on the validity of their historicity. The central group described within the Pentateuch and Deuteronomistic History is described as descendants of the character Abraham through his grandson, Jacob (later named Israel). This group is described early as the "sons of Israel," recorded in Exod 19:6, where they are also described as a "holy nation." The term "Nation of Israel" does not occur in the biblical texts. Instead, the terms "sons of Israel" and "Israelites" occur most frequently to address or identify this group. The closest use of this phrase is γένος Ἰσραήλ, translated as "Nation of Israel" in the NASB. This translation is a divergence from the ESV, KJV, and NIV.[2]

Though the term "Nation of Israel" does not derive distinctly from biblical literature, it is a widely used and accepted term within the realm of biblical scholarship. Examples include its use by Walter Brueggemann in *Prophetic Imagination*, Walter Kaiser Jr. in *The Coming Millennial Kingdom*, Brevard Childs in *The Bible as Scripture*, and Robert Alter in *The Wisdom Books*. The general connotation of this term used by these scholars is in reference to the sect of people descending from Abraham's grandson, Jacob (later named Israel) as described in the Pentateuch. The term distinguishes this described culture of people from other groups described in the Pentateuch and Deuteronomistic History such as Canaanites and Edomites.

The scope of this research does not allow for argument concerning whether this group existed or the likely time period that aligns with the biblical literature discussed herein. It is acknowledged that strong contention exists between the ideological description of this group in biblical literature and the archeological support of its discrepancies. The term Israel is used in the inclusive sense of the initial recipients of biblical literature. Since it is beyond the concern of this research, the debate on the historicity of Israel will not be further addressed. The reference to the "Nation of Israel" is used to indicate the group mentioned above as a separate entity from other groups described within the Hebrew Bible such as, but not limited to, the Egyptians, Canaanites, and Philistines. Since the term "Israelites" is used within the Hebrew Bible, this term and "Nation of Israel" are used interchangeably within this book.

---

2. See Phil 3:5.

LITERARY VERSUS HISTORICAL APPROACH TO INTERPRETATION

Literary, historical, and theological approaches are often the three interpretive methodologies currently used in contemporary biblical studies. The historical validity of narratives within the Pentateuch has caused questions among scholars. The onset of the Documentary Hypothesis disturbed conservative Christians believing that it inundated the historicity of the texts. Historical truthfulness was questioned based on the considerable time lapse between the event's occurrence and documentation.

Wilhelm de Wette argued that the Hebrew Bible lacks historical validity and should be categorized as myth. However, he attempts to compensate for this dogmatic theology by going on to say that the Israelites used these myths as their vehicle to truthfully convey their religious ideas.[3] De Wette carefully tied his belief to thorough scholarship, forcing his critics to disprove his opinions through their own scholarly calculations. August Tholuck attacked the opinions of those who sought to dehistorize the Hebrew Bible. He was supported by many like-minded academicians who sought to devastate the criticism used by de Wette and his followers.[4]

Gerhard von Rad also maintains that the stories recorded in the Hebrew Bible were founded on actual events. However, he correctly argues that it is impossible to construct an accurate picture of the history.[5] "An elusive, but real, historical event results in a tradition modified through time to meet different theological needs. At some later date that tradition is incorporated into Israel's reconstruction of her story of salvation."[6]

Albrecht Alt brought attention toward the historical accuracy of the Pentateuch in his essay, "The God of the Fathers," by stating that the religion portrayed by the patriarchs in Genesis is typical of semi-nomads. He further questioned the historical validity of Genesis by pointing out that these narratives were not recorded by the J and E sources until a thousand years after the patriarchs.[7] He further demonstrates that two types of law used in the Pentateuch, case law ("if a man does . . . ") and apodictic law ("thou shalt not") are borrowed from the Canaanites and did not originate with Moses.[8]

---

3. Bray, *Biblical Interpretation*, 276–77.
4. Ibid., 281.
5. Rad, *Old Testament Theology*, 1:116.
6. Routledge, *Old Testament Theology*, 36.
7. Wenham, *Exploring the Old Testament*, 171.
8. Ibid., 172.

Later scholars such as William Albright, Ephraim Speiser, and Cyrus Gordon try to reinforce the historical trustworthiness of the Pentateuch. John Bright also affirms its accuracy despite the later recording of events when he writes, "We can assert with full confidence that Abraham, Isaac, and Jacob were actual historical individuals."[9] The overall consensus of historical accuracy continues through the mid-twentieth century. However, this consensus begins to fade in the later part of the twentieth century.

The continuous activity of Israel borrowing and appropriating adds to the difficulty in determining historical accuracy. Generally, the nearer the record of the event is to its occurrence, the more likely its historical accuracy. Yet it is also regarded that the Hebrew Bible is as an entire act of imaginative remembering. Thus, the overall focus is not that of historical evidence but rather a narrative account of Yahweh. The development of the Hebrew Bible's collection of narrative stories is first and foremost for the purpose of describing Yahweh and His relationship to humanity. The intentional purpose is not to provide a historical account. This is evidenced by several examples of events purposely extracted from chronological order in order to better detail the theology behind the events. The question of historicity then becomes futile in that it misrepresents the overall purpose. On the other hand, stating that the purpose is not historically accurate does not denote that the historical details are reduced to subjective myth or whimsical storytelling.

The literary approach was pioneered by Erich Auerbach in 1947.[10] Its influence continues among current biblical scholars including Robert Alter and Tremper Longman.[11] While discussing the difficulties of a historical approach to the Hebrew Bible, Alter explains the historical approach is limited by what can be verified by archeologists and historians. The literary approach to interpretation, on the other hand, is not indifferent to history but purposefully focuses on the text itself and:

> ... directs attention to the moral, psychological, political, and spiritual realism of the biblical texts, which is a way of opening ourselves to something that deserves to be called their authority, whether we attribute that authority solely to the power of the human imagination or to a transcendent source of illumination

---

9. Bright, *History of Israel*, 91.

10. Bray, *Biblical Interpretation*, 467.

11. For an extensive list of literary critics and philosophers, see Bray, *Biblical Interpretation*, 467–75.

that kindled the imagination of the writers to express itself through these particular literary means.[12]

This literary approach of biblical interpretation is accepted and used within this book. Authenticating the historical accuracy is beyond the scope of this book and does not substantiate whether or not teaching paradigms are present within the biblical texts. Therefore, the literary approach was selected to validate the presence of pedagogical features and determine whether editors purposefully inserted or emphasized their presences in the biblical texts discussed within this book. Though not indifferent to historical events, the focus of this research is centered on the literary descriptions of actions described within the Hebrew Bible. Descriptions of pedagogy are examined based on their literary context and usage as well as the religious ideals that are often described in connection to these examples of instruction.

Related to a literary approach of biblical interpretation is reader response and interaction with a biblical text, or reader response criticism. Scholarly debates remain ongoing regarding the reader's role and freedom to relate himself or herself into the texts' world. More radical views of reader response criticism discredit the text altogether and construct a hermeneutical approach entirely on the reader's interpretation, where the reader is the absolute source for meaning. When using the literary approach for research in this book, it is noted that it is impossible to become completely objective to the text. Any biblical interpreter naturally reads and interprets through personal presuppositions and preunderstanding. However, the text must remain the central concern. This enforces the necessity of a literary approach where emphasis is on the words and content of the text rather that the subjective arguments presented through a historical approach.[13]

The literary context refers to the knowledge that may be learned from the surrounding subject matter of a given passage. The writers and editors of the Hebrew Bible used literature as a medium for moral instruction and training learners in the tenants of their worldview, including religious education and pedagogy for the future training of these religious ideals. The text itself is used as a structured means for locutionary acts with language to describe a localized setting and intentions for described acts.[14] In other words, authors used literature to engage readers through characters and their actions to define the author/editor's ethos and mythos. Therefore, a

---

12. Alter, *World of Biblical Literature*, 203–4.

13. For additional analysis of reader response criticism, I recommend Paulian-Timotei Petric's article, "The Reader(s) and the Bible(s) 'Reader Versus Community' in Reader-Response Criticism and Biblical Interpretation."

14. Vanhoozer, *Is There a Meaning*, 325.

literary approach specifically addresses the function of the texts addressed in this book. The nature and function of selected texts are identified to demonstrate this ethos of pedagogy as well as its intentional inclusion within the Hebrew Bible.

The incorporation of described events and religious principles to form narrative accounts were later accumulated into larger collections, initiating the canonical formation. This formation was an extremely complex process of tradition. Walter Brueggemann uses the term "imaginative remembering" when referring to this process. By this, he describes the act of remembering and storytelling that transpired intergenerationally within this community as parents and grandparents tell and retell their stories to the younger generations. This is demonstrated in texts such as Exod 10:1–2; Deut 6:20; and Josh 4:21. He goes on to describe this act of *imaginative remembering* as a trustworthy voice of faith and that as literature, it is not merely descriptive of the common world but vouches for the religious commitment of the characters described. "The theological aspect of this imagination is that the world is articulated with YHWH as the defining character, even though this character in all holiness defies every attempt to make this character available or accessible in any conventional mode."[15] This imagination involves a theological dimension that renders a world defined by God's character interrelated with a rich artistry lived through a reality of written word.[16]

Some scholars, such as Gerhard von Rad, see this act of remembering and storytelling as trustworthy and reliable[17] while others, such as William Dever[18] and James Barr[19] remain skeptical of the historical claims. With this in mind, modern readers of the Hebrew Bible must remember that the imposition articulated by Brueggemann, "[the] modernists tests of reliability on the text has been deeply wrongheaded and has asked of texts what they did not intend to deliver."[20] Therefore, events related by parents to their

---

15. Brueggemann, *Introduction to the OT*, 10.

16. The collective memory of the Israelite community plays an important role in the preservation of stories considered important. Birger Gerhardsson's study on *Memory and Manuscript* was previously discussed in chapter 1. Within his study, Gerhardsson discusses the community's responsive ability to memorize key events and texts as a direct result of the story's prominence within the culture and religious identity. Pnumonic devices such as song, alliteration, and chiasm were utilized as a means for accurate memorization and recitation of key details within the account. As stories become recorded, the collective memory of the community fuses the amassed accounts of cultural and religious heritage.

17. Rad, *Old Testament Theology*, 1:105–15, 1:302–5.

18. Dever, *What Did the Biblical Writers Know*.

19. Barr, *History and Ideology in the OT*.

20. Brueggemann, *Introduction to the OT*, 8.

children as standard belief were, at some point, canonized as part of the holy text through long normative usage. They are saturated with meaning of the God of Israel, the principle character, who providentially operates in these narratives that are reliable depictions of reality.[21] An important example of this is the story of the Passover, recorded in Exodus 12. Parents are encouraged to retell this account to their children for the purpose of illustrating an act of salvation by their God.

The literary approach selected for this research helps validate the presence of pedagogical features and determines whether editors purposefully inserted or emphasized these features in the biblical texts discussed herein. The studies presented in this chapter pertaining to the literary approach will be used as the foundation for chapters 3 through 5. In these latter chapters, textual evidence is discussed that supports the extent that editors of the Pentateuch and Deuteronomistic History draw the readers' attention to pedagogical features by rearranging texts or inserting key phrases to emphasize important pedagogical features.

Biblical Narratives

Several scholars have written on the subject of the use of narrative storytelling in the oral tradition of Israel's history. It is already well documented that this was one of the primary means for preserving the historical heritage and religious beliefs of this group. The very didactic purpose of scripture is to instill theological truth and moral character to its readers. The narrative is then one part of the cohesive whole that guides readers in this educational journey. This genre dominates the writing style of the Hebrew Bible, making up 40 percent of this literature. Here, history and theology come together within a story. Ideals are preserved within the characters and outcomes of the stories. Narrative stories are presented as a means of persuasion. Even the characters within the stories are persuaded by stories other characters tell.[22]

A narrative is a discourse affirming facts associated in sequential order with an underlying link. A discourse is how a story is told and the story itself is the truth a narrative relates.[23] The story is the content related through means of the discourse which links with other analogous discourses to form the narrative. Grant Osborne has also noted the varied use of narratives.

---

21. Ibid.
22. Amit, *Reading Biblical Narratives*, 1.
23. Marguerat and Bourquin, *How to Read Bible Stories*, 21.

They can be studied on both the micro (individual story) and macro (story of an entire book) level.[24]

The ethical ideas (or ethos) of the storytellers are embodied in the characters represented in each story. They encompass a transparent expression of human frailty that makes them appealing and applicable to their audience. Their characteristics mirror modern readers in their own ignorance, viciousness, pride, wisdom, esteem, and morale. These characters also learn through various modes within the stories, including the unfortunate consequences of poor or ill-informed decisions. Even the biblical heroes suffer shame when they disobey Yahweh's commandments. These characters, then, are a contrast to the immutable Yahweh they seek to know and conform to. Through this, hearers and readers learn vicariously through the success and failures of these characters.

It is widely accepted that Israel took part in oral tradition. The stories that taught the basics of their cultural and religious beliefs are repeated by mouth from one generation to the next.[25] Tayla Fishman also attests the substantial use of oral tradition in the development of Jewish culture and faith.[26] Other Scholars who agree with the use of oral tradition include Brevard Childs,[27] Martin Noth,[28] Walter Brueggemann,[29] and Robert Alter.[30] That is, the community's ethos, mythos, and logos are preserved and passed on from one generation to the next through spoken stories. It is believed that this is one of the intrinsic factors that aided in preserving the narrative accounts in Genesis and Exodus prior to their formal written recording at a later date. Parents then used these stories for instructing their children.

A close look at the descriptive plots within biblical narratives reveals the present imagery included within the story. Examination of the plot itself brings forth the transitions between time, locations, and characters. These changes take place by the "telling" of the narrator or the "showing" through the personae themselves. Though both instances are the work of the narrator, the "showing" has a far more dramatic impact for the reader.[31] Though biblical narratives are always a combination of the narrator's "telling" and personae "showing," "the more the author wishes to make the

---

24. Osborne, *Hermeneutical Spiral*, 158.
25. Jaffee, *Torah in the Mouth*, 4.
26. Fishman, *Becoming the People*, 243.
27. Childs, *Memory and Tradition*, 17.
28. Noth, *History of Pentateuchal History*, 3.
29. Brueggemann, *Introduction to the OT*, 9.
30. Alter, *Art of Biblical Poetry*, 27.
31. Amit, *Reading Biblical Narratives*, 49.

story dramatic, the more he reduces the narration and allows the personae to speak for themselves."[32] Additionally, a writer rarely leaves the location of narrative events unspecified. Naming the location for events helps them to feel real. Thus, the biblical authors offer geographical locations that may also include the historical significance of a particular location such as the description of Kiriath Arba (Hebron) in Gen 35:27.

The role of a narrator in the Narrative genre is an informant. He moves the plot forward through his description of events. Jan Fokkelman describes the narrator as the veritable ringmaster. Readers only "hear" the voices from characters that the narrator chooses to allow speak.[33] The narrator is synonymous with the biblical writer who "draws his material from events and characters in national history, but is not overly concerned with the strict requirements that historiography has to meet in the 20th Century."[34]

Therefore, the example narratives and their descriptions used within this book were purposefully written with didactic intentions. Writers specified elements within the stories to help the readers draw appropriate conclusions and draw inferences from the details contained within them. Specific to this research, the details pertaining to pedagogy, within these narratives, are useful for drawing conclusions on how the writers recognized the educational process of children, adults, and resident aliens. Beyond the expectation that these stories would be continually taught, they included descriptions on how these stories should be taught.

Authorship of Pentateuch

The importance for the discussion of Pentateuchal authorship relates to the research question concerning the extent later editors are responsible for the material directly associated with pedagogy. Within this book, it is advocated that later editors are largely responsible for inserting, rearranging, or emphasizing pedagogical features related to the active learning model proposed by Fleming. Therefore, this section is utilized to validate the basis that the Pentateuch is not the product of a single author but rather a compilation from several authors and editors that was not finalized until the Babylonian captivity or later.

Existing studies articulating the editorial activity of the Pentateuch are strongly established by scholars such as Antony Campbell and Mark O'Brien. Interest in editorial activity pertains to the third research question

---

32. Ibid., 51.
33. Fokkelman, *Reading Biblical Narrative*, 56.
34. Ibid., 57.

on whether or not there is textual evidence within the Pentateuch and Deuteronomistic History to suggest that editors purposefully inserted or brought attention to pedagogical features. Two major studies influenced the conclusion to this research questions, *The Bible with Sources Revealed* by Richard Friedman and *Unfolding the Deuteronomistic History* by Antony Campbell and Mark O'Brien. Both of these studies address the process of integrating multiple sources into the present final form of the Pentateuch and Deuteronomistic History respectively. They were used as a means to support the claim that major texts relating directly to pedagogy were later additions by editors.

Friedman's approach analyzes and seeks to identify the individual sources that combine to form the present final form of the Pentateuch. He addresses textual anomalies such as divergent uses for the name of Yahweh, contradictions of fact, repetition of details, and disproportionate phrases to account for distinctions in sources. It is regretted that Friedman offers sparse scholarly dialogue regarding his research and conclusions. It is also unfortunate that he does not critically engage the prior writings from Frank Moore Cross, Martin Noth, John Van Seters, or Julius Wellhausen. Though these sources are included in his bibliography, they are not brought to the readers' attention, within this text. Again, the addition of scholarly dialogue and critique would have greatly enhanced his work. During the course of this research, Friedman's sources were checked with the earlier research of Antony Campbell and Mark O'Brien in their 1993 book, *Sources of the Pentateuch*. Unlike Friedman, Campbell and O'Brien discuss their review of other scholarly activity pertaining to their research. The rare instances when these two sources differ are documented and discussed within this research.

The Pentateuch is traditionally referred to as the "Law of Moses" or "Book of Moses" based on the examples used in Ezra 6:18 as well as other texts. This title is used to describe portions of the Pentateuch, as seen in 2 Kgs 14:6, as well as all five books in Mark 12:26. Though there are portions of the Pentateuch that report Mosaic authorship for a given segment, the work as a whole is anonymous. Mosaic authorship is explicitly affirmed in Philo, Josephus, and the Talmud. This thought remained unchallenged in the Christian church until the seventeenth century AD.[35]

Rabbis of the Talmud, writing between 200 and 500 AD, discuss the Pentateuch's transmission to Moses in a series of small scrolls implying that the Pentateuch was written progressively and accumulated from a variety of documents over time. R. Zev Wolf Einhorn points to instances of Moses quoting Genesis prior to his theophany on Mt. Sinai. He suggests that Moses

---

35. Weiser, *Old Testament*, 72.

possessed certain documents authored by previous Patriarchs that he used when redacting the Pentateuch.[36]

Accounts such as 2 Macc 2:13 attribute to the traditional assumption of the Old Testament books maintaining unbroken continuity between the writing and the collecting of these books. "In the mid-second century BC we have evidence of all five books, including Genesis, being attributed to Moses (see Aristobulus, as cited by Eusebius, *Preparation for the Gospel*, 13.12)."[37] Elias Levita[38] further developed a theory that the men serving under Ezra established the Hebrew Bible and divided it into three parts. His theory was widely accepted by Jews and Christians until the latter part of the nineteenth century.[39] This sacred book of annals was preserved and considered an uninterrupted succession of authentic divine writing.

The patriarchal narratives were primarily preserved through oral tradition during the Egyptian captivity. They were then put into written form during the Mosaic period.[40] Later accounts such as the Exodus and wilderness experience were likely added early during the Davidic period. After gathering several compilations, the documents from the Mosaic age may have taken a final form under the direction of Ezra in the fifth century BC.

In 1651 Thomas Hobbes challenged the Mosaic authorship of the Pentateuch by pointing out some anachronisms and specific texts that he believed could not have been authored by the prophet. Other scholars, such as Isaac de la Peyrère, Baruch Spinoza, Richard Simon, and John Hampden came to the same conclusion. However, their works were condemned resulting in many of them receiving imprisonment.[41]

Baruch Spinoza was an unorthodox Jew who published *Tractatus Theologico-Oliticus* in 1670. In this document, he points out that the Pentateuch speaks of Moses in the third person as well as uses late names for some of the locations visited by Moses. He further suggests that the Pentateuch was put together by more than one editor based on the inconsistencies in some of the stories. Though he believed several sources were responsible for bringing together the Pentateuch, Spinoza believed there was a main editor from the fifth century BC, namely Ezra.[42] Baruch Spinoza was sharply

---

36. Student, "On the Authorship of the Torah."

37. Bruce et al., *Origin of the Bible*, 56.

38. Elias Levita (1469–1549 AD) was a Hebrew grammarian during the Renaissance Period.

39. Childs, *Introduction to the OT*, 51.

40. Albright, *Archeology of Palestine*, 225.

41. Miller et al., *Dating the Bible*, 65.

42. Wenham, *Exploring the Old Testament*, 162.

criticized for his publications to the extent of some critics attempting to kill him for his beliefs.

Concerned about the denial of Mosaic authorship, Jean Astruc constructed an explanation for the apparent inconsistencies within the Pentateuch. Attempting to refute the work of Hobbes and Spinoza, Astruc implemented literary analysis being used with other Classical texts, such as the *Iliad*, to examine the divergences and discover the genuine text. In his 1753 work, *Conjectures on the Original Memoirs that it Seems Moses Used to Compose the Book of Genesis*, he observed some of the repetitive stories and different names for God. Using these as criteria, he split Genesis into four separate sources, two longer and two shorter, then arranged them into four parallel columns. He concluded that these four sources were later combined, by Moses, into one document creating the repetitions and inconsistencies that are apparent in Genesis. Though Astruc's work did not convince many people, his methodology for analyzing the literature was widely accepted. Based on his findings, it became widely accepted that the Pentateuch was based on a variety of sources that were later redacted together.[43]

The documentary theory or documentary hypothesis was developed during the eighteenth and nineteenth century AD as a means to explain the literary complexities of the Pentateuch. This theory began under the scholarship of Alexander Geddes, Johann Severin Vater, G. H. A. Ewald, and W. M. L. de Wette but was established and popularized under Julius Wellhausen. The documentary hypothesis seeks to separate the assorted "sources" within the modern text. Whereas Jean Astruc supposed that Moses had combined the varying sources, advocates of the documentary hypothesis believed that a series of editors worked to integrate the sources into a single document.[44] It argues that the Pentateuch is derived from originally independent narratives that were later combined by editors or a series of editors. This hypothesis usually distinguishes between four sources represented in the Pentateuch, though this number is not a critical component of the hypothesis. Scholars who accept this theory believe it reconciles some of the biblical inconsistencies by showing that the Pentateuch was woven together from independent (and sometimes conflicting) documents.[45] Though Julius Wellhausen did not conceive of the documentary hypothesis, it is often credited to him due to his contribution of chronologically ordering these sources as JEDP and giving them a coherent story within the context of Israel's history.

43. Ibid., 162–63.
44. Ibid., 165.
45. Miller et al., *Dating the Bible*, 63.

The first source is the Yahwist narrative, or J source (from the German spelling *Jahweh*). This is believed to be the oldest source and encompasses Genesis 2 through Numbers 24, though some believe the record of Moses' death in Deuteronomy 34 was also part of the original J document. J was written between 950–850 BC and emphasizes God's nearness by describing Him in human terms, or anthropomorphisms. This source also emphasizes the continuity of God's providence from creation through the monarchy.[46]

The second source is referred to as the E source due to its preference of the name Elohim for God prior to the revelation of God's name to Moses in Exodus chapters 3 and 6. After this encounter, E employs both Yahweh and Elohim interchangeably when referencing God. This source parallels the J source, however, it highlights the tradition of the northern kingdom. E's narratives begin with Genesis 20 and are therefore somewhat later than J's. This source is dated between 750–700 BC. Since the E source is extremely fragmented, Martin Noth suggests that an editor supplied J with material found in E. If this suggestion is true, then recovering the E source is unfeasible.[47] Gordon Wenham gives an earlier date of 800 BC for the E source.[48]

The third source makes up the core of the material comprising the book of Deuteronomy and is thus referred to as the D source. The literary nature of this source is distinct from the previous two with its wordiness and prosaic mannerisms. Prosaic mannerisms are defined as literary characteristics that resemble prose. It is can also refer to literary features that lack imagination and interest. Also due to its distinctive style, wherever this approach appears in the Old Testament, it is referred to as Deuteronomistic. This source is attributed to the shaping of not only Deuteronomy, but extends into Joshua through 2 Kings. D emphasizes purity of worship. "Several scholars have postulated that the core was collected and composed in the early seventh century BC. This core was found during the renovation of the temple under Josiah;[49] it then gave practical direction to that reform."[50]

The final source identified in the Documentary Hypothesis is the Priestly source. Abbreviated as P, this source is a historical narrative expanded with legal texts and other material. P focuses on things such as genealogies, cultic laws, covenants, holy days, cultic buildings, and ceremonial procedures. Yahweh's holiness, sovereignty, and transcendence is also emphasized along with the establishment of worship led by the priests.

---

46. LaSor, *Old Testament Survey*, 10.
47. Ibid.
48. Wenham, "Pentateuchal Studies," 3.
49. 2 Kgs 22.
50. LaSor, *Old Testament Survey*, 11.

Sections of the Pentateuch such as Genesis 1, Leviticus 1–7, and Leviticus 17–26 are examples of material identified from the P source. "The ground source of P is often dated to the middle of the Exile (ca. 550 BC); and its final compilation sometime before the end of the fourth century BC."[51] Most other scholars give an earlier date for P, no later than 450 BC.

The importance of Wellhausen's theory, as it relates to this book, is the indication of purposed editorial activity and later phases of editing that offers textual evidence of later writers adjusting the narratives to make them more relevant to later audiences. This directly corresponds to the third research question that seeks to determine whether there is evidence of later editors who either insert or emphasize pedagogical features for religious instruction. While the details of Wellhausen's documentary hypothesis theory remain debated, its concept remains relevant and accepted among scholars.

S. R. Driver further advocated the documentary hypothesis. Two basic criteria for source analysis are the use of divine names and duplicated material. Driver also accounted for differing linguistic styles. For example, he notes the "P" source often uses jurist rather than historian language. In contrast, "D's" rhetorical writing style is similar to oral presentation.

Though these four sources were originally four separate sources; it is not believed that they were edited together to form a single document at the same time. Instead, it is believed that they were incorporated at different times by different editors. The oldest source, J, was combined with the second oldest source E to form a combined document, JE. The new JE document was then later combined with D to form JED. The JED document would finally be combined with P to form the present Pentateuch and the alleged JEDP document. The following diagram, used by Wenham,[52] further represents this formation:

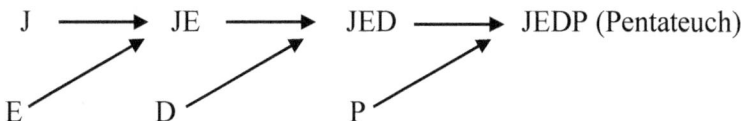

The editing phases of JE, JED, and JEDP are approximated as 750, 600, and 450 BC respectively. Differing scholars adjust the dates within a half century of each other. It is again asserted that arguing specific dates is not the focus of this writing. Here, dates are presented solely as a means of demonstrating multiple editorial revisions and discussing dates offered by other scholars.

51. Ibid.
52. Wenham, *Exploring the Old Testament*, 168.

Wellhausen furthermore examines the development of five areas of religious practice including place of worship, sacrifice, festivals, priesthood, and priestly income. He contends that these five areas vary throughout the Pentateuch in a parallel fashion to their variance in Israelite history. He argues that this further justifies the four sources and identifies approximate dates in which the editing may have taken place.[53]

Beginning with the place of worship, Wellhausen shows that Israelites worshipped and offered sacrifices at many different locations such as Ophrah, Manoah, and Mount Carmel during the time of the judges and early monarchy. During the late monarchy period of King Josiah, this custom changed and all the places of worship were destroyed outside of Jerusalem. Jerusalem then became the exclusive place for worship. Soon after Josiah's death, Jerusalem lost its exclusivity and the pagan shrines were restored until the Babylonian exile, when they were once again abandoned. Upon the Israelites' return from exile, Jerusalem was again recognized as the only acceptable place to worship. A pattern thus emerges within the historical books that the Israelites could worship at the place of their choice until the time of King Josiah (622 BC) when an attempt to centralize worship was made. Though this attempt failed in its infancy, it was later accepted by the post-exilic community.[54]

Wellhausen asserts that this same pattern is recognizable in the sources and editing of the Pentateuch. Patriarchs offer sacrifices in a variety of locations throughout both the J and E sources. As these two documents were edited together, it is understood that sacrifices could be offered wherever God made his presence known.[55] This parallels the early monarchial practice prior to Josiah.

Later in Deuteronomy, Israel's worship must take place in the location God will choose and not at the Canaanite shrines.[56] This notion parallels that of Josiah's attempted implementation of centralized worship in 2 Kgs 22:8–20. This connection of Deuteronomy and Josiah's reform allows a more precise date than other Pentateuchal sources.[57]

Finally, the P source describes the rituals of the tabernacle in such a way that it presumes a single location for worship. This complements the prevailing attitude toward worship following the release from Babylonian

---

53. Ibid.
54. Ibid.
55. Exod 20:24.
56. Deut 12:4–6.
57. Wenham, *Exploring the Old Testament*, 169.

captivity. Therefore, Wellhausen argues that this is likely the last of the sources.[58]

Additional elements within the Pentateuch also bear the marks of Israel's faith development through the differing phases of its editing. Writers such as James Sanders note that Deuteronomy ends with Moses' death and the Israelites still outside of the Promised Land but with a hopeful expectation of immanent entrance. This too parallels the hopeful expectation experienced by a landless exiled country throughout the Babylonian captivity as they make editorial revisions to reimagine their stories through the lens of their newer experiences.[59] The editing of the literature again leaves a residue of the mindset of a nation that waits in hope and coheres with the characteristics of this community of faith where history has not become fully visible in that they still await in expectation that the promises of God will be fulfilled. " . . . while the traditioning process is complex and long-term, it is now accepted by scholars that the final form of the text reflects the work and conviction of *two great theological-interpretive trajectories* working in and around the exilic period, both of which have deep roots in earlier phases of Israel's life and faith."[60]

Rather than seeking to provide a chronological historical account of humanity's relationship with Yahweh, the Pentateuch utilizes theological themes to propel the stories. This thematic development is noted by both Robin Routledge and Walter Brueggemann. Gerhard von Rad may have been the most obvious when he discusses the impracticality of placing Israel's creedal statements in chronological order in that merely Genesis through Joshua offers remarkable differences in structure than one would rarely venture beyond arguments of dating the narratives.[61]

As an editorial achievement of the Priestly and Deuteronomistic traditions, the final form of the text exposes the worldview of these faith communities. The Priestly tradition, or P source, is primarily conscientious of holiness and recognizes the cultic practices that lead to and develop this holiness. Keeping in mind that the literature contained in P is edited during the Babylonian Exile, a period when this faith community is under threat, one may note the commitment and focus on traditions such as the Mosaic Covenant and Exodus events that are prefaced with narratives that

---

58. Ibid.
59. Brueggemann, *Introduction to the OT*, 97.
60. Ibid., 98.
61. Rad, *Old Testament Theology*, 1:vi.

authorize the Sabbath[62] and circumcision.[63] In contrast to P, the Deuteronomic tradition, or D source, introduces covenant. Here, attention is given to the correct ordering of the political-economic practices of Israel.[64] During Noah's covenant, the Israelites are given a sign of the covenant within the rainbow between God and the earth.[65] The idea of a covenantal sign is witnessed again with circumcision in the Abrahamic covenant.[66] During the Mosaic Covenant, the Israelites are told that the Sabbath will serve as a sign.[67] Though these signs are attributed differently, they are all associated with God's promise to maintain order and are a sign of the grace belonging to His covenantal people. Now, at this injunction of turmoil and theological confusion, traditions are ordered in such a way that Israel's understanding of its special relationship, calling, and distinctiveness are highlighted alongside of their covenantal obligation to hear and obey God. From infancy this nation bore the sign of belonging to God and now, though they are experiencing Exile, they are reminded of their outward sign of inward consecration.[68]

Finally, the evidence of the plot development of the Pentateuch is shaped around a theme that moves from God's creation and ordering of *earth* (אֶרֶץ, *'erets*) to *the land which He promised* (אֲשֶׁר־דִּבֶּר אֶרֶץ *'erets*).[69] Traditioning takes place again as a focus on Israel's future moves from a different landscape of *'erets* as "earth" to *'erets* as "promised land." This movement takes place through the narratives of Genesis 12–36, where the patriarchs are assured of the promise of a special land. Though they inhabit the land for a short season, it is not possessed at the end of Deuteronomy. A parallel is drawn between a land of abundance that flows with "milk and honey" that is described as a "good land" in Deut 1:25 as representative of creation, which God called "very good" in Gen 1:31.[70]

The land plays an integral role in Israel's understanding of its relationship with God. The occupation and blessings of land are conditional upon Israel's obedience to God. C. H. Wright discusses the significance of land in his book *God's People in God's Land*, where he links covenantal theology

---

62. Gen 2:1–4a.
63. Genesis 17.
64. Brueggemann, *Introduction to the OT*, 99.
65. Gen 9:13.
66. Gen 17:11.
67. Exod 31:13, 16–17.
68. Routledge, *Old Testament Theology*, 167–68.
69. Deut 9:28.
70. Brueggemann, *Introduction to the OT*, 99–100.

with the nation's relationship with God. The occupation of land, or lack thereof, was a direct symptom of the nation's moral slide.[71]

This exilic community finds itself dangerously exposed and vulnerable to losing their cultic traditions. It is therefore plausible that the community begins to resolve to preserve its heritage through a written validation for their identity and praxis. Their Pentateuch then becomes a script for the displaced community wherein we see, as previously mentioned, and an illuminated connection in Deuteronomy 34. The death of Moses marks the end of a normative period and Israel is ready to enter the land of promise, but still landless. This narrative thus becomes particularly relevant to an exiled community who is also poised to reenter the land, but is still landless. Propelled by theological intentionality, the narratives and traditions of the Pentateuch take shape as ongoing relevant material to those of both Jewish and Christian faiths.[72]

The documentary hypothesis is governed by a concept of progressive development of Israel's faith. This imaginative remembering brings forth the tradition of telling and retelling the stories in order for faith to be possible for subsequent generations. Each generation retells the stories, believing it to be correct and final. However, rather than the final story, it is intertwined with other aspects of the tradition and memory. This traditioning process has come to constitute the church's Scripture and is an intentional advocacy for the conviction of faith.[73] It was this very adaptability of the authoritative Scriptures that "allowed them to serve as authoritative texts within the Jewish community."[74]

Though the documentary hypothesis dominated biblical scholarship through much of the twentieth Century AD, it began receiving strong criticism during the latter part of the century. This hypothesis rests largely on two main assumptions of sources and their dating. Both of these areas are currently under scrutiny. First, the criteria for distinguishing the separate sources has been relegated as invalid and some see this as more of a unified document. Second, those who do still distinguish the four sources have questioned the dating previously assumed.

This skepticism was initially led by J. Van Seters, then later supported by scholars such as Erhard Blum, Baruch Levin (sometimes spelled Levine), Rolf Rendtorff, Thomas L. Thompson, and Roger Whybray. Though they disagree about the nature of the Pentateuch's composition, they do agree on

---

71. Wright, *God's People in God's Land*, 71.
72. Brueggemann, *Introduction to the OT*, 22.
73. Ibid., 9.
74. McDonald, *Biblical Canon*, 12.

the rejection of the Documentary Hypothesis based on dating the J source to the sixth century BC or later.[75] Unlike his predecessors, Van Seters argues that the only clear marker for different sources is the duplication of episodes such as that demonstrated in Genesis 12 and 20 or 15 and 17. He goes on to state that repetitions within the story are more likely literary style, rather than proof of assimilated material.[76] "He regards the P material essentially as a supplement to J and dates it to the postexilic period. He holds that chapter 14 is later still, and that Genesis reached its present form about 300 BC."[77] Continuing to argue a later date for Genesis in *Prologue to History*, Van Seters contemplates the primeval history contained in Genesis 1–11 and demonstrates how both Near Eastern and Greek mythology are incorporated in the narratives. Van Seters goes on to suggest that Israelites could have encountered these ideas as well as other Mesopotamian sources during their Babylonian exile.[78] He argues for a theory that is now referred to as Supplementary Model. In this, he believes that the Pentateuch was based on an original document, identified as J, composed during the seventh or sixth century. This document was then expanded and achieved its final form in the fifth century BC.[79]

Though Van Seters is acknowledged by scholars such as Blum and Levin, Gordon Wenham disagrees with his treatment of patriarchal narratives as well as the primeval history in Genesis. "The closest non-biblical parallels to this material come from the period 2000–1500 BC in Mesopotamia and it is most unlikely that these traditions could have been transmitted to Israel after the second millennium."[80]

Rolf Rendtorff also challenges the documentary hypothesis as well as Noth and Rad's methodology for form criticism. Though they affirm that oral traditions were eventually collected into literary sources, Rendtorff asserts that these stories remained short and independent until a single editor combined the separate blocks.[81] This theory is also referred to Fragmentary model and was also endorsed by Erhard Blum. The Pentateuch then became a much slower process of accumulation. Fragments, rather than documents were gathered, edited together, and perhaps later revised. Wenham summarizes Rendtorff's arguments when he states, "It must be conceded that

75. Wenham, "Pentateuchal Studies," 4.
76. Ibid., 5.
77. Ibid., 5.
78. Ibid.
79. Seters, *Prologue to History*, 310–11.
80. Wenham, "Pentateuchal Studies," 5.
81. Rendtorff, *Problem of the Process*, 113, 118.

we really do not possess reliable criteria for dating of the pentateuchal literature. Each dating of the pentateuchal 'sources' relies on purely hypothetical assumptions which in the long run have their continued existence because of the consensus of scholars."[82]

R. N. Whybray also argues against the validity of the documentary hypothesis in his book *The Making of the Pentateuch: A Methodological Study*, where he states that it fails to achieve the very objective it lays out.[83] He further points out that the documentary hypothesis holds that the original sources were non repetitious or contradictory yet in its reconstruction of the sources has made them both repetitious and contradictory. Whybray's second main objection is in the use of the divine names for God as signaling for source changes. He retorts that since this faith community used a variety of names for God, varied uses of these names should be expected in the literature and thus does not provide proof of multiple sources or editing. Finally, he states that repetition in the text was often a case for emphasis or other stylistic reasons and again, does not necessitate that editing has taken place.[84]

Though the documentary hypothesis is repeatedly challenged, it remains the starting point for modern Pentateuchal studies. It is through the documentary hypothesis that questions regarding anachronistic names and inclusion of pagan myths are answered. In spite of its problems, this theory gives direction and solutions for a variety of questions placed on the text that cannot be answered by naming Moses as the single author or even limiting him as the main author of the texts. Furthermore, biblical evidence for the collection of smaller literary units into single units occurs much earlier than Van Seters and Rendtorff allow for.

The importance of the above discussion begins the foundation for responding to the research question concerning the extent later editors are responsible for the material directly associated with pedagogy. The previously established studies discussed in this section are used as the basis for forming the supposition that the Pentateuch is the compilation of several authors and editors. In chapter 3, the role of later editors who emphasize pedagogy within the biblical texts is supported.

---

82. Wenham, "Pentateuchal Studies," 6.
83. Whybray, *Making of the Pentateuch*, 18.
84. Wenham, "Pentateuchal Studies," 7.

Authorship of the Deuteronomistic History

Similarly to the previous section, the importance of this discussion of the authorship of the Deuteronomistic History directly relates to the research question concerning the role of later biblical editors regarding pedagogy. Therefore, the previously established studies related to the authorship of the Deuteronomistic History are discussed. This becomes the basis for the supposition of later editors who inserted, rearranged, or emphasized pedagogical features related to the active learning model proposed by Fleming. Research in chapter 4 supports this.

The Deuteronomistic History refers to the canonized books, Joshua, Judges, 1–2 Samuel, and 1–2 Kings. This collection of texts is attributed to the same writer of Deuteronomy due to their similarities in writing style and theological concerns. Martin Noth advanced this hypothesis in the 1940s and it was later modified by Frank Moore Cross. Cross agreed with Noth's original concept but disagreed with his dates. Believing the writing of this historian occurred later. Susan Niditch affirms the arguments of Noth and Cross by distinguishing between two phases. The sixth century exilic historian who likely wrote large portions of Deuteronomy and took responsibility for editing the Torah together as a cohesive literary unit is referred to as Dtr2. The earlier seventh century historian, who is responsible for Joshua through 2 Kings, also revises the work of the Dtr. This historian is believed to have worked during the reformation of King Josiah and is referred to as Dtr1.[85]

This dual redaction is widely accepted, though not universally agreed upon. Over a century ago, Abraham Kuenen identified meticulous layers within the book of Kings which he observed as confirmation that some realities were no longer accurate for the post-exilic Israelite community. He attributes key phrases, such as the reoccurrence of "until this day," as strata that are affixed to the very structure of the book, a structure Kuenen attributes to a Deuteronomistic editor.[86] Kuenen's conclusion of a Deuteronomistic editor was later embraced by Julius Wellhausen and combined with Martin Noth's research to lay the foundation of Frank Moore Cross's theory of Dual Redaction of the Deuteronomistic History.[87]

Richard Nelson's suggestion of the main composition of the Deuteronomistic History occurring during the reign of Josiah and revised during the early exile is highly supported by his peers. Antony Campbell and Mark

---

85. Niditch, *Judges: A Commentary*, 10.

86. Kuenen, *Historisch-kritische Einleitung*, 1:90–91, cited in Geoghegan, "'Until This Day,'" 201.

87. Geoghegan, "Until this Day," 201.

O'Brien also allude to this hypothesis as they highlight the various sources and plausible redactions of the texts in their work, *Unfolding the Deuteronomistic History*. On the other hand, Jeffery Geoghegan is contentious of an exilic editor and favors the pre-exilic redaction of the Deuteronomistic History. Among these changes include a shift in focus from the temple and cultic reform to theodicy, identity, and restoration.[88] On the other hand, Nelson agrees with Geoghegan's argument for the pre-exilic use of the phrase, "until this day." Both Geoghegan and Nelson attribute the use of this phrase to a pre-exilic editor who incorporated his personal witness to the continued existence of authentic objects and locations described within the narrative accounts. Nelson states, "This phrase is incorporated into every source known to have been employed by the historian."[89] Nelson further asserts that the optimism toward the monarchy indicates pre-exilic editing. However, the numerous negative passages toward the monarchy belong to later transmitters of the Deuteronomistic History. This reality is completely neglected by Geoghegan during his insistence on a single pre-exilic editor. Among these pessimistic insertions are examples such as 1 Kgs 9:6–9, 2 Kgs 17:13–14 and 21:8–9.

Frank Moore Cross also supports the notion of a later exilic editor who edited and supplemented the Deuteronomistic History material. As his successors, Cross contends that the intention behind this final editing is to "Bring it up to date in the Exile, to record the fall of Jerusalem, and to reshape the history, with a minimum of reworking, into a document relevant to exiles for whom the bright expectations of the Josianic era were hopelessly past."[90]

Due to the lack of consensus surrounding the editorial phases of the Deuteronomistic History, this study uses Campbell and O'Brien's treatment of these texts which allow for the final form of the Deuteronomistic History to be a revision during the exilic period.[91] Campbell and O'Brien's publication pertaining to the sources contained within the Deuteronomistic History continues to be regarded highly among their peers. The general introduction offers a sound review of major trends in scholarship since the publications of Martin Noth. It is admitted that redaction criticism of the Deuteronomistic History is difficult due to similar language among the sources. Campbell and O'Brien are conservative in their approach and plainly state when textual evidence is too vague to adamantly determine

---

88. Nelson, "Double Redaction," 324.
89. Ibid., 326.
90. Cross, "Themes of the Book of Kings," 285.
91. Campbell and O'Brien, *Unfolding DH*, 13.

its source. With minor reservations, their study is highly respected among scholars. Interest in the Deuteronomistic History for this book revolves around the final form of these texts, rather than the stages of its process. Therefore, the discussion of the pedagogy of the Deuteronomistic History in part 3 will look at the editorial activity of the Deuteronomistic History without further concern or pinpointing which editor made the revision.

As previously stated, the final forms of the Pentateuch and Deuteronomistic History are a literary achievement operating through a long and complicated traditioning process. It was accomplished through the gathering, appropriating, and reshaping of narrative stories, legal documents, some of which existed outside of Israel's history. Though both written and oral material was included, it is important to recognize that the final forms of these documents have been extensively restructured and recontextualized.

The importance of the above discussion regarding the authorship of the Deuteronomistic History is the basis for responding to the research question concerning the extent that extent later editors are responsible for the material directly associated with pedagogy. The previously established studies discussed in this section are used to support the supposition of the final form of the Deuteronomistic History as the result of multiple editorial revisions. In parts 2 and 3, the role of later editors who emphasize pedagogy within the biblical texts is supported.

SUMMARY

Without a scholarly consensus concerning the various editorial phases of the Hebrew Bible, readers must be cognitive enough to not merely pile theory upon theory that continues to fall short of validity and proof. The more difficult of a reconstruction hypothesis, the more difficult it is to prove. Modern studies consistently insist on the later date of the sixth century BC as the time frame when the final form of the Pentateuch took shape and improvable speculations are discouraged. This is also valid for the ongoing discussions surrounding the editor and dual editor theories of the Deuteronomistic History.

As the scholarly community continues to debate the matters of form and source criticism, the key objective to maintain is the function of the Hebrew Bible as a whole. Though it is a compilation of books and sources, nonetheless the final literary form has a specific aim for an intended audience. William LaSor may have stated it best when he insists that the canonical shape of each book be respected and the concern of exegesis is prime over a rigid distinction between diverse literary sources.[92] He summarizes that the final form function of the Hebrew Bible is the diverse truth applicable to the faith communities who received it. "Thus the Pentateuch in its final form, by being set outside the Promised Land, was designed to bring its primary message to the Jewish exiles in Babylonia. The Hebrew Bible provides both a stable text and a flexible capacity for adaptation in its interpretation."[93]

The major characteristic of the Hebrew Bible is the communication passed on to each new generation that continues to provide sustenance and life to a stabilized text. The instruction preserved offers the guidance necessary to properly anchor the newer believers of the faith tradition into the heritage of the faith community. For this reason, it is incumbent that the research within this writing focus on the literary nature of this communication rather than seeking historical validity of the events described.

As discussed throughout this chapter, the stories contained in the Pentateuch and Deuteronomistic History continued to adapt as the faith community evolved. The transmission of sacred texts begins at an unknown date but becomes traceable by the second century BC when the oldest fragments began to survive to modern excavations. The faith communities identified particular narrative accounts that preserved the identity and understanding of their God, Yahweh. In this transmission process, the stories themselves endure an imaginative process. By this, the narratives are told and retold intergenerationally from older generations to the younger. The stories allow for modest transmission modifications to occur to clarify archaic expressions so that the younger generation could understand them. However, this is delicately balanced with a firm understanding that freelance alterations were unacceptable. Storytellers could not alter a tradition or the text in such a way that it became unrecognizable to the community. The necessity of community recognition stabilized the textual integrity at all stages of transmission. In this, two responsibilities are accounted for. First, as oral tradition becomes written text, it is formalized and stabilized. Newer Israelite stories and adapted material from other cultures are slowly grafted into the traditions of a present Israelite generation so that the younger generations will continue in the faith of their elder ancestors. Though accounts from pagan cultures are adapted into Israelite tradition, they are reimagined in such a way that they highlight the providence of sovereignty of Yahweh. Excerpts from pagan folklore are reconstructed to convey theological truth

---

92. Lasor, *Old Testament Survey*, 604.
93. Ibid.

of Israelite faith. The purpose of this record is theological revelation rather than historical record, though historicity is not necessarily violated.

Historical accounts are preserved, but this was secondary to the preservation of national identity and concepts of covenant, land, and religious cult. At the final stage of this process is a nation in Exile, struggling to maintain this heritage. Now that cultural and religious identity is on the line, the community once again uses its traditions and orders them in such a way that hope is once again identified. Similarly to the survivors of the Egyptian captivity who learned of their calling and covenant with Yahweh at Sinai, so the survivors of the Babylonian captivity, are called to remember who they are and the unignorable outward sign of circumcision that marks them as belonging to Yahweh. Though they are presently landless, they too hope for entrance into a land of Promise.

Along with theological themes, the Israelites also preserved native teaching techniques and pedagogy. These features then become the primary tools for preserving national, cultural, and religious identity. It is these basic features that storytelling was built upon as well as later wisdom writings. This precedent is further discussed in the following chapter. The research in the following chapters will also show, teaching techniques and pedagogy are purposefully integrated in the text and, at times, highlighted by later editors through purposed reordering of the text or editorial insertions to draw attention to significant events or evidence of religious locations. Given the ongoing discussion of authorship and dating of the Pentateuch and Deuteronomistic History, only the final form of the texts are discussed in the following chapters.

In order to respond to the research questions, this chapter focused on the literary approach of interpreting the Hebrew Bible because is more readily concentrates on details pertaining to the biblical texts such as locations, characters, and descriptions of events rather than a preoccupation with historical data that cannot be conclusively proven. The literary approach selected for this research facilitates the exploration of the presence of pedagogical features. This approach supports whether editors purposefully inserted or emphasized pedagogy within the Pentateuch and Deuteronomistic History. The studies discussed in this chapter are used as the foundation for parts 2 and 3, where the textual evidence that supports the extent that editors insert or draw attention to pedagogical features is discussed as well as how these features relate to Fleming's VARK learning theory and the larger conceptual framework of active learning.

Part Two

Pedagogy of the Pentateuch

Chapter 3

Pedagogy of Deuteronomy

INTRODUCTION

The preceding chapter discussed some of the previously established studies related to the prevalence of editors of the Hebrew Bible. This chapter will begin to address the informal instructional methods that can be observed in the Pentateuch as well as textual evidence for editors who either insert or emphasize pedagogical features for religious instruction. The data presented within this chapter will support that later editors purposefully include or bring attention to examples of visual and kinesthetic teaching methods for religious education.

    One's understanding of self, community, and religion must be communicated with the proceeding generation to avoid losing identity and relationship. Without this continual instruction, new generations must repeatedly re-learn the knowledge already gained from older generations. The religious community of Israel adamantly assumed the responsibility of educating itself with the intention of lasting for many generations to come. As the people of this nation made observations and identified weaknesses, they incorporated them into their teaching praxis. They observed chief, pivotal actions taking place and recorded them in such a way that these events would instruct future generations about their inheritance as a race and religion. Mythos (basic values of a people) and logos (divine word) thus come together in the education of a faith community. As Crenshaw explains, "This symbiosis of human effort and instinctual memory suggests that knowledge participates in the sacred."[1] Though not always explicit, this educational process is nonetheless present in the Pentateuch and serves as an infrastructure upon which to build further pedagogy. In addition to storytelling, the Pentateuch illustrates various types of pedagogy. This chapter will argue that the final editors of the Pentateuch purposed to gather the narratives in such a way that they demonstrate a particular means for teaching the religious expectations to later adherents of their faith community.

The collected literature of the Pentateuch depicts a compilation of narratives determined essential for portraying the wisdom, purpose, and instruction of Israel's God. Due to the richness of its content, the authors determined that it applied to every aspect of their lives as individuals and a society. This literature teaches the religious expectations and cultural normality associated with their religious ideals. Included in this literature are narratives that describe interaction between Yahweh and humanity. One of the earliest examples appears in Gen 2:7, where Yahweh breathes into Adam's nostrils and is observed as the Creator. By virtue of Yahweh placing Adam into the garden, Adam seems to understand his role is subservient to Yahweh's. The first noted point of communication between Yahweh and Adam is in Gen 2:16, where Yahweh instructs Adam on what can and cannot be eaten. The prohibition focuses on the penalty for violating this command rather than the rationale. The narrator, then, makes a conscious effort to focus the readers' attention on obedience to the instructions themselves. Readers must then assume that some type of communication took place between Adam and Eve, who is later created in verse 22. Since she came after Yahweh's initial instruction, it is plausible that Adam was responsible for communicating, or teaching, this command to Eve. A transmission of information occurs as a party, who did not participate in the initial experience, gains knowledge of the expectations pertaining to a particular command.

The Pentateuch offers didactic examples of instruction through the portrayal of events within its narratives. This is established through the command for the Israelites to teach later generations of its occurrence. Knowledge is gained from the memory of sayings and stories. The means by which the characters help others remember their religious and cultural obligations becomes part of an amassed series of narratives that demonstrate a strategic method of passing on information.

The writers and editors of the Hebrew Bible take the responsibility to record their events as well as assimilate stories from foreign nations to creatively integrate these actions in such a way that they are theologically retold in a manner that represents and glorifies Yahweh. These writers focus on

---

1. Crenshaw, *Education in Ancient Israel*, 27.

their basic knowledge of Yahweh, covenant, and law and incorporate these visions of reality together with the literary subtleties of individual and collective literary talent. Integrated with the writing process, is a commission to teach their children and surrounding nations. This act of pedagogical activity is also integrated into their literature.

In the examples that follow, it will be established that the Pentateuch's editors deliberately used particular events to provoke natural human curiosity. As the Israelites engaged in worship, their worship became a pedagogical tool for engagement of those who sought information about Israel's God. These events become the tools used to instruct others in the normative expectations of Yahweh's law within the faith community. Smaller narrative accounts are purposefully selected to develop a macro-narrative that models the means for instructing later groups. As instruction is received, a binding of the generations takes place where the reality of the older generation is defined for the younger generation.[2] The macro-narrative is the maximal narrative, derived from a compilation of smaller stories contained within a literary work.[3]

Some tension may arise with concluding a pedagogical function of the Pentateuch verses a didactic function of the Pentateuch. Pedagogy is the specific act or practical method of teaching. This term is previously defined within chapter 1. Didactic is the inclination to teach or having an ulterior motive to instruct. The didactic nature of the Hebrew Bible is amply covered by previously published scholars such as Charles Isbell[4] and Christoph Levin.[5] The didactic nature of the Hebrew Bible is emphatically endorsed; the writers and editors of this literature had a fundamental didactic agenda for their work. The argument here is that, not only was the Pentateuch didactic, but it also carries an additional pedagogical function and conveys a specified manner in which Israelite children, adults, and resident aliens were instructed.

Throughout this chapter, observation and analysis of the Pentateuch will demonstrate a biblical example of religious instruction through patterns and practices. Evidence exists, within the Pentateuch, of an instructional process or pedagogy. The examination of specific examples of instruction practiced as they developed through the Pentateuch shows a larger cohesive structure of pedagogy.

2. Brueggemann, *Creative Word*, 15.
3. Marguerat and Bourquin, *How to Read Bible Stories*, 34.
4. Isbell, *Function of Exodus Motifs*.
5. Levine, *Old Testament*.

This chapter is structured to systematically address each of the books in the Pentateuch. The events presented in Deuteronomy describe the Israelites on the plains of Moab, awaiting entrance into the land promised to them. The character, Moses, is unable to go further with them and therefore leaves final instructions for them to continue educating the later generations of Israelites. In addition to this, Deuteronomy includes some of the clearest passages relating to education. Because of these two factors, Deuteronomy was selected as an accepted starting point for presenting the data related to the exploration of the research questions. Genesis, Exodus, Leviticus, and Numbers will then follow in Canonical order. It is arguable that this chapter could have started with Genesis and built toward Deuteronomy. However, this would have weakened the overall impact of the data. As presented, the content will begin and end with strong evidence of active learning pedagogical tools integrated into the texts of the final form of the Pentateuch.

Before the appraisal on the descriptions of pedagogy in these books, the two covenants that prompt the need for religious instruction are briefly discussed. The desire to teach their religious traditions is deeply espoused within Israel's religious texts. Therefore, the relational covenants between Yahweh and Israel that preempt their desire to teach their religious ethos are examined.

Rationale for Israel's Attentiveness to Religious Instruction

Abrahamic Covenant

Before discussing *how* this nation instructed members of the community, the question arises of *why* it concerns itself with religious education. The notion of training younger generations, adults, and foreign nations as a means of exemplifying Yahweh occurs in Genesis 12 as Abram enters into covenant with Yahweh. In this pericope, Abram represents the nation of Israel that was to come from his "seed." Yahweh speaks, telling Abram that he is to go into a foreign land where Yahweh will bless him and make him a great nation.[6]

Since this word first comes solely to Abram, he is thus subtly charged with the responsibility of conveying the importance of this blessing. In some manner, the later "nation" that results from this covenant, must be taught the roots of their inherited blessing. A form of education must transpire. Intrinsic to this education is the method of instruction. The narrator must

---

6. Gen 12:1–3.

now use Abram to formulate a pedagogy to teach the impending nation about this epiphany.

The universal direction of Israel's covenant with Yahweh is highlighted through the repetitions of this promise. Abram hears this covenantal promise again in Gen 15:1–5, and a third time in Gen 17:1–8. At this point, Abram's name is changed to Abraham and he is circumcised as a visible sign of this covenant. Yahweh reinforces the covenant to Sarah in Gen 18:18 after she had laughed at the thought of bearing a child at her age. It is confirmed again to Abraham in Gen 22:18 after he nearly sacrifices his covenantal son, Isaac, on Yahweh's behalf. During a famine, Isaac is tempted to move to a more fertile area; Yahweh then appears to Isaac in Gen 26:2–5 and instructs him to remain in the land shown to his father, Abraham. Here, Yahweh assures Isaac that the covenant spoken to Abraham is still intact. This blessing is then repeated to Jacob in Gen 28:14 prior to him leaving his father, Isaac, to find a wife in Paddan Aram. It is also restated to the tribes of Israel in Deut 1:8 as they prepare to conquer Canaan and take possession of the land originally given to Abraham.

As David Gunn and Daniel Marguerat both explicitly express, the narrative world is a verbal construct where life is the language itself. "All sorts of meanings and messages are found in the network of a text: theological and ideological themes, subtleties and polemics, social structures, symbols, metaphors, allusions."[7] Specific words are selected for a text to form patterns and textual significance. Furthermore, Hebrew prose purposefully uses verbatim repetition of a "word, phrase, sentence or set of sentences, or even the recurrence of words falling into the same semantic range can function to structure the story, to create atmosphere, to construct a theme or a character, to emphasize a certain point to the reader, or to build suspense."[8] Both repetition and variance evoke the reader to consider the significance of the similarities and dissimilarities.[9]

Centered within this Abrahamic Covenant are the phrases, "I will bless you . . . and so you shall be a blessing," in Gen 12:2, and "I will bless those who bless you . . . and in you all the families of the earth will be blessed," in Gen 12:3. Each of these phrases is derived from בֶּרֶךְ (berek),[10] the Hebrew word for knee. The word, "blessing" בָּרַךְ (bārak)[11] means literally to kneel. Though בֶּרֶךְ (knee) is unrelated to בָּרַךְ (bless), there is association between

---

7. Gunn and Fewell, *Narrative in the Hebrew Bible*, 147.
8. Ibid., 148.
9. Ibid.
10. Harris et al., *TWOT*, 285a.
11. Ibid., 285.

kneeling and receiving a blessing.[12] It is an act of adoration or passive receipt of praise. Abram then takes it upon himself to deliberately communicate this instruction he had received from Yahweh. It is observed in Gen 12:7 that Abram immediately builds an altar at the location where Yahweh had appeared to him. Thus, action is given a religious affiliation within the narrative and a visible altar is used to "record" and remember a religious event that occurred in a specified location. This is later used as a means, or pedagogy, of retelling (teaching) the importance of this event to someone who did not experience it firsthand. This particular point is discussed further later in this work where the Genesis text is discussed.

Mosaic Covenant

Similarly to the Abrahamic Covenant, a second covenant transpires that imposes the responsibility for instruction to those who are regulated by its precepts. The Sinai Covenant or more commonly, Mosaic Covenant, not only infers the responsibility for instruction, but demands accountability and thus the absolute necessity of its full knowledge and compliance. This covenant takes place in Horeb on Mount Sinai immediately following the escape from Egypt in Exodus 19–24. Within this covenant, the newly established Israelite nation is called to obedience to Yahweh's instruction,[13] which they agree to do in 19:8 and 24:3. This particular covenant sets Israel apart from all other nations as a specially selected people chosen to work on Yahweh's behalf. The Mosaic Covenant is a blood covenant[14] and is equally as binding as the Abrahamic Covenant. The anchor for the Mosaic Covenant is Yahweh's law given in Exod 20:1–17.

The Mosaic Covenant differs drastically from other covenants given in the Hebrew Bible. Whereas the Noahic, Abrahamic, and Davidic covenants are not conditional on the recipients' actions, the blessings of the Mosaic Covenant are contingent on Israel's obedience to Yahweh's law. This feeds in to the retributive theology observed throughout the remainder of the Hebrew Bible. Influenced by retributive theology, the Israelites believe as long as they observe Yahweh's law and are obedient, Yahweh's blessing is extended to them. However, when they neglect Yahweh's law and are disobedient, this blessing is withheld, which results in the nation experiencing oppression from opposing nations. This is further explained to the nation in Deuteronomy 28. As a bilateral agreement, both Israel and Yahweh are

12. Ibid.
13. Exod 19:5.
14. Exod 24:5–8.

obligated to one another. Israel is to be a light for the nations separated from Yahweh. Yet, it is their responsibility to be holy as instructed by Yahweh so that others would know they worship Yahweh, the covenant-keeping God. Because of this responsibility, Israel becomes liable for instructing, not only its own national members but now the foreign nations as well.[15]

Unequivocally, Israel has a monumental responsibility in its relationship and service to Yahweh. It is ambitiously charged with the assignment to be a holy nation. As a result, members of this formulating faith community must take it upon themselves to identify with the law of their God. It must become intrinsic to their identity as a nation. As they possess this knowledge, they must prepare a pedagogy in which they can train each member of their nation. As they continue to produce children, they must also determine a means by which their children can be taught the laws of their God. Finally, if they are commanded to train the foreign nations surrounding them, then they must also formulate a means to do so.

DEUTERONOMY

Pedagogical examples are found throughout the entirety of the Pentateuch. However, the structure and emphasis of Deuteronomy lends itself to be a primary text for examining these pedagogical features. More specifically, texts from the Shema and later speeches in Deuteronomy 11 and 31 present clear instructions for adults to accept the responsibility for the religious training of their children. Deuteronomy also includes specific instructions for teaching adults in chapter 31 and resident aliens in chapter 1. Therefore, this chapter begins with the text of Deuteronomy so that these commands can be considered first, prior to the ongoing examples of pedagogy found in the remaining books of the Pentateuch.

Instruction to Children

The most prolific format for instruction observed in the Pentateuch is that of parents and grandparents to children and grandchildren. In an effort to ensure that future generations would faithfully adhere to the Mosaic covenant, parents are instructed to teach the precepts of Yahweh's law to their children. This command is observed in several different references throughout the Pentateuch, though the more explicit instructions to teach children are found in Deuteronomy. In consideration of its agenda, Deuteronomy could

---

15. Enns, *Moody Handbook*, 57–62.

be called a community compilation or community modified document. This is based on the argument for its stages of development that was described in the previous chapter of this book. Dennis Olson describes the book as a "catechesis"; for him it is "a foundational and ongoing teaching document necessitated by the reality of human death and the need to pass the faith on to another generation."[16] Deuteronomy establishes a concentrated concern on instruction, not just for the general audience of the Israelite community, but the two generations that existed during its primary editorial phases. The first is the emerging community that experiences the conquest of the Promised Land. The second is the exilic community awaiting reentrance into the Promised Land. In both accounts, large portions needed explicit training on the religious expectations of Yahweh. According to Birch, "Yet, for all the focus on teaching, the book's basic concern is more explicitly religious; the tradition is not simply to be taught but inwardly appropriated."[17] Therefore, the means for teaching, or pedagogy, is also included within this document so that the members of the faith community could obtain the essential practices by which they could correctly convey their faith.

One of the clearest accounts of parents commanded to instruct their children is found in Deut 4:9–10. Prior to this passage, the Israelites were instructed to go and take possession of the land given in the Abrahamic Covenant.[18] They are then reminded of their lack of faith the first time Yahweh brought them to the Land of Promise and the resulting punishment of wandering in the wilderness, waiting for the faithless generation to die.[19] Moses then reminds the people of the many battles they have fought and favorably won because Yahweh was fighting for them.[20] In Deut 3:28, Joshua is named as the leader who will succeed Moses. Immediately after this, Moses begins speaking to the Israelites, reminding them that they have already learned Yahweh's statutes and are now responsible for teaching others. Present in this, they are told:

> Only give heed to yourself and keep your soul diligently, so that you do not forget the things which your eyes have seen and they do not depart from your heart all the days of your life; but make them known to your sons and your grandsons. Remember the day you stood before the Lord your God at Horeb, when the Lord said to me, 'Assemble the people to Me, that I may let them

---

16. Olson, *Deuteronomy and the Death*, 6.
17. Birch et al., *Theological Introduction to the OT*, 149.
18. Deut 1:8.
19. Deut 1:19—2:15.
20. Deut 3:22.

hear My words so they may learn to fear Me all the days they live on the earth, and that they may teach their children."[21]

This passage begins with a warning to "give heed to yourself and keep your soul diligently." The abstract nature of Yahweh in the Israelite religion and the absence of a physical representation of Him imposes difficulty when most other existing religions had physical idols. Counteracting this imposition, Moses goes on to reiterate, "so that you do not forget the things which your eyes have seen." They had never literally *seen* their God but they had seen the effects of His actions. Events such as the Exodus from Egypt and provision in the wilderness offered observations of Yahweh's work on behalf of His people. Therefore, their "seeing" was part of their religious experience rather than a literal representation of Yahweh. Furthermore, this seeing brings knowledge through experience. The memory of these experiences became vital to their religious life. As Peter Craige explains, "Religious life did not consist, however, only in remembering the experience of God in the past; memory, rather, functioned in order to produce the continuing obedience to the law of God, which in turn would lead to the continuing experience of the presence and activity of God."[22] Thus, the Israelites were not only warned to remember these events, but they were commanded to teach them to the future generations.

The phrase used in Deut 4:9, "make them known," begins a strong theme of educating the children that runs throughout Deuteronomy.[23] This theme derives from the context of covenant and the promise of land that began with Abraham, continued through Moses, and now extends to the future generations of Israelites. Yet this Abrahamic covenant merges with the stipulations set up in the Mosaic covenant where longevity in the land is contingent of obedience to Yahweh's commands. Thus forgetfulness is a premise for failure. It is vital that the Israelites not only remember their experiences, but ensure their children are thoroughly taught about Yahweh's actions within the history of their ancestors.[24] "Make them known" comes from יָדַע (yada'), "a root used in every stem and expresses a multitude of shades of knowledge gained by the senses."[25] This word means to teach, literally by showing. This word is different from the word used in verse 5, where Moses states that he has "taught" the Israelites. "Taught" in verse 5

---

21. Deut 4:9–10.
22. Craigie, *Book of Deuteronomy*, 133.
23. Deut 6:7, 20; 11:19; 31:13; 32:46.
24. Craige, *Book of Deuteronomy*, 133.
25. Harris et al., *TWOT*, 848.

is לָמַד (lamad)²⁶ and signifies a verbal instruction and is usually used in connection with learning Yahweh's laws. יָדַע on the other hand, denotes learning through observation and experience, generally through the senses. This word is used in Gen 18:21 in connection with knowing through seeing, knowing through hearing in Exod 3:7, and knowing through observation or experience in Gen 42:11. In addition to cognitive knowing, this verb also represents experiential knowledge as detected in its use in Gen 4:1, referencing Adam knowing or experiencing his wife Eve in a sexual encounter. It is likewise used in Gen 39:6 to demonstrate Potipher's lack of concern, or experience, of the events in his home.²⁷

The inherent intrinsic use of this word demonstrates tangible ascertaining, or learning through touch. Though the semantic range of יָדַע allows for instruction through verbal communication through a shared language, it more often reflects tangible experiential learning. Therefore, when this verb is used in Deut 4:9, it carries the basic lesson that Israel is to learn to fear and revere Yahweh through experiential learning, or more popularly known as active learning. Additionally, the audience is reminded to remember the things which their eyes have seen. This points to the experiences that this elder generation had already incurred. They themselves acquired information and made determinations in their faith toward Yahweh based on events they had seen with their eyes and thus experienced firsthand. As Deut 4:9 further depicts, it is through these tangible experiences that they are to likewise allow their sons and grandsons to experience by "making them known" (יָדַע). This directly references the event at Horeb where they experienced the theophany of Yahweh and his self-revelation in physical form.²⁸ Thus verse 9 implies that these Israelite parents and grandparents are to determine a means of relaying their reception of the Mosaic Covenant and Yahweh's revelation to their children and grandchildren.

This event is further described in verse 11, when they are called to remember physically standing at the base of Mt. Sinai where they saw the smoke with fire and heard the voice of Yahweh. A connection is necessitated for the parents to offer expressions or tangible memories of these experiences to their children. The existence of the nation depends on the education of the younger generation, since ignorance or blatant disregard of the covenant at Sinai produces communal paralysis from Yahweh. The retribution theology that was formed from the Mosaic covenant necessitated their need to teach younger generations how to obey the religious laws as well as

---

26. Ibid., 1116.
27. Vine et al., *Vine's Expository Dictionary*.
28. Exod 19:9—20:19.

the importance for obedience. The adults are particularly told to teach their children of the events experienced at Horeb. This location name is used interchangeably with Sinai. Therefore, Moses is referencing the Mosaic Covenant. The "only" in verse 9 links this emphasis of memory and teaching to the preceding blessings in verse 8. If they fail in this reflection and instruction, they will likely lose the greatness of their national identity.[29] This notion of educating one's children is strongly presented in Deuteronomy[30] and is important in the context of the covenant. The promise of land proposed to Abram was forwarded to Moses and is still a continued expectation for the Israelite community discussed in Deuteronomy. However, the fruition of the covenant and fullness of blessing is contingent upon the obedience of the people. It is therefore imperative that the adult community resolutely educate their children in the experiences of the elders so that the memory can pass to the proceeding generation.[31]

As this pericope moves into verse 14, Moses insists that he has diligently taught this current audience the statutes and judgments so that the Israelites were able to perform them. The word "teach" here is the same verb used in verse 5, לָמַד (lamad), carrying a strong implication of goading in the educational process of an oral instruction. This now goes further as Moses depicts the outcome of this learning as the performance of these laws. It was not merely the acquirement of information that was sought but knowledge that produced physical action. The object of this instruction is oriented to the future obedience within the Promised Land. As Moses speaks to a post-Sinai generation of Israelites, his address to the people is itself an example of the assertion given in verse 9 to teach their children and grandchildren anticipates the future tasks of teaching the laws and religious practices. This same idea is also reflected in Deut 4:1, where the expectation for action follows the knowledge gained by the Israelites from Moses. Following the theophany received at Horeb, Moses was told to "teach them the statutes and the laws."[32] The purpose of this initial instruction was to prepare the Israelites for their future relationship contained within this new Mosaic Covenant and observance of these laws within the land promised to them. The recollection of the teaching in Moses' present task anticipates, once again, the teaching of statutes and laws prior to the Israelites' entry into the Promised Land. As Craigie explains, "Thus the address of Moses was itself an example, on a grand scale, of the injunction given in verse 9 to teach the

---

29. Ridderbos, *Deuteronomy*, 84.
30. Cf. v. 10; 6:7, 20ff.; 11:19; 32:46.
31. Craigie, *Book of Deuteronomy*, 133.
32. Exod 18:20.

children and grandchildren, for the people now standing before him were a post-Sinai generation."³³

Several concepts are operative in Deut 4:1–14, beginning with the imperative command to instruct their children. Two different verbs for "teach" are used in reference to the parents and grandparents teaching their children and grandchildren, יָדַע and לָמַד. The former verb represents a tangible experience and the latter an audible instruction or reinforcement of their skill.

This is further emphasized through the translation of the Septuagint (LXX). In Deut 4:9, the LXX translates יָדַע to συμβιβάζω, which carries the notion of concluding in one's mind or to demonstrate.³⁴ This latter definition adheres more intimately with the rendering of יָדַע as experiential learning. Likewise, לָמַד in 4:10 is translated as μανθάνω (learn) and διδάσκω (teach). Μανθάνω is usually understood as the acquisition of knowledge, though it may also refer to knowledge gained from experience.³⁵ Διδάσκω is the act of instruction or explanation through a verbal exchange.³⁶

Second, a possible pattern is presented for the instruction of adults. As observed in Deut 4:3 and 10, the adult community is instructed to remember an event previously experienced. First, in verse 10, they reflect on their encounter with Yahweh in Horeb when the Mosaic Covenant is initiated. The record of this event is located in Exod 19:9—20:19. Here, prior to receiving instruction, the adults first saw smoke and heard the voice of Yahweh.³⁷ Thus their first exposure to the Mosaic law encompassed more than mere verbal instruction, but instead included multiple senses that deepened its impact to their memories. It is only after this experiential learning that לָמַד (*lamad*) later occurs. This same paradigm is also observed in Deut 4:3 as Moses references the Israelites' experience at Baal-peor. He uses this incident of the deaths of twenty-four thousand Israelites, who died as a result of sinning against Yahweh, to remind them that their lives depend on their obedience to their God.³⁸ They are required to remember their experiential learning from their own history to retain prominence of the oral instruction they have also received. The Israelites who leave Egypt in the Exodus event are given several experiences that come prior to oral instruction from Yahweh through Moses. These instances of learning vicariously through

---

33. Craigie, *Book of Deuteronomy*, 134.
34. Strong, *Biblesoft's New Exhaustive Strong's*, G4822.
35. Ibid., G3129.
36. Ibid., G1321.
37. Exod 19:9, 18–19.
38. Num 25:1–9.

vivid events are then later reinforced verbally through oral instruction from Moses.

The two phrases in Deut 4:10, "so they may learn" and "they may teach their children," both use the root word לָמַד (*lamad*).[39] Therefore, the expression used in Deut 4:5–10 is that this adult community, who has already received verbal instruction from Moses as well as personal observation of Yahweh during their desert excursion is now endowed with the obligation to model this information before their children and grandchildren so that they can likewise learn these same truths. As will be discussed, unique, observable (יָדַע) learning opportunities were continuously presented to the children that provided occasions for parents to verbally (לָמַד) instruct their children in Yahweh's law, using a similar pattern to that which Moses has just modeled and reiterated in 4:14.

A second example of parents explicitly told to instruct their children is located in Deut 6:7. Here two different words are used for this instruction, שָׁנַן (*shanon*) and דָּבַר (*dabar*). The former of these literally means to sharpen. It is most commonly used in the reference to sharpening a weapon but is also used metaphorically for sharpening one's tongue, as demonstrated in Ps 7:12. The piel, or intensive stem, is used for this verb in Deut 6:7 and is therefore properly translated as diligent instruction.[40] In its context, it refers to diligent instruction in the word of Yahweh. This word more readily enforces the manner in which children were to be taught which was earnestly and frequently. Parents are to repeat and repeatedly iterate. Similarly the sharpening of a weapon that requires consistent and continual friction, testimonies of Yahweh must be diligently taught in an effective manner by the parent to the child. In its simplest definition, דָּבַר on the other hand, means to speak.[41] The commands of the covenant were to be the subject of conversations and permeate every sphere life.[42] In and of itself, Deut 6:7 does not offer further explanation of the manner or pedagogy in which this teaching took place. Instead, it emphasizes the notion that Yahweh's commands were not to be merely enforced but woven into the practicality of everyday living, training, and conversation.

Yet, as the pericope continues, another observation is noted. That is, at some point, the children are provoked to ask questions of their parents, who are then required to answer. This is evidenced in Deut 6:20–21. Here, the parental responsibility to pass the religious stories of the faith community

---

39. Harris et al., *TWOT*, 1116.
40. Ibid., 2422.
41. Ibid., 399.
42. Craigie, *Book of Deuteronomy*, 170.

on to the children is reiterated. The cause of these questions seems to come from actions that the children have observed from their parents as well as the rest of the Israelite community. Verses 10–19 indicate that the blessings of Yahweh would be upon Israel as the nation obeyed the precepts of the Shema and commands from the Mosaic Covenant. The children would then monitor the obedience of their community to the commands, testimonies, and precepts of Yahweh.[43] In response, they are roused to question their parents as to why these actions take place. The availability of questions and answers between children and parents demonstrates a working relationship between these individuals. The positive nature of the question identifies that the child has some type of introductory comprehension of covenant and has already received preliminary instruction in obedience. As he or she observes the actions of the parents and likely the surrounding Israelite community, the child demonstrates a desire to know the meaning and significance of the commandments that shape daily life.

This question then necessitates an answer from the parents and an opportunity in which the children actively sought the information from their parents. The child's question is similar to that seen in Exod 13:14, but focuses on the meaning of the commandments. As shown in Deut 6:21–24, the answer given to a child's request for information contains a condensed account of the principle elements for the Israelite faith. They first recount the previous situation of the vassals of the Egyptian pharaoh.[44] Second, they recited the revelation of God in history from their experiences of the deliverance at Egypt, Yahweh's judgment and how he dealt with Egypt,[45] and the purpose of Yahweh as he granted the Israelites the Promised Land.[46] The fifth, and final, aspect of this answer contains an emphasis on Yahweh's law and the condition of obedience and reverence that it accentuates.[47] This pattern is also observable within the Psalms, demonstrating that the recitation of the religious story likely originated within the worship community.[48] More specifically, the parents respond to their children's questions by repeating their own visual and tangible experiences they personally encountered[49] as well

---

43. Deut 6:17.
44. Deut 6:21.
45. Deut 6:22.
46. Deut 6:23.
47. Craigie, *Book of Deuteronomy*, 175.
48. Pss 78, 105, 106.
49. Deut 6:21–23.

as the later commands or oral instruction they received.[50] As a result of this instruction, they too continued in the obedience of Yahweh's commands.[51]

This question and answer format is important as it embodies the motif of teaching the next generation and preparation for the "days to come." Through this, the pattern from these verses indicates the parents observed and were then orally instructed, which then caused an active demonstration of the information learned. Likewise, the children observed before requesting oral instruction that then resulted again in an active demonstration of the information learned. As previously noted from Deut 4:14, an intentional instructional method, or pedagogy, is formulated for the articulation of religious expectations. In the same manner in which God revealed himself to the adult community through both action and word, the replication of the covenant theology is taught through both action and word. The expected outcome of following this pedagogy is stated in verse 25, "It will be righteousness for us if we are careful to observe all this commandment . . ." In this context, righteousness describes the relationship with their covenant God. Thus, the answer to the son's question focuses on the appropriate relationship between humanity and Yahweh and the fruit of that relationship.[52]

Deut 6:4 is repeated in 11:19, though a different word is used in place of שָׁנַן (shanon). Here, לָמַד is once again used as a general reference to the activity of teaching and the role of parents instructing their children. As before, the LXX also translates this using διδάσκω. Deut 11:19 maintains the word דָּבַר (dabar) from 6:4. The LXX renders this from λαλέω, which is also a clear word for speech.

The rationale for parents instructing their children is specified earlier in chapter 11. Beginning in verse two, the audience is told that since their children had not personally experienced the actions of Yahweh, the parents are obligated to express these stories to their children.[53] Those who were privileged to gain firsthand experience of Yahweh's power are obligated to recount their testimony. The parents are pressed to recount their conception of the redemptive acts they witnessed. In doing so, the parent communicates the critical importance of the event to the child. As a result, the child gains perspective of the profound religious connection between the actions of Yahweh and the relationship developed with His people. These events are

---

50. Deut 6:24.
51. Deut 6:25.
52. Craigie, *Book of Deuteronomy*, 175.
53. Deut 11:2–7.

then assimilated into the child's own memory along with their significance for religious affiliation and community heritage.⁵⁴

Beyond this notion of testimony, Deuteronomy 6–11 both promote systematic religious instruction from parents to children in an informal setting of the natural occurrences and daily patterns of living. In a similar manner in which language and cultural norms are exposed to children, religious ideals are also expected to be repeated within the home for the purpose of training one's children.

The final observation of the command for instructing children is located in Deut 31:11–13. However, this passage carries a small variance in that there is not a specific reference of the parent teaching the child. Instead, the children are assembled along with the adult community to hear the law read in their presence. However, the word translated to "children" in the NASB comes from טַף (taph), which may also refer to the collective family that includes members younger in age.⁵⁵ The LXX more readily refers specifically to children by using ἔκγονος. This is further clarified in verse 13 where בֵּן (ben) is used in reference to the younger audience.

Several observable factors are present within these verses. First, the law is read so that the audience may "hear." This is שָׁמַע (shama') and means to hear intelligently and implies obedience to that which is heard.⁵⁶ The purpose of this hearing is again לָמַד, to become an expert or skilled in the knowledge gained. Additionally, this reading of the law and obedient hearing causes moral reverence. Two more effects of this reading are שָׁמַר (shamar) and עָשָׂה ('asah). The former carries a dominant meaning of guarding or watching over but may also refer to keeping or obeying.⁵⁷ The latter is to accomplish or apply.⁵⁸

The outcome or purpose for this is further demonstrated in verse 13. The children (בֵּן) who had not yet ascertained this may also hear intelligently (שָׁמַע) and become skillful (לָמַד) and likewise morally revere Yahweh. Within this act of listening intelligently is the inherent expectation of obedience, obedience that would then perpetuate the above cycle of instruction.

The context of these statements is that Moses is handing over the written instructions to the Levites who are then to read it in the presence of the people every seven years at the feast of Tabernacles/Booths when they

---

54. Lowe, "You are My Witnesses," 49.
55. Strong, *Biblesoft's New Exhaustive Strong's*, H2945.
56. Harris et al., *TWOT*, 2412.
57. Ibid., 2274f.
58. Ibid., 1708–9.

appeared before the Lord.[59] It is entrusted to the priests and elders as the spiritual leaders of the faith community.[60] This reading is closely connected to the festival itself. Its purpose was to refresh the heart and quicken the adoration of Yahweh's commands. Though this takes place initially, in Deuteronomy, prior to a major conquest, the described renewal would be educational with the purpose of the people assembling to hear and learn.[61] Consequently, the audience not only includes the men from the community, but women and children as well, who were permitted to hear and learn the words of their God. Here connection between the festival and oral hearing is established. The Feast of Tabernacles is one of three pilgrimage festivals for the Israelite community. The pedagogy of this festival is fully discussed with its instructions in Leviticus. For now, it is important to point out that this appeal within Deuteronomy 31 for the septennial reading of the law is established within the context of a festival. Within this, the noted pedagogical pattern of visual observation alongside audible instructions is demonstrated.

Instruction to Adults

The pedagogy for adults differs somewhat from that of children. Whereas the children often received instruction within an environment that employs multiple sensory contributions, such as sight, touch, and sound, the adults did not always receive instruction using multiple sensory modes. On the contrary, the vast majority of instruction to Israelite adults takes place in a "general assembly" where they audibly receive instruction. Three main words were used to describe these settings: קָהָל (kahal), מִקְרָא (mikara'), and עֲצָרָה ('atsarah). The first of these words is most often used as a general term of a multitude or local congregation of people. The Hebrew Bible contains 123 occurrences of קָהָל.[62] מִקְרָא is used more specifically within the Pentateuch. Though this word occurs twenty-three times within the Hebrew Bible, twenty of these are contained within the Pentateuch. This word more specifically refers to a public meeting.[63] However, it must be observed that each time מִקְרָא appears within the Pentateuch, it is used in conjunction with the word holy so that it is translated as "holy assembly" or "holy convocation." This is altered in the three uses of the word outside the Pentateuch.

59. Lev 23:34.
60. Deut 31:9.
61. Deut 31:12.
62. Harris et al., *TWOT*, 1991a.
63. Ibid., 2063d.

After Deuteronomy, מִקְרָא is no longer described as "holy."[64] The final word, עֲצָרָה, only occurs three times within the Hebrew Bible.[65] All three of these are found within the Pentateuch. This word specifically refers to an assembly on a festival or holy day.[66]

Deuteronomy only uses the terms קָהָל (*Kahal*) and עֲצָרָה (*'Atsarah*). The use of עֲצָרָה in Deut 16:8 was previously discussed. It is translated as "solemn assembly" and is in the context of Moses' instructions to the adults to annually observe the Passover, where they will eat unleavened bread for six days, followed by the solemn assembly to the Lord, where they will refrain from work. In this setting, עֲצָרָה refers to an observance that the Israelites are to keep rather than a reference for a means of instruction. The most specific examples, within Deuteronomy, of the manner in which the adult Israelites were instructed are the references to Moses' address to the Israelites such as those found in Deut 1:1, 3; 4:45; and 31:1. It demonstrates that the Israelite adults often gathered for audible instruction that was not, in that setting, accompanied by visual stimulant.

Reinforcing this notion is the word repeatedly used as Moses appeals to his people to "hear" the words he is proclaiming. This repetition is found in 5:1; 6:3-4; 9:1; and 20:3. In 31:9-13, the Levitical priests are then charged with the responsibility to read the Torah, or Pentateuch, before the people every seven years at the Feast of Booths. The literal phrase used in 31:9 is "this law" (תּוֹרָה) (*Torah*). It is arguable as to what constitutes "torah" at this point in the literary development. The LXX confirms the focus as the book of the law with its translation, νομου τουτου εις βιβλιον (*nomou toutou ein biblion*). This existence of a written law has been presupposed since Deut 17:18 but has not previously been explicitly described as authored by Moses. The implication is not that he has authored the work in its entirety but rather that this writing was a part of a series of events that led to the established recorded covenant.[67] In the context, the covenant reaffirmed in Moab in Deut 29:1 is likely in view. The pluperfect verb tense "Moses had written" better portrays this assessment.[68] The Mosaic Covenant given at Horeb, where the commandments are recorded on stone tablets, and this Moab covenant, where Moses has recorded the words, are thus paralleled by an author/editor. The Levitical priests who were charged with the tablets within the ark are also charged with keeping the "Book of the Law." Yet the

---

64. Neh 8:8; Isa 1:13, 4:5.
65. Lev 23:36; Num 29:35; Deut 16:8.
66. Harris et al., *TWOT*, 1675c.
67. McConville, *Apollos OT Commentary*, 439.
68. Sonnet, *Book within the Book*, 137–38.

addition of "and all the elders of Israel" further secures the responsibility for teaching and implementing the law by focusing the readers' attention on the command to read the law in the presence of the people during the feast of Tabernacles.[69] This command highlights the critical link between hearing the words bound within the Pentateuch and a sustained religious future for the Israelite community. The close connection of reading the law and festival gives the adult community an opportunity to associate the imagery and actions of the festival with the blessing of the law. The festival itself stands as a commemorative testimony of prior events and blessings that resulted from obedience. The newer audience, who may not have experienced the original event, can now relate a religious experience (festival), to oral instruction (law) and determine the benefit of the blessing of the law that comes from obedience and celebrate it within their experiences as demonstrated by David in Ps 19:8–15. They can then conclude that future obedience to this same law will end in future blessing. This is further established by the acceptance of women and children, in addition to the male community, at the reading of the law.[70] As Kevin Vanhoozer explains, "A similar relationship between reading/hearing the words of 'this torah' and future well-being is expressed in [Deut] 17:19, where Moses explicitly charges future kings to read the torah so that they may embody the covenant fidelity he has espouses in the plains of Moab."[71]

The final instruction regarding the training of the adults is located in Deut 31:19, where Yahweh tells Moses to write a song that is to be taught to the adults, who are then responsible for teaching it to the later generations. Both Campbell and Friedman agree that this final appeal to instruction is likely a part of the sixth century revision.[72] Not only this, but the appeal to add another element to assist with the memorization of the content further suggests that the sixth century editors were particularly concerned with the suggested pedagogy defined within the Pentateuch. The content of the song itself is found in chapter 32. Its central theme is the apostasy of Israel which results in God's judgment. It emphasizes the inconsistent religious adherence of the nation in contrast to Yahweh's steadfast attention. Here again is a suggested example of the final authors bringing material together to present a pedagogical document that teaches its readers distinct features of Israelite culture and religious heritage.

69. McConville, *Apollos OT Commentary*, 437.
70. Deut 31:12.
71. Vanhoozer, *Is There a Meaning*, 72.
72. Campbell and O'Brien, *Unfolding DH*, 92; Friedman, *Bible with Sources*, 359.

Instruction to Resident Aliens

Interlaced with the material that addresses the instructional format for children and adults is the pedagogy related to resident aliens. There are several types of aliens referenced throughout the Pentateuch and specifically Deuteronomy. The first is found in Deut 1:16, where גֵּר (ger) is used to describe those who are temporary inhabitants within the land. This term can also refer to non-Israelites who were new to the area.[73] This word is used dominantly within Deuteronomy when referencing non-Israelites who live among the Israelite people. Another form of "stranger" is referenced in Deut 32:16. Here, זוּר (zuwr)[74] is used to describe the proprietors of the various gods that Israel would lust after once they resided in the Promised Land. The few times this word is used in Deuteronomy, it is always in connection to foreign (strange) gods or those who possess these gods. Therefore, this word will not be discussed further in relation to pedagogy. נָכְרִי (nokriy) is used five times in Deuteronomy.[75] This term is used to differentiate the Israelites from the non-Israelites with respect to actions that the Israelites are restricted from because of the distinction that Yahweh has placed upon them. Rather than stating a restriction, Deut 29:22 uses this word when discussing those not under the Mosaic Covenant who inquire of the observable consequences for those who neglect the laws of Yahweh. As previously stated, the prevalent word used in the Deuteronomy text is גֵּר. Some non-Israelites were given certain rights in accordance to their dedication to Israel's God, Yahweh. Additionally, some were even extended the privilege of participating in some aspects of Israelite worship. This participation then necessitated some time of instruction to inform these foreigners of the importance of worshipping Yahweh and the attributes associated with this worship. Other specific privileges extended to resident foreigners included: the provision of food,[76] participation in the Sabbath rest,[77] participation in festivals,[78] and the ability to offer burnt offerings.[79] However, the availability of this participation is often limited to those who choose to obey Israelite

---

73. Harris et al., *TWOT*, 330a.
74. Ibid., 541.
75. Ibid., 1368c.
76. Deut 20:21–22.
77. Exod 20:10; 23:12; Deut 5:14.
78. Deut 16:11–15.
79. Num 15:14–16.

law.⁸⁰ He is even granted the opportunity to participate in the ongoing religious instruction of their children during the septennial reading of the law.⁸¹

One of the first Deuteronomic verses that subtly documents this instruction is 4:6. Here, the Israelites are told to keep the commands of Yahweh so that other people would see the wisdom of the Israelites and perceive their prominence. The requirements of the law are placed within an international context using a vocabulary reminiscent of the expectations found within the Wisdom Literature (notably, Proverbs, Job, and Ecclesiastes). The point of this statement is not to make a systematic connection between the Torah and Wisdom. The "people" (אַם) are likely the non-Israelites who are on the verge of being driven from the homes in Canaan. Furthermore, the repeated term "great nation" in 4:6 and 4:7 distinguishes the Israelites whom Yahweh has called "great" and the other nations who make unsupported claims of this same title.⁸² The admiration acquired from surrounding nations results from their acknowledgement that no other nation can be called "great" in the same sense as Israel.⁸³ As verse 6 describes, Israel's greatness is not observable in the same way that countries such as Egypt or Babylon were viewed. Israel would not be known for its wealth or military prestige. Instead, it would be known for its wisdom and discernment, a direct product of its obedience to the laws of their God.⁸⁴

Though the context of Deut 4:6–7 indicates the instructions to Israelite adults for compliance to the Mosaic law, it also addresses a secondary audience of non-Israelites. Rather than direct instruction, this passage relates information gained through visual observation of action and outcome from the Israelites. Through this observation, the distinct relationship specified in verse 7 is learned. The established relationship through covenant with Yahweh further distinguishes Israel from its neighbors.⁸⁵ The clear connections between obedience to the law and outcome of covenant relationship are described in verse 8 and will be observable by those that surround the Israelite faith community. Thus, a subtle witness takes effect in which foreigners gain understanding of the Israelite God and make a connection between law, relationship, and greatness.

It is further evident that non-Israelites participated in the oral recitation of the law and instructions every sabbatical year during the Feast

---

80. Lev 16:29; 17:8.
81. Deut 31:12–13.
82. McConville, *Apollos OT Commentary*, 104.
83. Ridderbos, *Deuteronomy*, 83.
84. Craigie, *Book of Deuteronomy*, 131.
85. Ibid.

of Booths, as demonstrated in Deut 32:12. It is important to note that this ceremony took place at the sanctuary where both the written law and tablets containing the Sinai law were kept. This commemorative event was used to educate the people. It served as a memory renewal for the elder generation and a point of novel instruction for younger or recent converts into the faith community.[86]

Nothing is stated about who is responsible for reading the law. It is plausible that it was a member of the Levitical tribe or elder of the nation based on their reference in verse 9. Ridderbos notes the interesting use of singular "you" in the command, "you shall read this law." He further notes that this is more suitably idiomatically rendered "the law is to be read."[87] Also ambiguous within this command is whether this occasion constituted special obligation to appear at this festival. The purpose of this septennial instruction is to further advocate the general aim of instruction articulated in Deut 6:6–9 and "build the law into the worshipping life of the community in perpetuity, so that those who have not previously 'known' (13) may not fail to do so."[88]

The narrative setting of this instruction to foreigners in Deuteronomy 32 therefore demonstrates that they participated in the Feast of Booths, where they were able to observe the Israelite's temporary living arrangements within the booths and likely hear the rationale and connection to the wilderness sojourn. They then could combine this visual observation with the reading of the law and further connect the affiliation between Yahweh's providence to His covenant and the expectations therein. Similarly to the Israelite children, who receive their introduction to the event and its historical significance, these foreigners are also introduced to concepts and stories that distinguish the heritage of Israelite faith. They too begin to share the ideals of this faith community as the instruction is passed from one generation to the next or from one nation to another.

Material relating to commands for parents to train their own children in pertinent religious affairs and historic events is found largely in Deuteronomy. The exception is found with the specific texts in Exodus that pertain to instructions for the Passover.

According to Friedman, the passages discussed above from Deuteronomy 4, 6, 11 and 31 all derive from the Dtr1 text. This is the material from the original Deuteronomistic history formed during the reign of King Josiah. On the other hand, Exod 12:24–26 is excerpted from E, as is 13:8,

---

86. Ibid., 371.
87. Ridderbos, *Deuteronomy*, 275.
88. McConville, *Apollos OT Commentary*, 439.

14. This would then pose a later date for these passages during the interlude of the existence of the northern kingdom before its fall to the Assyrians. It is therefore considered that the Dtr2 artisan from the exilic period was not directly responsible for recording these specific text selections.

The repetitious theme of learning through experiential learning, illustrated in Deuteronomy, parallels Fleming's description of learning through kinesthetic experience. Within Deuteronomy, the characters are held responsible for remembering their experiences and instructions from Moses in order to pass these religious traditions on to their children. The word used in this context is יָדַע (*yada'*), meaning "make them known" and carries the connotation of learning through experience. Additionally, the characters are told to respond to questions with a condensed account of principle factors for their faith as illustrated in Deut 6:21–24. The expected outcome for teaching children was found in Deut 31:13. Children are to observe the actions of their faith community (visual) and witness the resulting blessing. They then also hear the accounts (aural) that produced the faith in their elders so that they would likewise morally revere Yahweh, become obedient, and thus likewise also experience his blessing (kinesthetic). Their obedience to his laws then perpetuates the cycle of instruction for later generations. The adult faith adherents were not to merely tell of Yahweh's blessings as the result of obedience, they were to model it. In doing so, the younger faith adherents see and experience the religious ethos for themselves.

Additionally, Fleming's VARK learning theory is represented in the pedagogy of Deuteronomy through the description of pneumonic devices such as the song (aural) described in Deuteronomy 31:19 and kinesthetic learning illustrated in the participation of the Feast of Booths that precedes the oral reading of the law described in Deuteronomy 31. These examples offered from Deuteronomy support that the pedagogy illustrated reflects the active learning theory of visual, aural, and kinesthetic learning documented by Neil Fleming. The examples that follow will continue to support this as a strong pedagogical theme throughout the entirety of the Pentateuch.

Chapter 4

Genesis

From the Pentateuch, Genesis includes the least number of examples of pedagogy. However, it does include specific examples that continue to support the pattern for active learning that coincides with Fleming's VARK learning theory.

INSTRUCTION TO CHILDREN

The research completed for this chapter concluded that there are no specific references for the instruction of children within the book of Genesis. There are neither explicit instructions for elders to teach children, nor are there any narratives that demonstrate the education of children. That said, it is observable that proceeding generations do express their knowledge of religious adherence to a belief in Yahweh. This is more readily observed throughout the narratives of the Patriarchal history that begins in Genesis 12. Though readers are not told how Abraham teaches Isaac, it is apparent that some type of religious training has taken place in chapter 24. Here, Abraham makes a pledge with Eliezer that a bride for Isaac would be selected from the women of the territory of Abraham's descendants. Eliezer complies with Abraham's request and selects Rebekah, Abraham's niece from the city of Nahor. As Eliezer and Rebekah return, they find Isaac meditating. The text is ambiguous as to the purpose and subject of this meditation. Though meditation on his belief in Yahweh is likely, it remains speculative and thus will not be addressed further. A more specific example of learned faith occurs in Gen 26:2. Here, Isaac receives a vision and warning from Yahweh. Furthermore, the Abrahamic Covenant is repeated by Yahweh to Isaac. The outcome of this episode is Isaac's obedience to not travel further into Egypt but remain in the area of Gerar. This scene demonstrates a pre-formed religious identity with Yahweh. As previously stated, the text does not mention when or how Abraham taught Isaac about his knowledge of Yahweh. Yet the observable condition that Isaac demonstrates an understanding of Yahweh's existence points to a conclusion that, at some point, this religious training transpired.

A similar demonstration occurs in Genesis 27. This narrative encompasses a scene of deception of Rebekah and Jacob toward Isaac. In the midst of stealing Esau's blessing from Isaac, Jacob disguises himself as Esau. When Isaac questions how quickly Jacob was able to hunt wild game and bring it to him to eat, Jacob responds, "Because the Lord your God caused it to happen to me."[1] This statement relates that Jacob identifies the God of his father. A more prominent example is noted in Gen 28:10–17. Here, Yahweh speaks to Jacob in a dream and refers to himself as the God of Jacob's ancestors. As with Isaac, the Abrahamic Covenant is reaffirmed to Jacob. When Jacob awakens, he confirms his belief in Yahweh and refers to the location as the house of God and gate of heaven.[2] Once again, the Genesis narratives do not account for how Jacob acquired knowledge of Yahweh. However, it is evident from these scenes that religious training has occurred. The knowledge gained by his father and grandfather has been passed on to Jacob.

While Genesis does not describe any specific pedagogy for training children, it does allude to the fact that educating one's children is a reoccurring factor throughout the recorded generations of the patriarchal history through the lineage of the Abrahamic Covenant. It is a perplexing obscurity as to why the pedagogy of children is readily described and even commanded within the other four books of the Pentateuch but omitted from Genesis. It is further interesting that the initial command to teach children does not occur until the description of the eighth plague in Exod 10:2 and its connection to the Passover in Exod 14:24. It appears that this commemorative event of the birth of Israel as its own nation, upon its release from slavery, initiates the emphasis of training children regarding the mighty acts of Yahweh[3] and his work as their deliverer.[4] Since this is not the theological focus of Genesis, the emphasis of remembering and reteaching is excluded.

---

1. Gen 27:20.
2. Gen 28:17.
3. Exod 10:2.
4. Exod 14:24.

INSTRUCTION TO ADULTS

However, Genesis does describe kinesthetic learning taking place within the Israelite adult community. One of the first observable instances occurs in Genesis 17. Within this pericope, Abram is receiving a theophany where he is told that Yahweh will establish a covenant with him and his descendants. All who adhere to this covenant are to be circumcised in the flesh of the foreskin. Commitment to this act is established as a sign of remembrance of the covenant made between Yahweh and Abram, as stated in verse 11. This action is to be carried out on all male children, including the descendants of Abram as well as any servants who are a part of his household. In obedience to this command, Abraham has all of the male servants, their children, and his own son, Ishmael, circumcised that same day as seen in verses 26 and 27. This action, along with the instructions he received, would commemorate the material learned through this event. Thus, action is joined with the audible transmission of instructions.

Source critics are nearly unanimous in their identification of the promise to Abraham contained in chapter 17 as representative of the P source while 16 more accurately reflects the vocabulary consistent with J. Within the chapter 17 narrative, the language of verses 6 and 20 assimilates Abraham's fruitfulness with the command for Adam's fruitfulness in Gen 1:28. Thus, Abraham is presented as the bearer of what was intended in creation. Furthermore, he is purposefully situated in a trajectory of promise as this narrative connects him to the lineage of David, promise of future kings,[5] and "eternal" promise.[6] This text situates Abraham as an assurance of a fundamental relationship between Yahweh and His people through the statement "I will be their God" in verse 8.[7]

> This is a promise more fundamental than even the land. While the action is singularly unilateral and talks only of God's commitment to Abraham, the formula clearly presumes the unspoken counter-theme, 'You shall be my people' (Cf. Exod 6:2–7 for the full formula of P. . . . It is evident that this formula became crucial for Israel . . . precisely in the sixth century exile when normal external supports were collapsing.[8]

Present within this text is the change in Abram's name that occurs in 17:5. Here, Abram's promise of descendants is universalized to "father of many."

---

5. Gen 17:6, 16, 20.
6. Gen 17:7–8, 13, 19.
7. Brueggemann, *Genesis*, 153.
8. Ibid., 154.

Introduced closely with this is the custom for circumcision. Abraham's experience with God moves more specifically to his affiliation with adherents to this faith tradition and custom. Circumcision becomes the seal of trust. Eleven verses are devoted to this inaugural event, elevating its central importance to this pericope.

This tangible mark becomes a witness to identify those in covenantal relationship with Yahweh. It solidifies this union of faith for a formulating faith community. As demonstrated, Genesis 17 permits a reflection of the significance of visual and kinesthetic religious practice and symbolism within the teaching practices of the faith community. As Abram, now Abraham, conveys his expectation of a son from Sarah, a decisive moment of instruction inevitably takes place as to how he can expect such a preposterous outcome. Connected to this instruction, is an event that would undoubtedly solidify the instruction through the experience of circumcision. While evidence exists for circumcision beyond the Israelite culture, in exile, circumcision of later adherents of Yahwistic faith helped give identity to those who belonged to this heritage and distinguish them from the "outsiders" of Babylon.[9]

Though the covenant with Abraham is arguably the strongest recurring mention of covenant in Genesis, it is not the first mentioned. Preceding the Abrahamic covenant is the Noahic covenant that begins in Genesis 6. Here, the reader is introduced to the term בְּרִת (*berit*), covenant, in verse 18. Its use here expresses a relationship or agreement.[10] Scholars debate the intended covenant mentioned here. The notion that this covenant in chapter 6 references the Abrahamic or Mosaic covenant, established much later in the metanarrative, is not natural to this text. The immediate context goes on to mention the expectation of Noah's entrance into the ark and is strongly connected to a "lasting covenant" at the conclusion of the narrative account. This is further supported by the characteristics of source P and its emphasis on "lasting covenant."[11] The purpose of this covenant is to establish an agreement that Yahweh would spare Noah and seven members of his family when He destroyed the rest of humanity. Noah's salvation is contingent on his belief and obedience to Yahweh's instructions.

The narrator presents Noah as the main character moving the plot forward. To him, the covenant is announced. J describes Noah as finding

---

9. Ibid., 154–55.
10. Harris et al., *TWOT*, 282a.
11. Aalders, *Genesis*, 165.

favor[12] while P plainly states, "I will establish my covenant."[13] The narrator purposefully draws attention to the personal character of Noah as a conduit between creation and creator, where an alternative outcome becomes plausible.[14] He models faith that has not yet been presented within the Genesis narrative.

Also established within this narrative is the pathos of Yahweh. Genesis 6:6 describes Him as grieved (עָצַב, 'atsab).[15] Thus, the judgment rendered to humanity is not a product of his anger, but rather a saddened heart. The "pain" he had originally conferred on the woman in 3:16 is now the affliction of Yahweh Himself. His response to the sins of humanity is not indignation but rather brokenness.[16]

The conclusion of this narrative offers the hearers of this story an opportunity to connect its details and moral to a visual symbol of its account. As this covenant is mentioned again in chapter 9, it is now closely connected to the symbolism. It begins with a blessing pronounced by Yahweh to Noah and his family in verse 7. The inclusion of a sign for this covenant begins in verse 12 as an ongoing reminder and assurance of this promise. Regardless of whether or not the rainbow existed prior to its acknowledgement in Genesis 9, it is used by the editors of the text as a visual religious symbol to remind its adherents of a moral shaping story within their tradition. The first established covenant is represented by a visual symbol. Upon the sighting of this phenomenon, elder members of this faith community are presented with an opportunity to remind younger adherents of a man's faith that brought salvation and a grieving God who preserves his relationship with an elect people.

The narratives compiled in Genesis 6–9 are a combination of the J and P documents. These documents are separable by the different references to the deity. The J flood account refers to Yahweh by name, whereas the P document uses the generic title, God. Genesis 6 begins with J; beginning in verse 9, a portion of the P document is infused but preceded by a quick introduction of the material using the editor's formula, "These are the records of . . ."[17] This formula is used again in 10:1.

Contrasting endings are noted between the J and P accounts. The outcome of the sacrifices offered in J's document in 8:20–22 is exceptionally

---

12. Gen 6:8.
13. Gen 6:18.
14. Brueggemann, *Genesis*, 79.
15. Harris et al., *TWOT*, 1666.
16. Brueggemann, *Genesis*, 77.
17. Friedman, *Bible with Sources*, 42.

different from that of P. Here, readers are merely told that ground will no longer be cursed on account of humanity, an echo from Genesis 2. However, this message was "said in Yahweh's heart." The characters themselves are not told of this outcome. Instead, they merely leave their sacrifices and began to farm the ground. The establishment of the covenant in 9:8 occurs within the P portion of the combined narrative. The expectation stated in verses 1 and 7 to "be fruitful and multiply" is an unmistakable reiteration of the blessing established in Gen 1:28. The strong theological implication of verses 12 and 13 affirms Yahweh's commitment to humanity.[18] Instead of a silent change of lifted curse, the editors have chosen to leave the readers with a final, audible blessing and visual representation of Yahweh's promise.

Within the Hebrew Bible, sacred pillars are often associated with idolatry. Moreover, the Israelites are forbidden to erect them[19] and are instructed to destroy existing sites.[20] However, Jacob erects a sacred pillar at Bethel,[21] Moses erects twelve pillars at the base of Mt. Sinai,[22] and Joshua erects a pillar at Shechem.[23] Given the above mentioned sites and the absence of any textual data that demonstrates adverse reactions from Yahweh toward these particular sites, it is reasonable to suggest that the abhorrence of sacred pillars is directed only to those connected with idolatry. Robert Alter further addresses the contradiction of the Patriarchs erecting altars and the specific instruction to refrain from this practice in Deut 16:22. Alter asserts that the development of the pillars as a Canaanite practice led to Yahweh's hatred of them and thus the restriction placed in Deuteronomy, which was not asserted during the practice of the Patriarchs.[24]

Twice, Jacob is recorded as erecting a sacred pillar at Bethel. The first instance occurs in Gen 28:18–22. Here, Jacob is on his way to Paddan Aram to seek a wife. Along the way, Yahweh speaks to him. In order to mark the occasion, he uses the rock he had slept on to complete the pillar as a monument for the location where Yahweh had spoken and promised Jacob land and a multitude of offspring. A second pillar is erected at Bethel in Gen 35:14 by Jacob. As in chapter 28, the pillar is not built until after Yahweh speaks to Jacob. Following the blessing spoken to Jacob by Yahweh, Jacob

---

18. Campbell and O'Brien, *Sources of the Pentateuch*, 26.
19. Deut 16:22.
20. Deut 12:3, Hos 10:1–2.
21. Gen 28:18.
22. Exod 24:4.
23. Josh 24:26.
24. Alter, *Five Books of Moses*, 962.

first builds an altar and then builds a sacred pillar. Unlike the previous account, oil is poured on the pillar described in Genesis 35.

A similar construction is described in Genesis 31. Here, a covenant is made between Laban and Jacob as Jacob prepares to leave the territory of Laban with Laban's daughters, who have been taken as wives for Jacob. As the covenant is made, Jacob sets up a stone as a pillar. Following this, the two gathered additional stones to form a mound as a "witness" or a testament of the new covenant established between the two men. Specifically, the pillar and mound of stones were to be a reminder for both men. In the event that either journeyed toward the other with malicious intentions, they were to pass by these two landmarks and remember their covenant with one another at Mizpah.[25]

All three of these accounts point toward the use of visual reminders of verbal accounts. The pillars made at Bethel represent a reminder for Jacob of the blessing spoken to him by Yahweh at that location. Similarly, the pillar and mound of stones at Mizpah remind both Jacob and Laban of their verbal agreement to bring no further harm to each other. Alter points out the additional significance for the pillar at Mizpah. The repetition and rhetorical composition of Laban's speech clearly characterize the binding terms of the treaty. This narrative further serves as a record of origination within political history as the designation of an international border.[26] Though it is not specifically stated, in connection with these narratives, the pillars likely stood as monuments where participants could return to remember the original purpose or intent of the pillar. As in these accounts, they were fixed, visual reminders of an event that transpired at that location. It is plausible that these were used to recount to the story of the original event to later passersby, similarly to what is demonstrated with the mound of stones positioned after the crossing of the Jordan river as the Israelites enter into Canaan. Within the narrative of Joshua 4, Yahweh instructs the Israelites to gather stones from the bottom of the Jordan and stack them as a monument at Gilgal. Here, the established pattern is repeated. The stacked stones would provoke their children to inquire of the purpose of the stones, thereby presenting parents with an opportunity to retell the story of the mighty and merciful acts of Yahweh as they crossed the Jordan and previous ancestors had crossed the Red Sea.[27] The inherent purpose of the stones at Gilgal is to connect an oral story with a visual reminder of its occurrence. It is likely that the stones at Mizpah and Bethel serve a similar purpose. Concern for

---

25. Gen 31:52.
26. Alter, *Five Books of Moses*, 175.
27. Josh 4:21–24.

the educational process is intrinsic within these accounts. Interest for the unknown serves to evoke a teachable moment where dialogue is offered to connect the object of curiosity (i.e., a pillar of stones) to its religious significance.

The use of stones piled as a memorial continues further into the Deuteronomistic History. Three instances of Samuel's erection of stones pillars occur in 1 Samuel. The first occurs in 1 Sam 4:1 when the Israelites camp at Ebenezer. Ebenezer is a transliteration from אֶבֶן הָעֵזֶר (`*Even Hatsezer*), which means, "stone of help." This particular memorial marks the site, north of Jerusalem, where Israel is defeated by the Philistines. This memorial is mentioned again in 1 Sam 5:1. A different stone memorial is mentioned in 1 Sam 7:12. This site is also built by Samuel and is also named Ebenezer. The reuse of this name indicates the reversal of the events occurring in 4:1. This time, since the people of Israel have recommitted themselves to Yahweh, they are given favor and, with their God's help, gain victory of the Philistines. Once again, the pillar is utilized as a visual reminder of religious significance. Obedience to God's laws determines whether or not their God will allow them to gain control over their enemies. The two sites of Ebenezer mark both sides of this religious understanding. One marks their site of loss due to religious disobedience; the second site marks the site of their victory, due to religious obedience. As before, a visual marker aids in their remembrance of these events as well as offers an opportunity to teach this religious lesson to those who inquire.

SUMMARY

Though infrequent, Genesis includes multiple pedagogical examples of active learning such as the description of the visual reminder of the Noahic covenant and the construction of pillars as visual reminders of locations where religious experiences occurred, as described in Genesis 28. Kinesthetic learning accompanies Abraham's oral instructions of his Covenant in Genesis 17. This particular example offers reoccurring teaching opportunities as it is repeated for the ongoing generations. It also acts as a visual reminder for those who have accepted the obligation of the covenant. Here, the pattern of visual and/or kinesthetic pedagogy is used in conjunction with oral instruction. This correlates with Fleming's learning theory of visual, aural, and kinesthetic learning styles that are incorporated in the larger conceptual framework of active learning.

Chapter 5

Exodus

SIMILAR TO THE PREVIOUSLY discussed literature of Deuteronomy, Exodus also contains explicit examples of parents instructed to teach their children the elements of their religious faith. Active learning is repeatedly utilized as the main teaching technique for the religious instruction of children, adults, and resident foreigners.

INSTRUCTION TO CHILDREN

A prime example is located in 10:1–2, where Yahweh speaks to Moses, strengthening his faith, by telling him that the hardening of Pharaoh's heart was the result of Yahweh's involvement so that Moses could tell his own children and grandchildren how Yahweh made a mockery of the Egyptians in order for the Israelites to know the supremacy of their God. Within this context, Moses is used as a representative for all of the Israelites. Therefore, the command for Moses to tell his children is related as a commission for all Israelite parents to retell this event to their children and grandchildren. Pss 78:43–53 and 105:23–38 narrate how this account was retold to the later generations. יָדַע (*yada*) is used in verse 2, "that you may know." Thus, experiential learning is used in connection with the retelling of this event. However, particular to this passage, יָדַע is not used with a description of any visual or kinesthetic events within the immediate context of the word. Friedman and Campbell disagree on the source for this section. Friedman attributes Exod 10:1–2 to E while Campbell follows Noth and attributes it to J. Bénédicte Lemmelign, arguing the literary criticism of the Plague narratives extensively, concludes that Exod 7:14—11:10 is composed of multiple text fragments. Lemmelign presents the argument that 10:2 is a later expansion of the Samaritan Pentateuch[1] to the original narrative in order to demonstrate that it was the command of Yahweh that brings the results of 10:3–6. She points out the reference to Aaron with verbs in plural form beginning in 10:3 that represent a linguistic change from 10:2.[2] Lemmelign also contends that "the results of one specific study cannot be taken as decisive or final."[3] Edgar Kellenberger, in a review of Lemmelign's research, compliments her detailed focus to the specified text and importance to the scholarly community. However, he also attests to inconsistency in the textual witness. Kellenberger states, "in most instances concrete manuscripts form the foundation of this study, but for the LXX the eclectic text of the Göttingen edition is used. This limitation restricts Lemmelijn's critical remarks (on p.215) about an eclectic text which did not exist in antiquity."[4] While it is acknowledged that Exod 10:2 does seem to interrupt the thought of verses one and three, it is not enough to conclude that it was intentionally placed for the purpose of pedagogy. Instead, it is possible that the expansion was asserted to convey the expectation that the religious function of plague narratives was to be communicated with later generations. With limited, expanded, scholarship on this specific text, it is difficult to ascertain whether Lemmelijn is correct in her assertion of the expansion of 10:2. If it is an inclusion from the SamP4Q material, as she argues, then it is probable that it was edited in with the E collection of narratives, thus validating Friedman's position that Exodus 10 is from E with repeated refrains in 9:35; 10:20; and 10:27 from R with a final insertion of R in 11:9–10.

The command to teach their children, "that they may know that I am Lord," is clearly expressed in 10:2. Verses 1–2 form an addendum to the previous statement from 9:16, "But indeed, for this reason I have allowed you to remain, in order to show you My power and in order to proclaim My name through all the earth." Here, the text indicates the primary purpose of the plagues is for the Egyptians, as well as the Israelites, to recognize the supremacy of Yahweh. Though the context of 10:1–2 does not describe a visual or kinesthetic opportunity, when it is used in connection with 9:16, the plagues are a visual presentation for the original audience. The impact and religious implication gained by the original audience is then to be repeated to the proceeding generations. As noted earlier, there is no altar or specific event mentioned in chapter 10 that will connect with the plagues

1. Specifically, SamP4Q.
2. Lemmelijn, *Plague of Texts*, 204.
3. Ibid., 117.
4. Kellenberger, Review of *Plague of Texts*.

and provoke questions from the later generations. As discussed later, the Passover celebration likely served in this capacity, particularly with its association with the inaugural Passover and the tenth plague on Egypt recorded in Exodus 11.

Festivals

In addition to the direct instructions to teach their children within the book of Exodus, Israelite parents are given specific cases or times when their children should be taught. These are recorded within the descriptions of the main religious festivals.

Children were invited to participate in the religious festivals of Israel's faith community. This included holy days such as Passover, Pentecost, and Feast of Booths. This is supported by statements such as Exod 13:14, where the parents are instructed to answer the questions of the children who are present during the ceremony. Moreover, the parents are told to purposely include their children in the observation of ordinances.[5] This participation was purposefully interwoven within these events and is observable in several areas. As portrayed in the literature, three of the festivals required all the males of Israel to travel to the Temple in Jerusalem.[6] These included: The Feast of Unleavened Bread, The Feast of Pentecost, and The Feast of Booths.

According to Harris, the Hebrew designation of festival is the word חג (khag or hag) which originally implied a led chorus and processional around a shrine or altar. It was later used as a reference to the specific religious festivals that corresponded with pilgrimage to Jerusalem, listed above.[7]

Passover

The Passover is a festival that is repeatedly discussed within the Pentateuch. Our discussion here will begin with Exod 12:24–26. Prior to this passage, Exodus has described all ten signs, or plagues, given to the Egyptians. In conjunction with the tenth and final sign, the first Passover feast is observed in the first pericope of chapter 12. The Feast of Unleavened bread is then discussed in 12:14–22 and is then followed by the command in 12:24–26 that the Israelites are to observe these events (Passover and Feast of Unleavened bread) annually forever as an observable reminder for the Israelites

---

5. Exod 11:24.
6. Exod 23:14–19.
7. Harris et al., *TWOT*, 2282.

and their children. They are also told to be ready to teach their children when they ask questions about the observation of this event. When this happens, the older generation of parents and grandparents are to testify to their children concerning Yahweh's goodness to Israel.

The celebration of Passover would have provided several teachable opportunities to describe Israel's past oppression under the Egyptians as well as Yahweh's deliverance of the Israelites from Egypt. Additionally, Yahweh's character would likewise be revealed through the retelling of this event through the symbolism embedded within the annual commemoration of the event. The name alone, פֶּסַח (*pesach*) means to pass over or through as a means of mercy or sparing. The mere name of this event gives insight into its distinct pedagogical use. Some believe its name derives from its root word פֶּסַח (*pesach*) as a reference to passing through the Red Sea. Philo supports this in his use of διαβατήρια as does Gregory of Nazianzus, who uses διάβασις. Others argue that the true sense of this word is found in Exod 12:27, where it clearly implies a leaping over rather than passing through.[8]

This event is celebrated on the fourteenth day of Nissan, and the event is the first annual religious festival on the Jewish calendar. Four days prior, the head of each household is to select the paschal (Passover) yearling lamb or goat. Some believe the four-day headway is in recognition of the four generations that had elapsed since the Israelites had come to Egypt. This animal would then be killed on the eve of the Passover and its blood painted on the doorposts and lintel using a hyssop. This made it obvious to others who passed by which homes were celebrating the event. The slaughtering and eating of this animal was the introductory celebration for this event.

There are a few key references for instruction within the Exodus 12 text. The first is located in verse 3 where Yahweh directs Moses to "tell" the entire community of the initial Passover. The word used here is דָּבַר (*dabar*). It is a common verb that means to tell in relation to informing the hearers; it is instruction through declaration.[9] Moses is commanded to stand before the whole community in order to instruct them in the details for this event. In its entirety, the community would have included men, women, and children.

Moses then tells the community that every year thereafter they will celebrate this event again. Furthermore, they were to hold a public meeting on the first and seventh day of the celebration. The word translated as "sacred

---

8. McClintock and Strong, *McClintock and Strong Encyclopedia*.

9. Strong, *Biblesoft's New Exhaustive Strong's*, H1696. Cf. Harris et al., *TWOT*, 1696.

assembly" in the NASB comes from מִקְרָא (*miqra'*).[10] It is a somewhat rare word that only occurs twenty-three times in the entire Hebrew Bible. מִקְרָא comes from the root קָרָא (*qara'*), which means to call out or to recite.[11] In the case of its usage in מִקְרָא, the reading is intended for a specific audience and is intended to elicit a specific response or a calling to a specific task, as it is demonstrated in Exod 2:7 when the maidservant of Pharaoh's daughter is sent to "summon" (קָרָא) a nurse. Nothing further describes the public meetings within the context of Exod 12:16. However, מִקְרָא is used in Neh 8:8, where it refers to a "reading" of the law that likely included an explanation of its meaning. This word is used exclusively for religious convocations. It may refer to a weekly Sabbath as used in Lev 23:2, but it is more commonly used for special convocation Sabbaths. For example, the Passover and Feast of Tabernacles were opened and closed with special convocation Sabbaths.[12] Given the context of its root, קָרָא, and the purpose for which this sacred assembly met, it is plausible to infer that the instructions given by Yahweh concerning the Passover were recorded and then orally read and explained during these annual celebrations. This becomes even more plausible given the instructions that occur in verses 24–27.

Beginning in verse 24, the Israelite community is instructed to "observe these instructions." The word "observe" is translated from שָׁמַר (*shamar*). As stated earlier, it carries a dominant meaning of guarding or watching over but may also refer to keeping or obeying.[13] The basic idea of its root is to take great care over. It can express careful attention to the obligations of a command, as seen with its use in Exod 20:6 and Lev 18:26. In these two verses, as with its context of Exod 12:24, it highlights perfunctory compliance with Yahweh's commands.

The same word is used in verse 25 for "observe this ceremony." Once again, שָׁמַר is used. However, an interesting change occurs for the word translated in English as "ceremony." Instead of the expected מִקְרָא (*miqra'*) that was used in verse 16 for "sacred assembly," a different word is introduced, עֲבֹדָה (*'abodah*). This word means to labor or serve. It is used to describe laboring for an agricultural harvest[14] as well as constructing the tabernacle.[15] When עֲבֹדָה is used in connection with service to Yahweh, it is in response to obedience, as demonstrated in the bringing of sacrifices in Josh 22:27.

---

10. Harris et al., *TWOT*, 2063d.
11. Ibid., 2063.
12. Ibid., 2063d.
13. Ibid., 2414.
14. Exod 1:14.
15. Exod 35:25.

The LXX translates this word as λατρία, which better describes the thought as divine service or worship.[16] This is different from the LXX translation of "assembly" in Exod 12:16, where κληθησεαι from καλέω is used. Καλέω is a far different idea with its reference to calling aloud or summoning.[17] This is evidenced in texts such as Matt 20:8; 22:39; and Luke 19:13, where it clearly refers to a summons before a crowd.

The audience is offered an important directive for instructing their children in Exod 12:26. The text first carries the expectation that the children will be provoked to ask questions as they take part in this annual celebration. Specifically, the parents are told that their children will likely ask about the significance of the ceremony itself. The parents are then told to be prepared to answer their children in verse 27, where it states that they are to "tell them, 'It is a Passover sacrifice to the Lord who passed over the houses of the sons of Israel in Egypt when He smote the Egyptians, but spared our homes.'" The word "tell" is אָמַר ('amar), which is a broad term that allows for some liberty in its translation. Some of its variances that could fit the given text include: say, report, answer, boast, and declare.[18] The statement is recorded two more times in Exod 13:8 and 14. In verse 13:8, a new word for "tell" is introduced. Here, the word נָגַד (nagad) is used. The simple definition of this word is to explain. It has a clear designation of communication by word of mouth.[19] However, in verse 14, אָמַר ('amar) is used.

Once again, a pattern becomes evident. The pedagogy for children represented in Exod 12:1–28 shows that the children will first actively participate in a festival. Through this engaged activity, questions surface which are directed toward their parents. *After* the child asks a question, the parent then begins to teach the child about the particular ceremony and the historical event that prompted the memorial. A tangible, kinesthetic environment produces an opportunity for verbal instruction between the parent and child to take place.

The memorial of the Passover supper helps to preserve the story of the Exodus. After the inaugural event, Israel goes on to enter and conquer the Promised Land, where it would be easy for the people to settle into new homes and forget this great act of Yahweh. The annual observance of Passover offers Jewish parents another opportunity to teach their children the meaning of their national independence and the deliverance of Yahweh. Here, as well as in 13:8, 14–15; and Deut 6:20–25, the Pentateuch anticipates

---

16. Strong, *Biblesoft's New Exhaustive Strong's*, G2999.
17. Ibid., G2753.
18. Harris et al., *TWOT*, 118.
19. Ibid., 1289.

the inquisition of children regarding commemorative events as well as the meaning of laws.[20] The adult generation is charged with the responsibility to share the heritage of their religious faith with their children. The adult Israelites are to use these questions as opportunities to teach the children to be loyal to Yahweh based on what he has done on their behalf. This principle can also be observed in Pss 34:11; 78:1–7; and 145:4.

Feast of Unleavened Bread

The seven days following the Passover are celebrated as the Feast of Unleavened Bread. The instructions for this event are recorded in Exod 12:15–20. Observance of this event included the removal of yeast from the home and the participation in a public assembly. Because the instructions for this celebration are so closely connected with instructions for Passover, there are not any new details pertaining to the teaching aspects of this event that have not already been discussed in the preceding Passover festival.

INSTRUCTION TO ADULTS

Exodus also contains references for a kinesthetic teaching environment that involves the adult Israelite population in Exod 11:7. Here, Yahweh tells Moses about the tenth plague that will occur against the Egyptians. He then states, in verse 7, that the purpose of this plague is, "that you may understand how the Lord makes a distinction between Egypt and Israel." The word translated as "understand" in the NASB is the Hebrew word, יָדַע (yada). Primarily, this word means to ascertain by seeing.[21] Therefore, based on this verse, Moses would fully recognize or learn the distinction between Israel and Egypt by the visual education that would occur during the tenth plague on Egypt. Though this is stated to Moses, the fact that substantial turmoil continually disconcerted Egypt while the Hebrew people remained unscathed was nevertheless observable by all who occupied the area. All of the Israelites, adults and children, may have observed and concluded that they were distinct from Egypt. This plague is followed by the Passover event as previously discussed. It is important to note that the instructions for how to proceed with the Passover were orally given to the adults. In Exod 12:3, דָּבַר (dabar) emphasizes the audible command given to the adult Israelite

---

20. Josh 4:21–24.
21. Harris et al., *TWOT*, 848.

community. As a result of receiving these instructions, the people are then expected to actively engage in obedience to these instructions.

As separate events, it appears that the instructions for the Passover come without any initial sensory contribution. In other words, there are no visual or physical stimuli that precede the instructions for the Passover to emphasize its importance. A closer look at the activity of the editor, however, produces a different perspective. According to Friedman's analysis of the text, Exod 11:1–8 is derived from the Elohist source, while Exod 12:1 begins a section derived from the Priestly source. Connecting these two accounts are the inserted verses, Exod 11:9–10 from the editor. Thus, by bridging these two accounts, the pattern again resumes with a visual impression that precedes the oral instruction.

This combination of accounts occurs again in Exodus 19–20. Here, according to Friedman, several of the literary sources are operable. The setting for Exodus 19 describes the adult Israelites encamped around Mt. Sinai where they are able to visually see a mass of cloud. The purpose of this cloud is stated in verse 9; it is for the Israelite community to hear (שָׁמַע, *shama'*) the words of Yahweh to Moses. שָׁמַע means literally to hear but may also adequately mean to witness. Due to the combination of visual representation and audible representation, "witness" seems an adequate translation of this word in Exod 19:9. As the passage continues, the pattern of visual and auditory learning persists. In verses 10 and 14, the people are told that they must consecrate themselves. This is then followed by the instructions to wash their garments as an act of obedience and the symbolism of their lesser status in the presence of Yahweh. The two days of unusual preparation that bridged the inward preparation for meeting with Yahweh are paralleled in the outward action of cleanliness. This once again solidifies the significance of the instructions about to occur. Furthermore, the people are restricted from touching the mountain that Yahweh has descended upon. Disobedience for this command would result in death. Following the consecration, the Israelites then witness both fire and smoke upon the mountain as well as the sound of horns. Following this scene, Moses returns from the presence of Yahweh on the mountain to the encamped people at its base. Upon his return, he audibly speaks the Ten Commandments to the people. Much of Exodus 19 is a combination of the J and E sources, whereas the Commandments in chapter 20 originate with an extra-biblical source. Campbell affirms that the Decalogue was not likely original to the narratives but was a later insertion.[22] The transition between chapters 19 and 20 is the inserted sentence from a later editor in 20:1. When the audible instructions for the

---

22. Campbell and O'Brien, *Sources of the Pentateuch*, 188.

Commandments are placed against the witnessed events in chapter 19, the pattern of visual stimulation preceding audible instruction is again present to the reader.

Exodus 31:13–17 discusses the Sabbath as a sign of the covenant immediately following the revelation at Sinai. Here, the character Moses is instructed to speak (דְּבַר) to the Israelites and tell them that the observation of the Sabbath is a sign, or pledge, between Yahweh and the people that they would know that it was their God who sanctified them. The word, "know" in verse 13 is יָדַע, previously discussed as the word used for knowledge gained by experience. This command is previously recorded in Exod 20:11 and repeated Exod 35:1–3 and again in the Decalogue of Deuteronomy.[23] Its repetition and further explanation denotes the emphasis of this command. The statement was likely original to the P text of Exodus 31 and 35, while Exod 20:11 is an addition of the final editor to the Sabbath law in 20:10. The rationale for the Sabbath rest changes between the Deut 5:15 and Exod 20:11. The rationale for the Sabbath was not a part of the Exodus 35 record of this law, while it does appear in the P text of Exodus 31 where, like 20:11, it is a parallel for Yahweh's rest after Creation. Given the various sources of these texts, it seems possible that the Dtr1 source altered the purpose of the Sabbath to fit the existing religious mindset during its composition. Later, when the final editing of the Pentateuch is taking place during the exilic period, an editor added Exod 20:11 to the Decalogue to reiterate the original purpose of the Sabbath. The true "rationale" for the observation of Sabbath is not relevant to this argument. Regardless of whether it reminded the Israelites of Yahweh's rest or their deliverance from Egypt, in both adaptations for the law, the text demonstrates later writers and editors connecting a tangible experience with a religious affiliation. "That they might know" demonstrates that learning transpired through obedience to this command. The writer of Exod 31:15 included a repetition of שַׁבָּת (shabat) as an indicator of the superlative, or supremacy, of the event. Some translate the repletion as "high Sabbath." This perpetual covenant acts as another kinesthetic learning environment where adults learn through action. Through the observation of the weekly Sabbath, adults learn the means of their sanctification. Here within the context of Exodus 31, the Sabbath serves as a sign of Israel's relation with Yahweh by observing the example that he emulated in Gen 2:1–3.

The Tabernacle is described in Exodus 25–30 and 35–40. The word, "tabernacle" rightly means "the place of dwelling."[24] When Yahweh states, "Let them construct a sanctuary for Me, so that I may dwell among them."

---

23. Deut 5:12.
24. Harris et al., *TWOT*, 2387c.

The purpose clause of this statement is imperative to the text. The phrase, "so that" initiates the purpose of this structure is a location where Yahweh may dwell among His people. It is interesting Yahweh selects a tent structure to fulfill this purpose. Sandra Richter suggests that the tent structure of the Tabernacle was selected for its similarity to the tents that the Israelites also dwell within. Though there is nothing within the biblical texts to validate this premise, it is noted that Richter also points out that when Israel moves to more permanent home structures, Yahweh likewise moves to the semi-permanent structure of the Temple.[25]

Prior to the Tabernacle, the Tent of Meeting was used as a structure where the presence of Yahweh could be sought. The expectation of meeting with God in the Tent of Meeting was not exclusive to Moses. Instead, Exod 33:7 states, "whoever sought the Lord would go out to the Tent of Meeting that was outside the camp." In other words, anyone could seek communication with Yahweh. The original Tent of Meeting is contrasted from the Priests' Tent of Meeting, or Tabernacle, which was situated in the center of the Israelite camp, rather than outside.[26] The Tabernacle was comprised of three areas: the outer court, the holy place, and the Holy of Holies. As one passed from the perimeter, through the outer court, through the holy place, and into the Holy of Holies, greater levels of restriction were exercised. The reason for this restriction was the elevation in holiness as one moved toward the Holy of Holies, where Yahweh's presence resided. This holiness is further communicated by the reduction of size for these spaces and the elevation of costly materials used in their construction. Only priests were permitted to enter into the holy place, while others would die upon entrance.[27] Within the Tabernacle, the Ark of the Covenant resides and serves as the focal point of sacrificial ritual.[28]

Any ritually clean Israelite could enter the outer court, only priests could enter the holy place, and only the high priest could enter the Holy of Holies. Entrance into the Holy of Holies only occurred on the Day of Atonement. According to Exod 28:35, the High Priest was required to wear bells on the hem of his garment so that its sound could be heard when he entered the presence of Yahweh. It is quite possible that this initiated a heightened awareness of the day's significance and, more importantly, the significance of a human entering the presence of a holy God. Perhaps, select elders of the community silently listened for the ringing of these bells as the High Priest

---

25. Richter, *Epic of Eden*, 180.
26. Num 2:17.
27. Num 3:10.
28. Exod 29:1–42.

moved within the Holy of Holies, profoundly aware of the consequences if he was not properly prepared for this encounter. It is conceded that this remains imaginative speculation. Yet, coincidently, the basic matter of a tangible expression for religious belief is evident within this description. No doubt the ringing bells on the priestly garment drew attention from others and likely drew questions for those observing them for the first time. Once again, a teachable moment offers itself as elder Israelites are able to then teach on the significance of these bells as well as the significance of man entering the presence of God, and the escalating importance of a God who dwells among His people.

Additional religious symbolism was also integrated into the priestly garments. These garments were made from the materials received as offerings from the Israelite community.[29] Eight articles of clothing are described, four inner and four outer. Since footwear is omitted from the list, it is likely that this is not a full inventory of the regalia. Two examples of this religious symbolism are found within the breastplate. Twelve precious stones were integrated into the breastplate to represent each of the twelve tribes. When this article was worn by the high priest, it bore the names of the tribes to bring their remembrance before the Lord.[30] This breastplate also included contained the Urim and Thummin, or sacred lot used to make important decisions. Worn above the heart of the high priest, it signified that justice originates with God. The Pentateuch does not describe a formal pedagogy that resulted from the integration of symbolism with priestly attire. That said, it does offer a perfunctory conclusion similar to the symbolism of the festivals that does include pedagogy of a similar nature, namely the provoked questions from those who do not understand the purpose of the symbols and the resulting opportunity of an elder to retell the significance of the given symbols.

INSTRUCTION TO RESIDENT ALIENS

A more subtle form of witness took place within the Exodus literature by means of the Mosaic legislation that regulated the status of resident aliens or foreigners. As in Deuteronomy, the term used for this group is *gerim* from the singular noun, גֵּר (*ger*). Two types of these resident aliens are described in the Pentateuch, circumcised and uncircumcised. The defining difference in status pertained to one's ability to participate in the celebration of

---

29. Exod 25:2–7.
30. Exod 28:29.

Passover.³¹ Apart from this stipulation, Mosaic legislation conveys the same laws applied equally to foreigners and Israelites.³² By these means, Gentile foreigners were granted unlimited access into the daily routines and religious views of the Israelite social structure.³³ This access includes equality within the law and the right to asylum in cities of refuge,³⁴ the right to accumulate wealth and to own Jewish slaves,³⁵ as well as the right to offer sacrifices at the tabernacle and temple.³⁶ Because of this assimilation, resident aliens also received instruction in Israel's religious heritage and expectations.³⁷

The first fifteen chapters of Exodus form a coherent narrative dominated by various signs from Yahweh directed toward a non-Hebrew (alien) audience. The signs themselves served as a witness to Yahweh's supremacy over the foreign idols and gods they worshipped. Compounding the effectiveness of these signs, the Hebrew people discussed these signs among themselves as well as with the aliens who also witnessed them. Thus, they became a means of instruction.

Various words are used to describe miraculous displays of Yahweh's power. These include: אוֹת (sign),³⁸ פֶּלֶא (miracles),³⁹ מֹפֵת (wonders),⁴⁰ יָד (power),⁴¹ and כֹּחַ (power).⁴² Fundamental to the purpose of these signs is the demonstration of Yahweh's power and supremacy through the Hebrews' release from Egyptian slavery. Exod 6:4–6 links this commitment to Yahweh's covenant with Abraham. Here, Yahweh is described as acting on Israel's behalf by means of "great judgment." The word "judgment" is translated from שֶׁפֶט.⁴³ This term refers to the series of acts Yahweh preformed through Moses and Aaron to achieve the outcome of Israel's release from Egyptian control. The seven repetitions of the phrase, "I will," in verses 6–8 mark the personal involvement of Yahweh. Additionally, the text later clarifies that

---

31. Exod 12:48; Num 9:14.
32. Deut 1:16; 12:12; 14:2; 26:12; Num 15:15–16.
33. Lowe, "You are My Witnesses," 61.
34. Num 35:15.
35. Lev 25:47.
36. Lev 16:29; 17:8, 10, 12, 15; 18:26.
37. Deut 31:11–12.
38. Harris et al., *TWOT*, 41a.
39. Ibid., 1768.
40. Ibid., 152a.
41. Ibid., 844.
42. Ibid., 973.1.
43. Ibid., 2443a.

these acts would serve as a means for instruction for both aliens and future Israelite generations.[44]

Exodus 9:13–19 begins the third triad of plagues. Here, the rationale for the plagues is expanded. Five declarations are given to Pharaoh. First, he is told that the plagues demonstrate Yahweh's incomparable power so that His name and power would be known everywhere. Second, Yahweh declares that Pharaoh has been provisionally spared in order to demonstrate Yahweh's providential control of worldly affairs and positions of authority. Third, Pharaoh is reminded that, had Yahweh struck the people first instead of merely sending pestilence, they would have perished. Instead, Yahweh has been exceedingly gracious. Fourth, Yahweh declares that the impending weather would be beyond anything the Egyptians had previously experienced in their recorded history. Finally, grace is again afforded to the Egyptians with a means of sparing themselves and their property from the hail. Importantly noted, is that Yahweh wants to build His reputation throughout Egypt and the earth. Therefore, thus far, He has spared the Egyptians from terminal destruction. Verse 16 clearly states that the purpose of this grace is the demonstration of Yahweh's power so his name (reputation) may be made known throughout the world. Twice[45] the text makes the point that Yahweh had another purpose, beyond keeping His word to Abraham, for these displays of His power among the Egyptians. The location of these acts, Egypt, is only the stage, the audience is "all the earth" (repeated twice). This text is acknowledging the necessity of instruction about Yahweh's character beyond Israel. Furthermore, it also offers a means for this instruction. The Egyptians experienced mighty acts of Yahweh and gained firsthand knowledge of His grace. The result would be narratives that echo throughout surrounding nations who, in turn, hear of these acts and vicariously learn of Yahweh's grace and power. The word "know" in verse 14 is expectedly translated from יָדַע (*yada'*).[46] Exodus 9 is largely attributed to the E document with a brief inclusion from P.[47] Friedman notes an editorial addition in 9:35 before the transition into chapter 10. He also notes an anomaly within verse 30 where the term "Yahweh, God" occurs for the first time since Genesis 2.[48]

Later in the Exodus text, the law offered a provision for circumcised male aliens to participate in the Passover celebration.[49] The "foreigners" and

---

44. Lowe, "You are My Witnesses," 57.
45. Exod 9:14, 16.
46. Harris et al., *TWOT*, 848.
47. Exod 9:8–12.
48. Friedman, *Bible with Sources*, 135.
49. Exod 12:48.

"sojourners" were not permitted to participate. This stipulation seems to primarily apply to Israel's future settlement in the Promised Land, rather than their current circumstance in Egypt. These addendum laws are located within the P document. It differentiates between, בֶּן־נֵכָר (ben nekhar) in verse 43,[50] a word normally used for non-Israelites who were temporarily visiting a land and strangers, and גֵּר (ger) which refers to long-term foreign residents in verse 48.[51]

Interrupting the Elohist's literature within Exodus 12 and 13 is an insert from P. In 12:48, an abnormal concession for the inclusion of Gentile resident aliens to participate in the commemorative events of the Passover is found. The later literature of the Priestly source offers an integrated law that permits the aliens who live among the Israelites and undergo the covenantal sign of circumcision to partake in the annual event that recalled and retold the miraculous signs associated with Israel's deliverance from Egypt and to join in the celebration of Passover, "like one born in the land."[52] Since the Passover celebration is intimately connected to Israel's national experience of deliverance from Egypt, those who do not identify with the nation are ineligible to participate. Privately owned servants who had accepted the Israelite covenantal sign of circumcision could partake of Passover since they were long-term hired hands and were integrated as property. A resident alien (gerim) must undergo circumcision before making a voluntary sacrifice at Passover and become, "as a citizen of the country." In other words, he must commit to identify as an Israelite before he can participate in an Israelite ceremony. This is the only mention of cultural conversion in the entire Hebrew Bible. The only other means for a foreigner to become an Israelite is through marriage or the long process of ethnic assimilation that resulted in long-term residence within the land.[53]

Following the insertion of P's amendment to the Elohist's narrative of Passover, the editor inserts verse 51 to summarize that it was in that day of obedience that Yahweh brought the Israelites from Egypt. This is a refrain of verse 41. Following this summary, the text resumes with E's further instructions on consecrating the firstborn. This concession of allowing foreigners to participate in an Israelite tradition reflects a later religious tradition but is inserted within the earlier account to allow it to be associated with the Passover from the commencement.[54]

50. Harris et al., *TWOT*, 1368b.
51. Ibid., 330.
52. Lowe, "You are My Witnesses," 61.
53. Tigay, "Exodus," 131.
54. Campbell and O'Brien, *Sources of the Pentateuch*, 40.

The toleration of the Israelites for unconverted Gentiles indicates their intention of incorporating them within the Israelite culture. Through the assimilation process, resident aliens were repeatedly exposed to the recitation of Yahweh's actions during annual festivals[55] and in the temple through the singing of Psalms.[56] The expectation of newer legislation of Exod 12:48–49 was that these resident aliens would pledge obedience to Israel's religious laws and undergo the right of circumcision, whereby they would become full members of the covenant community. A remarkable feature of Israelite law is the provision of social rights to resident aliens. By the Gentiles allowing themselves to undergo ritual circumcision, they demonstrated their allegiance to the Abrahamic Covenant and thus identified themselves with the people of Israel and their God. Participation in the Passover further identified them with the events associated with the redemption of Israel.

Given the gravity of this process and the complexity of adult circumcision, this commitment was likely preceded by ample instruction from Israelite men. In this particular narrative occurrence, the pedagogy seemingly follows as verbal instruction followed by the kinesthetic events of circumcision and sacrifice. The culminating act of circumcision would no doubt seal the previously received instruction of Israelite cultural practices and the religious significance for circumcision. The significance of this cultural conversion was not indiscriminately hastened but rather a well-planned and deliberate action by those who chose to allow the rite of circumcision on their bodies. Similar to the sign of circumcision originally received by the adult men in Genesis at the conception of the Abrahamic Covenant, this was likewise a memorable event and religious experience that these resident aliens committed themselves to.

Another example of instruction to resident aliens occurs in Exod 22:21, where they are told to refrain from doing harm or oppressing strangers within their land. This command is repeated in 23:9. Friedman attributes both of these verses to the E source. Campbell disagrees with this classification. Instead, he contends that Exod 20:22—23:33 cannot be identified with P, J, or E. He further states that tensions between the text and source suggest that this portion of Exodus was not original to the above aforementioned sources. He therefore references Exod 20:22—23:33 as a non-source text.[57]

In the absence of a defined pedagogy for resident aliens, Exodus does offer a few laws concerning this group. Exod 12:19 relates that the aliens who live among the Israelites were to abide by similar ordinances for the

---

55. Deut 16:11, 14.
56. Pss 96:1–3; 105:1–4.
57. Campbell and O'Brien, *Sources of the Pentateuch*, 195.

Passover as the Israelites. Though these foreign residents were not obligated to offer a Passover sacrifice, they were obligated to refrain from yeast during the seven days of the Passover festival. According to Adele Berlin, this may be due to the sharing of bread between the Israelites and resident foreigners. Aliens must also refrain from yeast in order to avoid accidental contamination with Israelite food.[58]

Later in this same chapter, it is recorded that both Israelites and foreigners who convert to the Israelite religion are to abide by the same laws.[59] This was a means of offering equality to both groups. The word used here is *torah*, understood as "teaching" or "instruction."[60]

The last law occurs in Exod 20:10, where it is stipulated that all must observe the Sabbath rest, including resident foreigners. The Hebrew reads literally, "your stranger," which implies that it applied to those foreigners who were, in some way, dependent on an Israelite household.

Within the context of Exodus, there is little evidence offered to determine an appropriate means of instruction. Since the Israelites are instructed to treat these foreign residents, and more particularly, the proselytes, as equals, it seems likely that religious instruction occurred similarly to the adult Israelites. However, there is simply not enough textual evidence to fully support this hypothesis within the Exodus text.

That said, additional attention should be drawn back to the Israelite duty to foreign residents in Exod 23:9. The purpose for the well treatment by Israelites is not only a humanitarian effort, but also because the Israelites themselves know the frustrations and sorrows of being a stranger among another race. Within this particular verse, the adults are given a command that is then attached to a visual and kinesthetic reminder of an experience they have known. It is probable that this connection helped to solidify the importance of this command within their memories. Because they had physically endured a similar circumstance, they were better prepared to sympathize with other foreigners. Therefore, they are instructed, in Exod 23:9, to retain that memory in order to assist them with the fulfillment of their obligation to other foreigners.

SUMMARY

Exodus includes some of the strongest commands for parents to instruct their children such as those found in Exod 10:2; 12:24–26; and 13:14.

58. Berlin and Brettler, *Jewish Study Bible*, 127.
59. Exod 12:49.
60. Alter, *Five Books of Moses*, 384.

Included in these commands are also examples of the pedagogy that parents are to use. Alone, 10:2 offers only the command for oral instruction. However, in 19:16 it is established that Yahweh has shown himself to them through displays of his power. They were already given visual examples (and arguably kinesthetic examples) of Yahweh's supremacy. Now, it is the parents' responsibility to reinforce this truth through oral instruction (aural). Later, in Exod 12:1–28, this pattern of active learning through visual and kinesthetic pedagogical tools is established again through the use of religious festivals that will prompt the children to ask their parents questions concerning their significance. In response, the parents must testify of Yahweh's goodness. Similarly, parents are told to include their children in the religious ordinances which will provoke their children to ask questions. In Exod 13:14, the parents are instructed to respond and explain the religious ethos behind these ordinances. When instructing children, a clear pattern emerges in Exodus that coincides with Fleming's VARK learning theory for active learning. Oral instruction alone is not an example offered in this text. Instead, visual and kinesthetic learning environments are created that precede oral instruction.

This pattern is established again for the religious education of adults. Exodus 11:1—12:1 offers an example where editorial activity brings together two separate texts for the creation of an active learning paradigm. Here, the oral instructions of Passover that begin in 12:1 are joined with the visual/kinesthetic teaching tool derived from the experience of the plagues. The editor joins these two independent narratives together with his insertion of 11:9–10. Therefore, a pattern similar to the pedagogy for teaching children is established for the adults. Visual/kinesthetic experiences precede oral instructions. This pattern is found again in Exodus 19–20 where the editor brings together two independent texts so that the oral account of the law in chapter 20 is juxtaposed with the visual experience described in chapter 19. The editorial insertion of 20:1, identified by Friedman, Campbell, and O'Brien, again sets up the pattern for active learning that coincides with Fleming's theory.

Chapter 6

Leviticus

SEVERAL PEDAGOGICAL FEATURES ARE located in Leviticus that correlate with Gardner and Fleming's conceptual frameworks for active learning. Specifically, visual learning is uniquely incorporated into much of the religious attire and structures, while kinesthetic learning is integrated into the religious festivals and ceremonies. Leviticus integrates an expectation for innate curiosity and natural inquiry. The diverse learning strengths of learners, both child and adult, results in more diverse experiential learning activities integrated into the religious attire, symbolism, and participation of religious festivals.

INSTRUCTION TO CHILDREN

The third annual festival is the Feast of First Fruits, celebrated on the sixteenth day of Nissan but is also mentioned as celebrated on the sixth day of Sivan.[1] As stated earlier, Nissan corresponds with March and April on the Roman calendar, while Sivan corresponds with May and June. The Feast of First Fruits is described in Lev 23:9–14. Though children likely participated alongside of their parents, there is no explicit mention of children within the instructions for this event. Consequently, the pedagogical aspects of this event will be covered more thoroughly in the educational instructions for adults.

---

1. Num 28:26.

Festivals

Pentecost

Pentecost is founded as a celebration of the Israelites receiving the Ten Commandments at Mt. Sinai. The word "Pentecost" is a Greek word meaning "fiftieth day" and is attributed to the celebration for receiving the Ten Commandments fifty days after leaving Egypt. Within the Pentateuch, Pentecost is celebrated as harvest and the presentation of new grain to Yahweh. Lev 23:16 describes this event taking place between the celebration of the Passover and before the Feast of Booths. Additional names used for this festival are "Feast of the Harvest"[2] or "Feast of Weeks."[3] It is further described in Deut 16:9–12, where the Israelites are explicitly told to celebrate this event with their children. Once again, this text demonstrates that one of the purposes for this event is a memorial to the nation's slavery in Egypt. Thus, stories commemorating that event and testimony of events, circumstances, and epiphanies were likely told and retold as the experience of living within the booth is relived.

Feast of Booths

The Feast of Booths has several English variances for its title. It may also be referred to as the Feast of Tabernacles or Feast of Ingathering. All of these titles are derived from the original Hebrew title, *Sukkot*. This celebration builds for six days and reaches its height on the seventh day, when a procession circles the altar seven times[4] and "*Hosha'na*" (save now) is exclaimed. This event takes place on the fifteenth day of Tishrei, which corresponds to late September to late October on the Roman calendar. The word *Sukkot* is the plural form of *sukkah*, which translates as booth or tabernacle. The booth is a fragile dwelling consisting of tree branches. It was first used as a small hut that provided shade within the harvest fields.

The celebration of the Feast of Booths is first discussed in Lev 23:33–44 and is specifically celebrated for the training of later generations. During the celebration of *Sukkot*, people leave the dwelling of their homes and live within the *sukkah*. The purpose of this action is intended to remind those who participate in this event of the 40 year wilderness excursion prior to entering the Promised Land.

---

2. Exodus 23:16.
3. Deut 16:10.
4. Suk. iv. 5.

The induction of this event begins with Yahweh speaking to Moses, telling him to give this declaration (*dabar*) to the sons (*ben*) of Israel. Though, in its most literal sense, בֵּן refers to a son, it does not exclusively refer to male offspring. It may also carry a wider connotation that allows it to refer to both male and female collectively. It can be used colloquially as a synonym for people belonging to a particular group such as "sons of prophets" or "sons of Ammon." This is a common phrase used 630 times within the Hebrew Bible. In the context of Lev 23:34, the literal translation is "sons of Israel." Its use here is the idiomatic reference for people of Israel, or Israelites, rather than literal children. An equivalent expression is found throughout Ezekiel where the phrase "son of man" refers exclusively to an adult individual.[5]

The first day of the Feast of Booths is set aside for a "sacred assembly." As seen in Exod 12:16, the word מִקְרָא (*miqra'*) is used specifying that Moses is to publically meet with the Israelites. This further validates that the above phrase, "sons of Israel," refers to an adult congregation rather than children. Similarly, a second public meeting was held on the eighth day to formally conclude the celebration.

Leviticus 23:42–43 further clarifies the instructions and rationale for the booths. Here, it states that all native born Israelites are to live in these temporary structures, "so that your generations may know that I had the sons of Israel live in booths when I brought them out from the land of Egypt." דּוֹר (*dore*) is translated as "generations" in verse 43. The etymology of this word does not offer enough evidence to determine a particular, suggested age range. Instead, this is a broad scope that future descendants of the native Israelites needed to learn the purpose for this feast. However, the instructions for this annual event are repeated in Deut 16:13 and 31:11–13 where one's children are clearly included in the participation and receipt of instruction.

Leviticus 23 includes a model of instructions for both the adults and the children. The instruction for the adults will be discussed later in this chapter. The instruction for children during the Feast of Booths includes an aspect of the kinesthetic learning environment. They were likely included in the opening assembly on the first day of the celebration, where they were able to listen to the teaching that took place. This was then followed by them physically moving into the temporary shelter of the booth. Similarly to the Passover, when children asked their parents questions concerning the activities and symbolism of the festival, the parents have an opportunity to

---

5. Harris et al., *TWOT*, 1121.

teach their children, not only about the transpiring event but the history, tradition, and religious correlation with the event.

The connection of a pupil asking before the teacher offers an answer is referred to as a "teachable moment." This phrase was first popularized by Robert Havighurst in his book *Human Development and Education*. Here, he defines a teachable moment as a specific time which makes the achievement of a task possible. In reference to education, a teachable moment is the time at which learning a particular subject becomes possible or the easiest to retain.[6] More recent uses of this term define it as a significant event where the emphasis is on the "moment" verses the lesson. Students retain more information for a longer period of time when it is connected to an event.[7]

The notion of training connected to an event or "moment" is observable in the Leviticus 23 text with the expectation of the annual observation of the Feast of Booths and short term residency within the booth. The children participating in this were offered a teachable moment in which questions may have been provoked through the course of unusual events whereby the parents were given the opportunity to instruct their pupils.

Liturgy

Similarly to the religious festivals, liturgical events also offered circumstances in which questions were likely stimulated. The use of the term liturgy in this book, refers to the prescribed structure of public religious settings. This includes religious garments, altars, and locations stipulated within the Pentateuch. It is acknowledged that much of the material within this section will also apply to the instruction for adults. However, it is introduced here as it pertains to the training of children.

INSTRUCTION TO ADULTS

Leviticus is replete with examples of active learning pedagogy that engages the adult Israelites. The entire sacrificial system described involves the reinforcement of their religious ethos regarding the consequences of sin. The death and extraction of blood of the animals used for the atonement of sin offers repeated opportunities for kinesthetic learning. The rationale behind the laws pertaining to what is clean and unclean again likely provokes question and discussion regarding the religious ethos supporting their religious

---

6. Havinghurst, *Human Development*, 7.
7. Gladwell, *Tipping Point*, 55.

obligation to uphold these laws. Likewise, they offer ongoing kinesthetic reminders as the Israelites enforce and obey these laws. Through this, Israel comes to learn that their holiness depends on distinction. Just as they have been set apart by Yahweh from the other nations, so they must also discriminate the differences between clean and unclean, thereby reinforcing the oral instructions through active participation of obedience.[8]

Kinesthetic learning also occurs through the celebration of national festivals. Religious events such as the Day of Atonement, Year of Sabbath, and Year of Jubilee all employ active learning pedagogy through the participatory expectations. However, the pattern of active learning prior to oral instructions is more strongly illustrated through the weekly participation of the Sabbath day that also involves an assembly of the Israelites for instruction. Leviticus offers few details describing the content of these sacred gatherings and therefore it will not be belabored here except to assert again the pattern of kinesthetic learning preceding oral instructions.

With the exception of the frequent mention of "sacred assembly," the book of Leviticus does not make a specific reference to educating adults with explicit reference to how instructions are transferred from one person to the next. However, as stated above, this text offers multiple examples of kinesthetic pedagogical tools that reinforce religious laws, traditions, and ethos. Furthermore, several festivals include the assembling of the people for a holy convocation that credibly includes oral instructions. Additionally, the visual learning that is described as used for children in the above section is also an applicable pedagogical tool that reinforces the religious education of adults. Here again, the combination of festivals (kinesthetic), symbolism of the tabernacle (visual), and sacred assembly (aural) are used as it parallels active learning emphasized by Neil Fleming through the VARK learning theory.

INSTRUCTION TO RESIDENT ALIENS

Leviticus makes no specific references to educating resident aliens. However, it repeatedly refers to the fair treatment of aliens,[9] and expectation that the laws for foreigners should be consistent with those of Israel.[10] Furthermore, according to Deut 1:16, these resident aliens should expect the same judgment as Israel. Leviticus also addresses the expectation of Israel to nurture their relationship with the resident alien and to "love him as

---

8. Alter, *Five Books of Moses*, 634.
9. Lev 19:35.
10. Lev 24:22.

yourself."[11] Though it is not identified in Leviticus, it is rational to conclude that some type of education was offered to these residents who were to obey the religious laws of Israel[12] and accept responsibility for disobeying Israel's God. Given the expectation of consistency in laws, it is submitted that the religious education of these foreigners resembled the education patterns of Israelite adults.

SUMMARY

Active learning is presented in Leviticus through the visual and kinesthetic learning occurring through the religious attire, symbolism, and festivals. This integration of symbolism and experiential learning moves beyond passive learning of mere oral accounts of past experiences by drawing on the student's natural curiosity and participatory actions that further engage the learner in active learning. This involvement further acknowledges the significance of prominent religious events and increases the potential of retention through active participation of sensory and motor areas of memory.

---

11. Lev 19:33–34.
12. Lev 18:26.

Chapter 7

Numbers

THE NARRATIVE ACCOUNTS CONTAINED in Numbers portray a dying generation that has no option but seek ways to ingrain their religious ideals and experiences to their children. The imminent mortality for their lack of faith produces a new challenge for ensuring their memories of Yahweh's activities are remembered by the next generation. The pedagogy used is likewise recorded in these accounts. Visual reminders of lessons learned through their experiences are integrated into their religious stories and assimilated into their relics. Furthermore, the gathering of the people for oral instructions is assimilated with religious festivals as a means of connecting memory with active participation.

INSTRUCTION TO CHILDREN

It is interesting that the instructional focus is seemingly on the elder generation training the younger generation, who is to succeed them, yet, there are no specific narrative accounts within Numbers that address the training of children. Nevertheless, there are several occasions related in this book that the Israelite children would have undoubtedly observed and thus likely received some type of religious explanation as to the significance or rationale of the event. Events such as visual presence of Yahweh within the cloud over the tabernacle may have easily provoked questions from the children, enabling the parents to relate their religious understanding.

The account that may have offered a more structured approach for the training of the children is the rebuke of the adult Israelites after they complain upon hearing the spies' report of the Promised Land in Numbers

14. Following the intercession of Moses, the Israelites learn that all of the adults, with the exception of Joshua, Caleb, and Moses, must die in the wilderness and only their children will be permitted to enter this land. As this discipline is carried out, the adults are faced with the seriousness of passing on their knowledge, since there will be no tribal elders to assist this younger generation once the current adults die in the wilderness. These parents and grandparents must now formulate an intentional system of training their descendants in religious perceptions and the ideals of their ancestors.

Though the editors of Numbers did not include narratives that address this education, the book does offer occasions when these children would have been able to personally observe the supremacy of Yahweh and learn from their parents. These events may include the miraculous provision of manna and water within the dessert or the visual presence of Yahweh in the pillar of smoke and fire. Since the training of children within Numbers is not specifically addressed, speculations on pedagogy will not be entertained.

INSTRUCTION TO ADULTS

Within Numbers, visual reminders serve as a form of pedagogy. A story is recounted followed by a visual reminder. A trilogy of these reminders is found in Numbers 15–17, which includes tassels, bronze plates, and Aaron's rod. The first reminder is initiated by a problem recorded in Numbers 15, when a man breaks the Sabbath in order to gather wood. Since this is the first known disregard for the Sabbath, the people are uncertain of the consequences. The man is bound while Moses seeks the Lord's command. In response, Yahweh tells the Israelites to remove the man from their camp and stone him to death. They comply with this decree. Afterward, the Israelites are instructed by Yahweh to sew a blue tassel on the corners of their garments to remind them of the law.[1] This blue tassel serves as a dual reminder. First, it reminded the wearers of the commands of their God and thus the Mosaic Covenant. Second, it reminded them of their deliverance from Egypt by the providence of their God. Hereafter, this becomes a kinesthetic pedagogy whereby the initial generation, which participated in the stoning of the man, could retell later generations of the consequences of disobedience to the law. This visual reminder would act as a prompt for those who saw it to remember their need to obey God's commands. Additionally, it reminded them to trust in their God as their deliverer.

A different visual reminder is recorded in chapter 16. Here, the sons of Korah, a sect of Levites, rebel against Yahweh by refusing to accept the

---

1. Num 15:32–41.

priesthood of Aaron. This rebellion results in their death. An additional 250 Israelite men, not from Korah's clan, also join in Korah's rebellion. As a consequence, Yahweh kills them by fire. The firepots used by the 250 deceased men are then gathered, at the instruction of Yahweh, to be hammered into plating for the altar of the Tabernacle. Its purpose was to serve as a reminder that only descendants of Aaron could serve as priests and burn incense.[2]

The third reminder in this trilogy follows immediately after the Korah narrative. The acceptance of the Aaronic priesthood is still disputed. Therefore, Yahweh instructs Moses to gather the rods from each of the twelve tribal leaders, after they have written their names on them. The rods are then placed within the tent of meeting overnight. When Moses reenters to collect the rods, one had budded and bore ripe almonds. It is found, by the inscribed name, that this is Aaron's rod. Hereafter, this budded rod serves as a reminder of the election of Aaron's lineage to serve as priests. It further serves as a sign for those who rebelled against this decree to remind them that such rebellion is punishable by death, as evidenced by the preceding deaths with bodies engulfed by earth, fire, and plague.

The precedent continues for the use of visual imagery in pedagogy. Rather than simply issuing a command, the expectation is assimilated with a visual element that aided in the memorization of religious expectation. These reminders also likely became occasions for those who were not familiar with these figurative elements to ask questions and thus receive instruction and learn the relative incorporation of these visual reminders.

The narrative of the bronze serpent also includes the use of visual symbolism in Num 21:6-9. Within the context of the story, the Israelites complained about being bitten by snakes in the wilderness. It is recorded that many Israelites died as a result of these snakebites. The word used here for "serpent" is the same word used in Genesis 3. As the people are faced with the prospect of death from these bites, they appeal to Moses to intercede on their behalf. Yet, the language they use is reminiscent of terms used in Exodus. As in Exod 8:8, "Entreat the Lord that He remove the frogs," the Israelites now ask, "intercede with the Lord that he may remove the serpents."[3] Yahweh's response, however, is not the removal of the snakes, but rather an iconic means for the Israelites to be healed, once bitten. Yet, the presence of the bronze serpent that Moses is instructed to prepare is not enough to heal the people. Each individual must take the responsibility to look at it.[4] The importance of this event is in the use of the visual imagery to instruct the

2. Num 16:40.
3. Num 21:7.
4. Hamilton, V., *Handbook on the Pentateuch*, 343.

adult Israelites. Mark Hamilton explains, "Moses removing the source of the affliction would restrict Israel's opportunity to learn something important about the biblical God, namely that healing is contingent and salvation is conditional."[5]

Also within Numbers, a less specific teaching occurs during the מִקְרָא קֹדֶשׁ, often translated as "holy convocation" or "sacred assembly." Here, מִקְרָא (miqra') is a derivative of קָרָא (qara') and denotes an audible recitation or reading. Often addressed to a specific audience, its intention is the acquisition of a specific response. מִקְרָא is specifically used in the context of the cult, such as the weekly Sabbaths in Lev 23:2. Its usual meaning is reminiscent of the five annual feasts. These events require a special summoning of the Israelites and call to worship through the blasts of trumpets. This is recorded in Num 10:2, 10. Though only males were invited to attend,[6] physical presence was mandatory.[7] These holy convocations are depicted several times throughout the book of Numbers. The first appears in 28:18 during the observation of the Passover. Three are recorded in chapter 29 in observation of the feast of trumpets,[8] the Day of Atonement,[9] and festival of Succoth.[10]

A different assembly is mentioned in Num 29:35. Here, the word עֲצָרָה ('atsarah) is used. Though it is from the word עָצַר, "restrain," עֲצָרָה is properly translated as "solemn assembly."[11] Alter points out that the different word choice is meant to distinguish this assembly from those that use the countdown of the bulls. Here, the assembly is clearly joined with the cult, though only one bull is sacrificed.[12]

It is unfortunate that nothing further is recorded within the biblical text to describe what was recited during these sacred assemblies. The word choice of מִקְרָא leads me to believe the primary means of education was an audible teaching for the adult male Israelites. Since there is no further explanation, it can only be estimated that religious leaders or elders read, or recited from memory, the laws associated with the celebrated feast.[13] It is speculated that perhaps these males were reminded of the purpose for the

5. Hamilton, M., *Transforming Word*, 195.
6. Exod 23:17; 34:23.
7. Harris et al., *TWOT*, 2063d.
8. Num 29:1.
9. Num 29:7.
10. Num 29:12.
11. Harris et al., *TWOT*, 1675c.
12. Alter, *Five Books of Moses*, 837.
13. Gerhardsson, *Memory and Manuscript*, 95.

given feast through the stories that verified their importance and connection with their religious identity with Yahweh. Though the teaching itself was audible instruction or recitation, this teaching occurred in the context of the feasts. Therefore, it remains that the primary context for this education occurred within a kinesthetic environment. As these men participated in the events of feasts, they heard the accounts or instructions associated with these feasts, reinforcing their identity, religious heritage, and responsibility to the faith community.

INSTRUCTION TO RESIDENT ALIENS

Similarly to the accounts previously mentioned, Numbers also addresses the ability for resident aliens to participate in the Passover alongside the Israelites. Such residents were allowed to adopt the religious ideals of the Israelite faith community. Though there was no formal "conversion" ceremony, non-Israelites were required to be circumcised prior to participating in the Passover offering. This requirement is likely the referenced meaning of Num 9:14, "according to its law," though it is somewhat ambiguous in the text.[14]

It also appears that resident aliens who had aligned themselves with the Israelite deity were also allowed to participate in other offerings. This is evident in Num 15:14, where instructions are given for religious offerings to Yahweh by these resident foreigners. Verses 15–16 further regulate that there will remain one law to govern both the native Israelites and the resident foreigners within the assembly. Here, קָהָל (*kahal*) is translated as congregation or assembly and refers to the amassing of the people before Yahweh. Its root, קֹל (*qôl*), denotes speaking as the primary reason for this gathering. This is further reinforced by the LXX translation of קָהָל as ἐκκλησία[15] (*ekklēsia*).[16]

SUMMARY

Visual imagery and kinesthetic environments are repeatedly employed as pedagogical means of instructing children, adult Israelites, and resident aliens throughout the book of Numbers. There are no recorded instances of a formal assembly gathered that is not within the context of some type of

---

14. Ibid., 727.
15. Strong, *Biblesoft's New Exhaustive Strong's*, G1577.
16. Harris et al., *TWOT*, 1991a.

religious event or festival. Furthermore, visual imagery is repeatedly included within the narrative accounts as a means to help onlookers remember the importance of Yahweh's commands and prior accounts that contributed to their religious understanding. Though the occurrence of this symbolism is used in the context of the adult community, it is likely that the Israelite children and resident aliens would have also observed these symbols and likewise used them as a means for asking questions and acquiring religious principles.

Chapter 8

Part Two Summary

MATERIAL RELATING TO COMMANDS for parents to train their own children in pertinent religious affairs and historic events is found largely in Deuteronomy. The exception is found with the specific texts in Exodus that pertain to instructions for the Passover. This pedagogy was both explicit (such as direct commands to instruct children)[1] and implicit (such as the description of the Feast of Booths).[2]

As discussed within this section, teaching occurs in one of two modes: expository and hypothetical. Expository teaching emphasizes the skills and mastery of the subject matter by the instructor. The teacher's authority resides in the power of the example provided and his or her worthiness of emulation. Hypothetical teaching, on the other hand, challenges the student to seek answers. They are provoked to ask questions in their quest to discover knowledge.[3]

The centrality of the home and parents as the educators of children intentionally served as a means of witness to future generations concerning religious expectations. As discussed in chapter 1 of this book, the family unit is established as the primary means for teaching children through sensory affiliations followed by narrative instruction. The preponderance of admonitions for parents to instruct their children using visual and tactile methods in additional to oral narrative creates a suspected obligation of its continued use.

---

1. Deut 6:4.
2. Leviticus 23.
3. Crenshaw, *Education in Ancient Israel*, 27.

The primal mode of education adapted from the Pentateuch is traditionally the use of story. However, the use of visual examples as objects that first evoke curiosity and questions has remained overlooked. It has been demonstrated throughout this chapter, that physical symbolism is intentionally used as a means for reminding viewers of Yahweh's laws or his previous actions in the lives of the Israelites. Furthermore, festivals and religious events are utilized as a further means to engage children, Israelite adults, and resident aliens in the religious affairs of the faith community. These events offered a kinesthetic environment in which participants are actively involved. These events are also utilized as an occasion where the participants are vocally addressed and reminded of the religious laws and heritage of the Israelite people.

Parents are required to teach their children within the home. Yet, the children are also able to observe festivals and religious symbolism throughout the community. This offered abundant opportunities to reinforce their training and seek hypothetical teaching. On the other hand, adults and resident aliens learned primarily during the sacred assemblies where the laws and explanations were vocally given to all hearers. Though the instruction itself is audible, these assemblies occurred within the kinesthetic occasion of the festivals. Like the children, these adults also observed the routine symbolism permeating through attire, festivals, and religious locations. This symbolism was posed as reminders for the adults to reinforce the ethos of the faith community.

The final form of the Pentateuch is constructed as a paradigm of pedagogy for Hebrew children, adults, and foreign aliens. It demonstrates religious values through the lessons of faithfulness to Yahweh. Stories of past events are retold for theological perspective. Moreover, the Pentateuch demonstrates the purposed use of visual imagery and kinesthetic environments as pedagogical tools to incorporate into their religious training. The final editors of the Pentateuch carefully selected narratives that recount their religious ideals and theological perspective of Yahweh. Yet, in addition to utilizing these stories, they have also incorporated the means by which these stories are retold.

The final form of the Pentateuch has undeniable didactic value for religious training through merely reading its included texts. However, it also demonstrates further educational value by utilizing the varied means of education it described within those accounts. As they prepared for entrance into the Promised Land, the people of Israel determined the appropriate means for relating the mythos, logos, and ethos of their people so that the ideals would be perpetuated for many future generations. Likewise, the final exilic editors were once again preparing for entrance into the Promised

Land. It was therefore necessary to ensure that the returning people were able to reidentify themselves with the expectations of Yahweh and His covenant within the Promised Land. In order to do this, they utilized stories that offered tangible evidence of their God. Since the new readers may not have been eyewitnesses to the accounts recorded within these narratives, they pointed them to the tangible expressions, festivals, monuments, altars, and attire that were themselves a witness to the acts of their God—thus again connecting the visible with the invisible, testimony with adjudicators, and story with tangible truth.

Part Three

Pedagogy of the Deuteronomistic History

THE PREVIOUS SECTION INTRODUCED the rationale for Israel's emphasis on religious instruction as it related to the covenants established between Israel and Yahweh. It also discussed the examples of pedagogy described within the Pentateuch and their purposed inclusion, insertion, or emphasis by later editors. Part 3 will further investigate the Deuteronomistic History for its similar evidence of pedagogical features inserted or emphasized by later editors. Along with part 2, this section continues to establish that visual and kinesthetic instruction methodology is used in addition to oral narrative. Moreover, there is textual evidence supporting the role of a later editor who either inserts or emphasizes pedagogical examples for religious instruction.

The editorial activity within the Deuteronomistic History is uncontested by biblical scholars. Instead, the debate centers on the number of revisions and their timing. This deliberation does not affect the proposal of this book where the focus is on the editor(s)' activity and revision of material relating to pedagogy. Examples of the Deuteronomistic editor's interest in pedagogy are systematically discussed later in this section.

In part 3, the previous research carried out by Brevard Childs and other scholars from his same discipline is used to demonstrate how later editors of the Deuteronomistic History purposefully added and rearranged texts to draw attention to pedagogical features. Childs is one of the early scholars to draw attention to the Deuteronomist's use of the grammatical formula, עַד הַיּוֹם הַזֶּה, "until this day." In his 1963 article, "A Study of the Formula, 'Until This Day,'" Childs begins with the statistical use of the formula, stating that it occurs eighty-four times in the MT. He also highlights two important occurrences from the LXX that are absent from the MT, Gen 35:4 and Josh 24:30.[1] He then goes on to discuss the use of the phrase "until this day" in its etymological, ethnic, geographic, cultic, nature, political, legal, and sociological etiologies. During his discussion, Childs builds on the prior research of J. Fichtner and agrees with Fichtner's conclusion that the form of assigning names to a location in conjunction with the use of the phrase "until this day" is found in the earlier sources of the Pentateuch, particularly J. It noticeably decreases in Joshua and Judges before discontinuing altogether in the exilic redactions. The phrase continues in usage, though no longer appears in connection with a location. When it is separated from its etymological use, a different pattern emerges. Instead of decreasing, the phrase increases in frequency within Judges and finds its highest frequency in the writings of the DH.

> This means that the period in which the use of etymological etiology is dying out, the use of the formula increases in frequency. The implication would be that the formula no longer functions primarily within the etiology, but has assumed a different role.[2]

Childs challenges the presuppositions of Alt and Noth in their assessment of the formula's localization in etiological stories whose purpose was used "to explain and legitimatize a given practice or phenomenon by projecting its origin into the distant past, from which point a direct line of tradition could be traced "until this day." Instead, Childs concludes that the original etiological story is not always ascertainable given the alterations and adaptations of the source material. He further asserts that the "present literary composition is not primarily etiological in character."[3] He finally concludes that the phrase "until this day" is used as a personal testimony to confer a received tradition rather than justify an existing phenomenon through etiology.[4]

Childs makes no attempt to identify the era or number of Deuteronomistic History editors. He does however, assert that the phrase "until this day," "reflects the age of many different redactors,"[5] suggesting more than one revision. Unlike Childs, Jeffery Geoghegan is emphatic in his assertion of a single pre-exilic editor in his 2003 article, "'Until This Day' and the Pre-exilic Redaction of the Deuteronomistic History." Like Childs, Geoghegan

---

1. Childs, "Study of the Formula," 279.
2. Ibid., 286.
3. Ibid., 290.
4. Ibid., 292.
5. Ibid.

contends that this phrase was used as the editor's "own personal witness to geographical, political, and cultic realities mentioned in his sources that still existed at the time of his historical enterprise."[6] Geoghegan disagrees with Childs's observation that the phrase's occurrence in multiple sources is evidence of multiple editors. Instead, he purports that it may indicate a single editor with access to all of these sources and merely "inserted the phrase whenever he encountered something still existing at the time of his editorial work."[7] Geoghegan's perspective is worth consideration as he concludes that several editors using the same phrase with identical grammatical irregularities to confirm locations is peculiar and unlikely.[8]

Geoghegan further addresses the distinct geographical perspective of the Southern Kingdom, a subgroup of Israel, and the overwhelming use of this phrase in connection to locations and artifacts located in this region. He concludes that this is further evidence of a single pre-exilic editor since, "most, if not all of these items cannot properly be said to exist after Jerusalem's destruction by the Babylonians."[9] He states that "the phrase's redactional nature, its southern perspective, and its pre-exilic provenance are important starting points"[10] for his conclusion of a single pre-exilic editor. Rather than multiple editors, Geoghegan asserts that the doublets and textual differences are a product of the DH incorporating various sources.[11]

While Geoghegan's argument is valid, he does overlook several details. Most importantly, he does not address the deviations between optimism and pessimism toward the monarchy. It is plausible that he would include this in his category of "textual differences," however; these deviations present a significant change to the development of the Deuteronomistic History. The contribution of Childs and Geoghegan is their textual analysis of the repeated phrase "until this day" throughout the Deuteronomistic History. In conjunction with their suggestions of this phrase as a later textual addition, this research determined that the majority of these phrases are directly related to texts pertaining to pedagogy.

Richard Nelson identifies the development of the Deuteronomistic History in, *Double Redaction of the Deuteronomistic History*, where he proposes two editors. Nelson maintains the first editor is responsible for the editorial changes during the reign of King Josiah and is overtly optimistic toward the

6. Geoghegan, "'Until This Day,'" 202.
7. Ibid., 203.
8. Ibid., 205.
9. Ibid., 209.
10. Ibid., 225.
11. Ibid., 226.

monarchy and its religious reformation. The second editor writes during the exilic period with an obvious negative perspective of the monarchy.[12] Nelson begins his research with a brief survey of scholars who have contributed to the advancement of his hypothesis prior to his writing. He includes the arguments that he esteemed as valuable toward the work of literary criticism and those he established as of little value due to their poor argumentation. The work of Martin Noth and Frank Moore Cross is included in the scholarly work accepted by Nelson. Nelson then uses the next several chapters to support his hypothesis by systematically addressing particular texts within the Deuteronomistic History that support his proposal of these two editors. Grammar, syntax, and theology are all taken into account as Nelson addresses his theory.

Nelson reiterates his theory in his 2005 article, "The Double Redaction of the Deuteronomistic History: The Case is Still Compelling." Here, Nelson continues to affirm the strong argument for a Josianic DH made by Cross. He further agrees with Geoghegan's assertion that the recurring phrase "until this day" represents the contribution of a pre-exilic editor who uses the phrase to authenticate his sources.[13] Like Childs and Geoghegan, Nelson states that the use of this phrase occurs in every source utilized by the DH. Nelson emphasizes the pre-exilic interests that culminate during the reign of Josiah. This largely coincides with the argument presented by Geoghegan. However, Nelson correctly identifies textual abnormalities that cannot be convincingly attributed to a single pre-exilic editor. He observes, "Many themes important to the DH simply drop out in the material that follows Josiah's reform."[14] He includes examples such as the omission of dynastic promise to David in the final chapters of 2 Kings.

> The positive role of 'place' (2 Sam 7:10–11; 1 Kgs 8:29, 30, 35) and 'house' associated with Yahweh's 'name' (2 Sam 7:13; 1 Kgs 3:2; 5:17, 19 [et 3, 5]; 6–8; 9:3; 2 Kgs 21:7) is turned upside down. Now 'place' (2 Kgs 22:16–20) and 'house' (23:27; cf. 1 Kgs 9:7–8) become the target of threat and destruction.[15]

He also asserts that pessimistic passages toward the monarchy are later additions or alterations to the original narratives.[16] Nelson finally reasserts his previous conclusion, "The double redaction hypothesis of a DH

---

12. Nelson, *Double Redaction*, 126–27.
13. Nelson, "Double Redaction," 326.
14. Ibid., 330.
15. Ibid.
16. Ibid., 332.

composed in the time of Josiah with limited additions made by an exilic reviser accounts for the most striking and puzzling disparities in ideology within DH and provides a simple coherent basis in history to explain these differences."

The arguments made by Childs, Geoghegan, and Nelson all contain valid discussions. It is the assessment that Nelson's hypothesis most adequately aligns with the current studies by biblical scholars on the Deuteronomistic History. While Childs's argument asserts sound statements, his declaration of several editors is insubstantial. Geoghegan correctly addressed this statement in his rebuttal that the grammatical precision of this phrase is more likely attributed to a single editor's insertion. Nelson also supports this conclusion. Yet, Nelson follows through on Geoghegan's oversight of changes in attitude toward the monarchy and thematic focus. Since these elements remain unaddressed by Geoghegan, his final argument is inconclusive. Nelson's conservative view is widely accepted among his peers, including Campbell and O'Brien, who repeatedly reference his text in their work on the Deuteronomistic History described above.

Chapter 9

Joshua

THE USE OF STACKED stones as monuments was mentioned in chapter 4 in relation to narrative accounts in Genesis. This chapter will demonstrate that the stacking of stones, recorded in the Deuteronomistic History, served a variety of purposes that were mainly pedagogical in function. These include, but are not limited to, memorials, monuments, and graves for important officials, each retaining a pedagogical purpose. The practice is first found in Joshua 4. Upon the entrance to Promised Land, the Israelites are instructed to gather one stone for each of the twelve tribes from the bottom of the Jordan River as they miraculously cross this body of water. They then stack the stones at Gilgal. The purpose of this is found in 4:7. These rocks are to be a memorial (זִכָּרוֹן, *zikron*)[1] among the Israelites. It is meant as a witness and reminder of Yahweh's action in the lives of the Israelites. This particular account, however, has additional significance. According to the literary description, the adult generation of Israelites who personally witnessed the exodus from Egypt and miraculous crossing of the Red Sea have died in the wilderness, with the exception of Joshua and Caleb. Though it is plausible that some of the Israelites entering the Promised Land were children during the first miraculous crossing of water, four decades have transpired and possibly dulled the lucidity of that memory. Furthermore, many of the current Israelites were born during the wilderness excursion and therefore did not personally witness the Red Sea crossing. The oral stories have helped to maintain the significance of the account and identify the powerful deliverance enabled by Yahweh. Yet, as the Israelites prepare

---

1. Harris et al., *TWOT*, 551b.

themselves for entrance into the Promised Land, the narratives allow for a repeated occurrence of this significant event.

According to their tradition, the Israelites escaped from Egypt by means of Yahweh's deliverance. Within their immanent future, they will need this same assistance from their God as they battle the resident Canaanites. This account serves as an anchor between the exodus and crossing of the Jordan. As in the desert, they will experience periods when they are unsure of Yahweh's presence. During such times, they will need reassurance. When the presence of their God cannot be proven by their present experiences, this pile of stones will assure them of their past encounters and their ability to draw upon tradition and the religious ethos of their faith community.

Upon entrance into the Promised Land, Yahweh once again allows for the parting of water, thereby solidifying the timeless truths encapsulated within the stories of their ancestors. Indeed, the God who delivered the Israelites out of the Egypt is now with them to deliver them into the land promised to them. In order to further memorialize this event, a monument is erected as a testimony for future generations. Beyond the use of didactic stories, the pedagogical tool of a tangible object is formulated as evidence, a sign, of their God's work. It is expected that others will see this monument and inquire of its significance. Therefore, the Israelites are commissioned with the responsibility to answer these inquiries with their own testimony of participating in this event. A later editor then adds the final statement in verse 9, "and they are there unto this day," for future readers and hearers of this account to solidify the importance of this event and its continued importance in the religious history and identity of this people.

Jeffery Geoghegan is one of the recent scholars to address the significance of the phrase "until this day." He builds on previous publications by Abraham Kuenen and Brevard Childs, who also argue for the cause of this repeated phrase. Geoghegan argues that compelling evidence shows that this phrase is employed by a single editor "as his own personal witness to geographical, political, and cultic realities mentioned in his sources that still existed at the time of his historical enterprise."[2] Geoghegan's suggestion of a single editor utilizing this phrase deviates from earlier research by Brevard Childs, who concluded that the phrase "reflects the age of many different redactors."[3] Regardless of the final analysis for single or multiple editors who use this phrase, all parties are in agreement that this is a later addition to the originally recorded narratives.

2. Geoghegan, "Until this Day," 202.
3. Childs, "Study of the Formula," 292.

The editor draws further attention to the miraculous crossing of water through the repetition of response used with Rahab to connect the two extraordinary voyages across water. In Joshua 2, Rahab reports that the inhabitants of Jericho had heard of the miraculous crossing of the Red Sea which caused "our hearts to melt and no courage remained in any man any longer because of you; for the Lord your God, He is God in heaven above and on earth beneath."[4] This statement is an echo of Deut 4:39–40:

> 'Know therefore today, and take it to your heart, that the Lord, He is God in heaven above and on the earth below; there is no other. So you shall keep his commandments which I am giving you today and it may go well with you and with your children after you, and that you may live long on the land which the Lord your God is giving you for all time.'

Rahab's admittance of great fear, or terror, of the Israelites is also borrowed language from the Pentateuch. This phrase is found in Exod 23:27 to describe the terror that Yahweh will send ahead of the Israelites to cause confusion among the Canaanites so that they can be conquered by Israel. It is also found in Moses' song in Exod 15:15–16. As he celebrates the crossing of the Red Sea, Moses sings, "... the leaders of Moab, trembling grips them; All the inhabitants of Canaan have melted away. Terror and dread fall upon them ..." Thus, Rahab confesses the reaction that had been foretold. The editor has decisively selected the wording of Rahab's confession to ensure readers connect the two miraculous crossings of water. Rahab's account serves several functions within the narrative. From the literary context, Rahab serves as a parallel to Joshua in chapter 1. Both characters demonstrate faithfulness in Yahweh which leads to the salvation of those who are interested in serving Yahweh. Rahab's account in chapter 2 also affirms the theology of Israel's mission and confirms that Yahweh welcomes all cultures of people, provided they are willing to obey Him.[5] Moreover, Rahab's confession of fear is stated first in Josh 2:9 and then in reverse order in 2:11, demonstrating the narrator's focus upon these words echoed from the earlier Pentateuchal accounts. The editor uses the Rahab narrative to draw the readers' attention to the connection between the miraculous crossing of water recorded in Exodus and the second miraculous crossing recorded in Joshua. This connection is made through the repetition of response found in Exod 15:15–16 and Josh 2:9, 11. The editor is purposefully emphasizing these two accounts and preparing readers for the pedagogical tool of stacked stones that will occur in Joshua 4.

4. Josh 2:11.
5. Hess, *Joshua: An Introduction*, 81.

The narrator further ensures the connection of the two miraculous water crossings by a repetition found in 2:10 and 5:23. The verb translated as "dried up" is used for the first time in Joshua 2 to describe the Red Sea. Later, the Canaanite response to the crossing of the Jordan River is recorded in Josh 5:1.

> Now it came about when all the kings of the Amorites who were beyond the Jordan to the west, and all the kings of the Canaanites who were by the sea, heard how the Lord had dried up the waters of the Jordan before the sons of Israel until they had crossed, that their hearts melted and there was no spirit in them any longer because of the sons of Israel.

The descriptive language and repetition of the phrases "dried up" and "hearts melted" is a purposed attempt of the narrator to draw attention to the linkage of these events. Yahweh had used a visual means to teach both Israelites and non-Israelites of his might and providence. The response was twofold. Non-Israelites learned to fear the sons of Israel and their God. The cumulative effect of hearing that Yahweh allowed the Israelites to cross both the Red Sea and Jordan River on dry ground dismayed the hearts of the Canaanites. Yet for some, such as Rahab, it also provoked interest and ultimately salvation. On the other hand, this event brings assurance to the Israelites in the Power of their God. As previously mentioned, the newer generation of Israel is confirmed by the crossing of the Jordan. The story they had heard from their ancestors is now witnessed firsthand. In order to memorialize this event and ensure that it is not forgotten, a visual reminder of stones from the bottom of the river is stacked as evidence that it occurred.

The repeated reshaping of this account and fragmentary effect of this story is evident and discussed by Campbell and O'Brien. A closer examination of this story reveals an anomaly in the memorial erected and the plausibility of two memorials, one in the center of the Jordan[6] and the second at Gilgal.[7] According to Yahweh's instructions that initiated this action, the stones would be placed at the location of their lodging.[8] In Joshua's affirmation of this memorial in his speech recorded in verses 5–7, the specific location of the memorial is not mentioned. Campbell and O'Brien establish the likelihood that this is evidence for the combination of sources.[9] However,

---

6. Josh 5:9.
7. Josh 5:20.
8. Josh 5:3.
9. Campbell and O'Brien, *Unfolding DH*, 115.

they conclude that it is more probable that the actual location of the memorial was at one location or the other, but not both.[10]

In consideration of the final form of this text, Campbell and O'Brien's conclusion is incorrect. Based on the text, in its present form, two sites are clearly revealed. Joshua reports the compliance for the memorial at Gilgal in verse 8. The rationale for the memorial at Gilgal is also given in verse 8. It is to be a sign so that when their children inquire of it, the elders will be able to testify of their miraculous crossing. The second memorial site in the middle of the Jordan River is reported in verse 9 with its catechesis stated in verses 6–7. As with the memorial at Gilgal, the purpose of the mid-Jordan memorial is clearly pedagogical in nature. It too will invoke the curiosity of their children and require the elders to respond with a narrative accounting for their miraculous crossing of the Jordan River. However, it is significant to point out that this memorial also contains the reference that it remains "to this day." The addition of this phrase could have come at any point in the traditioning process of this narrative. The emphatic date of this supplementation is of no concern here. However, its use brings focus to the mid-river memorial site with the editor's emphasis on its authenticity. This authentication is missing from the Gilgal memorial. However, the Gilgal memorial remains prominent in the continuation of the narrative through its connection in the proceeding chapter of Joshua and the overall maintained importance of Gilgal, whereas the attention for the mid-river memorial is dropped from this point forward. It is therefore concluded that two memorials are likely. Both serve pedagogical purposes and provide a tangible object that will precede the oral narrative by provoking the curiosity of those who see it, namely children. The apparent resource of a later editor is also located within this pericope as attention is given to the authentication of the continued presence and purpose of this memorial for a later audience.

Following this episode is the recorded circumcision in chapter 5. Campbell points out that this chapter gathers three traditions that are affected by the transition from wilderness to Promised Land: circumcision after the wilderness sojourn,[11] conclusion of manna and observance of Passover,[12] and Joshua's encounter with the "captain of the host of the Lord."[13] For simplicity of explanation, focus first on the circumcision of male children born during the wilderness excursion. This sign of faith commitment to the Abrahamic Covenant had been ignored during their sojourn. As they

---

10. Ibid., 116.
11. Josh 5:2–9.
12. Josh 5:10–12.
13. Josh 5:13–15.

enter into the Promised Land, this religious act is reinstated. It is a sign of induction into the faith community of those who worship Yahweh and must be completed prior to one's ability to participate in Passover. Both Meyers and Hess allude to the clumsy editing of this text. Hess, in particular, notes that this is recorded as a successive circumcision in verse 2. He explains that his could be an address for the difference between Egyptian circumcision, which does not completely remove the foreskin, and the Israelite circumcision that does require its full removal. He also mentions the suggestion that Israelite circumcision was originally a rite of puberty and that the earliest forms of this narrative imply older ages of these participants.[14] This is also noted in Meyers's study.[15] Campbell discusses the unambiguous Hebrew that clearly states the Israelites are to be circumcised a second time. However, the later reference in verse 9 states that they were uncircumcised. Campbell assures that this is likely the LXX reinterpreting the convolution for its audience and therefore omits "a second time."[16] Hess goes on to state that this attempt for harmonization contains no explicit explanation within the text.[17] It is therefore contended that Campbell is correct in his assertion that any attempt to make an authorial attribute for Joshua 5 is imprudent.[18]

Regardless of when this chapter was included within the overall content of Joshua, it accurately re-establishes the necessity of Israel's covenantal responsibility and establishes the use of kinesthetic learning. It is unnecessary to argue whether male children were included based on redaction of the priestly source. Instead, the point is that this newer generation accepted the obligation of this cultic rite, no doubt solidifying the veracity of their commitment to Yahweh and his laws.

The emphasis of the text itself centers on the fact those who originally came out of Egypt were circumcised but had died in the desert. Both of these facts are mentioned twice in verses 4 and 5. Both groups are recognized in their totality in verse 5. Whereas all of the preceding generation had received circumcision, no one in the present generation had received it. Verse 6 adds that those who died perished because they were disobedient while the present generation participated in circumcision because of obedience. A purposed parallel is further drawn from verse 6. The text emphatically states that the elder generation had died because they did not listen. The word used is שָׁמַע (shama'). It denotes the expectation of obedience as a result of

---

14. Hess, *Joshua: An Introduction*, 118.
15. Meyers, "Joshua," 472.
16. Campbell, *Joshua to Chronicles*, 45.
17. Hess, *Joshua: An Introduction*, 119.
18. Campbell, *Joshua to Chronicles*, 118.

hearing.[19] The same word is used in the call to hear (obedience) in Deut 6:4. In essence, they had acted in opposition to Yahweh's first command, that they would hear the Lord. Verse 6 also references the land sworn to their forefathers. This is a connection drawn from Genesis 17 and the covenant made between Yahweh and Abraham. It is there that the first instructions for circumcision are given and promise of land is attributed to Abraham's descendants. Finally, Josh 5:6 references the land flowing with milk and honey. Though this is the only occurrence of this phrase in Joshua, it is used fifteen times in the Pentateuch to describe the profusion of agriculture in Canaan. It is associated with the covenants between God and Israel and the reward for Israel's obedience.[20]

As stated, the generation of Israel recorded in Joshua is depicted as obedient to Yahweh and sharply contrasted with the preceding generation who died because of disobedience. Chapter 5, like many others, uses the means of a tangible location to solidify the authenticity of this event. The location of this new mass circumcision is recorded as Gilgal. To further solidify the account, the editor also records that it is named "to this day" in order for his contemporary generation to recognize the validity and identify with the account.

Similar to the stacked stones from the Jordan River, a related action is taken in Josh 7:26. After the stoning and burning of Achan's body in response to his rebellion against Yahweh, he is buried and a pile of stones is built over his grave as a reminder to other Israelites of Yahweh's anger against such indiscretion. Without reservation, the memory in their participation of Achan and his family's stoning would be a permanent reminder of Yahweh's insistence on complete obedience to His instructions. For those who did not witness this occasion first hand, the monument would serve as a ready reminder. Though the specific statement "when your children ask, you will tell them" is absent from this narrative, it is certainly assumed. In addition to the stones, the area is named Achor, עָכָר ('Akhar), meaning "troubled," and permanently connects the outcome of Achan's rebellion with the location.[21]

The account of Achan in Joshua 7 serves a distinct literary objective for the book. It is connected to a larger meta-narrative that spans Joshua 1–9. Within these accounts, the narrator shifts the focus between events where Yahweh intervenes with Israel within their own camp and events outside their camp. In relationship to Yahweh's action within Israel's camp, prior to

19. Harris et al., *TWOT*, 2412.
20. Hess, *Joshua: An Introduction*, 121.
21. Harris et al., *TWOT*, 1621.

chapter 7, the reader has observed the selection of Joshua as the new leader,[22] the circumcision after crossing the Jordan River, and the judgment of Achan. Between these are accounts of God's actions outside of Israel's camp, including the spies' visit to Jericho, the defeat of Jericho, and the conquest of Ai.[23] The literary composition of these stories focuses the readers' attention on events within the Israelite camp in preparation for events that involve the foreign residents of Canaan as Israelites commence to take possession of it. Joshua 7 is then juxtaposed as a necessary suspension in the narrative between the victories at Jericho and Ai to demonstrate, again, the importance of complete devotion and obedience to Yahweh.[24] The commemoration of the pile of stones and naming of the area is a firm reminder of this expectation and serves as a pedagogical tool of two tangible locations that have the capacity to evoke inquisition and oral narrative while the proposed student is experiencing disequilibrium. Here, the visual and kinesthetic pedagogical features of the stones and selected name of Achor serve as a means for religious instruction that accompanies oral teaching.

Later, readers are reminded of the death of Achan in Josh 22:20. In the context of the latter narrative, the tribes of Reuben, Gad, and Manasseh have built an altar near the Jordan. Seeing it, the other tribes believe they are breaking the unity of the tribes and degrading their altar at Shiloh. They remind these three tribes of two preceding rebellious acts that had led to Yahweh's wrath. The first precedent is listed in Josh 22:17. The account of Baal Peor and the death of twenty-four thousand Israelites from rebellion is mentioned to remind these Transjordan tribes of the consequences for such action. This same account was also used by Moses in Deut 4:3 as a reminder for those preparing to enter the Promised Land. The second precedent listed is Achan's rebellion against Yahweh and the affect of his sin on the entire nation during their loss of the battle at Ai. This example is recorded in Josh 22:20. In response to these accusations, the three tribes evoke three different names as a superlative for Yahweh, recorded in verse 22, to demonstrate the invocation of Yahweh and deny the claims of the other tribes. The three Transjordan tribes attest to the supremacy of Yahweh. They go on to defend the purpose of this altar is a witness for the future generations of the three Transjordan tribes and those on the other side of the river, that all are required to offer sacrifices to Yahweh on the altar at Shiloh. The word "witness" is the same noun used to denote a human witness in court.[25] This

---

22. Josh 1:16–17.
23. Joshua 8.
24. Hess, *Joshua: An Introduction*, 156.
25. Lev 5:1; Deut 17:15.

replica at Gelioth Jordan is meant to visually remind all of the tribes of their religious identity and unity.[26]

A third pile of stones is described in Josh 8:29. When the Israelites are given victory at Ai, they kill its king and hang him on a stake as a trophy until dusk. In accordance with the law,[27] they then remove him, bury him, and place a heap of stones on the site as a visual reminder of this event and the consequences of rejecting Yahweh.

Additionally, the destruction of Ai is described as a permanent heap of ruins, and portrayed in 8:28 as desolation. This phrase only occurs one other time, in Deut 13:16. The inhabitants of Ai are punished because they failed to worship Yahweh. As in the chapter 7 account, a later editor has added the phrase "and it stands to this day" to the end of this account to serve as a dual reminder for later readers. Ai is a reminder of the Israelites' failure to destroy the city because of disobedience and a reminder to the non-Israelites of the consequences for rejecting Israel's God. This passage bears a clear affinity to the notice on Achan's grave: "They raised over him [Achan] a great heap of stones that stands to this day";[28] "and raised over it a great heap of stones that stands to this day."[29]

Moreover, the conquest of Ai is followed by the covenant renewal at Mount Ebal. Immediately following the description of Achan's stone grave marker is this renewal described in 8:30–35. Campbell highlights the prior research concerning this passage and notes its inclusion in two other textual locations. "The LXX places it after Josh 9:1–2; [while] a Hebrew text from Qumran, 4QJosha places it just before Josh 5:2."[30] Within this pericope, Joshua is described as building a stone altar and then proceeds to write "a copy of the law of Moses" on the stones. Afterward, Joshua reads these words "according to all that is written in the book of the law" to the assembly of Israelite men, women, and children as well as the foreign aliens. Here, a later editor uses the events of Joshua's central campaign to highlight his theological emphasis. Alongside this, the editor(s) record the pedagogical tools and examples for the continuation of this instruction. According to this passage, the editor indicates that the tangible locations, altar, and memorials still exist for elders to use as examples of Yahweh's providence to new or younger faith adherents. The example included a kinesthetic event, followed by a visible, tangible memorial, and concludes with the verbal instruction of a

---

26. Hess, *Joshua: An Introduction*, 292.
27. Deut 21:22–23.
28. Josh 7:26a.
29. Josh 8:29b.
30. Campbell, *Joshua to Chronicles*, 46.

leader to the assembly of people. Here, all three learning styles identified by Fleming are utilized as the active learning paradigm for instruction emphasized by the editor(s).

This ceremony re-establishes the relationships between Israel and Yahweh. Having addressed the concerns and consequences for violating the covenant in chapters 7–8, the close of chapter 8 and the literary unit brings the readers' attention to three theological themes. These three themes are identified by Richard Hess as, "the obedience of Joshua to the divine instruction, the participation of Israel, and the pre-eminent role of the Mosaic instruction in the ceremony."[31] An altar is built and sacrifices are offered, in accordance with the Mosaic Law. Following this, the narrative closes with the description of Joshua inscribing the words of the law upon the stone and then audibly reading them. Verse 35 describes the audience as the entire assembly of Israel, including the women, children, and resident aliens. Here, within chapter 8, the audience first sees the visual demonstration of covenant through the erection of the altar and sacrifices before they audibly hear the instructions of this covenant. It is closely assimilated with the victory at Ai in order for the participants to associate divine blessing with obedience.

The literary structure of the first eight chapters of Joshua offers a repetition of actions that shifts the focus to several characters who demonstrate the providential role of Yahweh with both Israelites and non-Israelites. Second, verbal cues are used to link the miraculous events of crossing water. Whereas the initial crossing of water demonstrates the defeat of an enemy, the latter crossing anticipates the defeat of the newer generation's enemy. Finally, the defeat of Ai concludes the narrative of the failed attack in chapter 7. Joshua's questions in 7:7–9 are resolved with the conclusion of chapter 8.[32] Overall, alongside of the accounts that demonstrate Yahweh's might, providence, and fulfillment of the Abrahamic covenant of land possession, the narrator has included several visual prompts for retelling these accounts. Monuments at Gilgal, Achor, Gelioth, and Ai all serve as reminders of Yahweh's action and intervention. Furthermore, they are intentionally placed as pedagogical tools so that passersby can inquire and thus hear the oral narratives of and theological training on the importance of obedience to Yahweh and the resulting benefits and consequences of one's choices. The editor draws the readers' attention to these sites by including the phrase "to this day" so that his own generation may also inquire of them to prove the validity of the stories and continue to use these visual reminders as instruments for instructing newer faith adherents. This reinforces for both the

---

31. Hess, *Joshua: An Introduction*, 172.
32. Ibid., 171.

original witnesses of the events and later hearers of the stories that although they cannot see Yahweh, they can see the effects of Yahweh and the results for those who either obey or disobey. Furthermore, the editor emphasizes the significance of the pedagogical features with his inserted phrase, "until this day."

Joshua 10 records the burial place of five kings that remains "to this very day." The documentation of this event shares an interesting connection with Achan's burial place in chapter 7. Both 10:27 and 7:26 testify of a memorial stone that remains for the present audience to verify. With the exception of the twelve stones used as a monument of the crossing of Jordan, these two grave memorials are the only stone memorials to said to exist "until this day." As previously mentioned, the statements, "They raised over him a great heap of stones that stands to this day,"[33] and "raised over it a great heap of stones that stands to this day,"[34] show strong resemblance with one another. Following the description of the burial of the king of Ai are the six verses describing the altar on Mt. Ebal and the renewal of covenant that specifically fulfills Moses' words from Deut 27:1–8. Geoghegan affirms the hypothesis of Martin Noth and concludes these ascriptions are probably later redactions from an earlier text.[35] The use of "until this day" brings an earlier matter of concern for the original DH to a central concern for the contemporary audience of the editor.[36] Here, the grave markers are integrated into the repertoire of visual aids used in the pedagogy recorded in Joshua as they validate the authenticity of the narrative and justify the religious ethos of strict obedience to Yahweh's commands.

The event of covenant renewal at Mount Ebal, described in Joshua 8, is repeated in Joshua 24. This time, the location is more explicitly specified as Shechem. The text employs the verb "presented themselves" (יצב, *yatsav*).[37] This verb is previously used in Exod 19:17, when the Israelites presented themselves to hear Yahweh's covenant, and in Deut 31:14, when the leadership transitioned from Moses to Joshua. Here, in Joshua 24, the verb is used in a dual role to imply both occasions. At the end of this chapter, Joshua will die and the leadership of the nation will transition to the "elders who survived Joshua." In addition, verse one uses the definite article before "God," an occurrence also found in Exodus 19 and 24.[38] This is followed

---

33. Josh 7:26a.
34. Josh 8:29b.
35. Geoghegan, "Until this Day," 212.
36. Ibid., 213.
37. Harris et al., *TWOT*, 894.
38. Hess, *Joshua: An Introduction*, 300.

by a lengthy recitation of Yahweh's redemption of Israel through their history and the establishment of the basis for Israel's loyalty to Yahweh on the merit of His care. This culminates at verse 14 with the stipulations of the covenant. The people are confronted to make a decision whether or not they will worship Yahweh exclusively. They respond affirmatively, resulting in the ratification of the covenant. However, before this occurs, Joshua surprisingly responds to their affirmation by questioning their ability to keep this covenant. He informs them that they must throw away their "foreign gods." This acknowledgment demonstrates two things. First, it acknowledges that Israel has disobeyed Yahweh through the creation of these foreign idols. Second, the action of destroying these idols would further solidify, for this generation, the acknowledgment of Yahweh as a jealous God[39] and reinforce their monotheistic religious worldview.

Shechem is mentioned a second time in verse 25, signaling the close of the pericope. Similarly to his actions in chapter 8, Joshua then proceeds to record the words of the Mosaic Law on stones. He then proclaims that these stones will be a "witness" (עֵדָה, 'edah) of their confession of religious exclusivity to anyone who passes by this location. This is the same word used in Genesis 31 when Jacob and Labon erect a pile of stones as a territory border (witness) between them. It carries the connotation of the testimony of an event.[40] Here it is used as a visual reminder or monument of this covenant affirmation prior to Joshua's death. These stones offer a visual and tangible reminder of the instructions they have learned from Joshua and the kinesthetic action of discarding their foreign idols for religious adherence that reinforced the aural instructions they had received regarding the importance of their monotheistic faith. Additionally, those who did not personally experience this event are left with the tangible memorial that served as a pedagogical tool for reinforcing this religious ethos.

Joshua 24 has received substantial attention regarding its dating and authorship. This arises, in part, from the description of gathering the Israelites in verse 1. Since the Israelites are already assembled together, according to 23:2, it is suggested that chapter 24 is a later addition to the text. The phrase "you will not be able to serve the Lord"[41] is also a textual anomaly that leads some to affirm a later date for this chapter.[42] Campbell and O'Brien agree with Nelson's assessment concerning the controversy and lack of scholarly consensus regarding the correct date of Joshua 24. Postu-

---

39. Josh 24:19.
40. Harris et al., *TWOT*, 1576c, 1576e.
41. Josh 24:19.
42. Campbell and O'Brien, *Unfolding DH*, 162.

lating a date is not necessary for the argument of this book. The relevancy of the agreement concerning the late addition of this chapter satisfies the purpose of its discussion here.[43]

SUMMARY

The allotment of land described within Joshua may present itself as tedious to some modern readers. However, these descriptions are theologically crucial because they demonstrate Yahweh's fulfillment of the Abrahamic Covenant, especially the promise that Israel would possess its own land. The detailed fulfillment of this promise expresses Yahweh's reliability and further strengthens the relationship between Yahweh and Israel.[44] The possession of land is a central concern that coincides with Israel's religious ethos. Deuteronomy serves as a pivotal text where Israel looks back on the promises described in Genesis and forward to their fulfillment. This fulfillment is experienced by the characters described in Joshua. Therefore, the educational ethos concerns itself with this land, in connection with religious identity. The writers and editors of Joshua purposefully use these narratives as a pedagogical tool for the teaching of religious culture. The attainment of the land itself serves as a tangible reminder that Yahweh has fulfilled His promises to their ancestors. As later generations hear the oral traditions of elder faith adherents, they may recognize the validity of these accounts by the mere acknowledgement that they themselves occupy the land described in these very stories. This lends itself to the importance of why the allotment of land is included in their religious texts. It is intrinsic to the basic pedagogy demonstrated by the DH.

In summary, the book of Joshua includes multiple examples of pedagogy. Instructional tools such as stacked stones (visual) and circumcision (kinesthetic) are used to reinforce the audible instructions the characters receive. Furthermore, monuments at Gilgal, Achor, and Ai serve as reminders of Yahweh's actions. Altars, such as the one erected near Jordan, are described as a witness of religious ethos to those who pass by. These are intentionally used as pedagogical tools so that those to see them (visual) may inquire of their significance and hear the story explained (aural). Therefore, active learning that corresponds with Fleming's VARK learning theory is used for the theological training on the importance of obedience to Yahweh. Finally, an editor emphasizes these pedagogical features by inserting the phrase "to this day" so that his own generation may also inquire and

43. Ibid.
44. Hamilton, M., *Transforming Word*, 248.

authenticate the existence of these locations and further learn theological truths from these pedagogical tools.

Chapter 10

Judges

THE PEDAGOGICAL INTENT OF the DH continues into Judges. The conquest of Canaan carries on as Judges 1 describes the defeat of additional cities. This chapter also serves as a literary bridge between the Joshua and Judges texts. The narrative of Caleb and his family is repeated from Joshua 15:15–19 almost verbatim. This is used to acknowledge the connection between these two texts as well as purposefully introduce readers to Othniel, the first judge. The use of land as kinesthetic evidence for the validity of didactic stories also continues in Judges. Chapter 1 explains why Kenites and Simeonites live in Judah's territory. It includes a series of accounts of the failure of the Israelites to eliminate Canaanites from their land.

Chapter 2 goes on to explain that the reason for their failure to rid the land of Canaanites is Israel's unfaithfulness to Yahweh. Judges 2:1 depicts "the angel of the Lord," who serves as the narrator to describe the vicarious position of Israel. Readers are informed that the audience of this angel is the "sons of Israel." As discussed in the previous chapter, this audience can reasonably suggest that only men attended this assembly but it is also possible that women and children were included. Through this messenger, readers learn that the Canaanites will become a burden to Israel because Israel has failed in their compliance with their Covenant with Yahweh. In response, those who heard this message wept over their actions and their consequences. Furthermore, they name the location Bochim, "weeping." As with prior texts, this location thus becomes a tangible memorial of this confrontation between Yahweh and the nation of Israel. Later generations may inquire about the rationale for giving this location such a disheartening name. In response, elders can share stories about the consequences of negligence toward Yahweh's covenant and further demonstrate the importance for future generations to act in compliance in order to not repeat the offense. The didactic narratives for this tradition offer explanations for the presence of Canaanites in the land possessed by Israel.[1]

Judges 2 repeats the death of Joshua, recorded in Joshua 24, and illustrates the contrast between the nation's faithfulness prior to Joshua's death and the lack of faithfulness during the present conditions described within the chapter. Whereas the book of Joshua demonstrates the victory of the conquest because of Israel's faithfulness to Yahweh, Judges 2 begins to demonstrate the contrasting shift toward the later generations and their lack of faith. The word "served" in verse 7 is used in connection with Israel's allegiance to Yahweh. However, when it is used again in verses 11, 13, 19, and 3:6, it is in the context of serving other gods.

The previous generation, who witnessed entrance into the Promised Land, experienced vivid examples of Yahweh's redemption. They devoted themselves to their God. The newer generation depicted in Judges is seemingly ignorant of these experiences. The latter part of chapter 2 recounts how Israel forgot Yahweh's actions on their behalf. The narrator describes them in verse 10 as a generation who did not know Yahweh or his actions; 2:11–19 then serves as an overview of the organized accounts extending from 3:12 to 8:35. The organization of these accounts is determined by the framing of each activity to express its theological relevance and educational value in Israel's religious worldview.[2] Gerhard von Rad and Antony Campbell disagree on the purpose of these accounts. Rad articulates their purpose as Israel's ordering under Yahweh's authority. As with Plato's *Republic*, it defines justice and political theory.[3] Campbell, however, demonstrates the importance for reading these narratives as a witness of Joshua's failure in leadership.[4] Campbell's assessment is incorrect. While Joshua was certainly imperfect in character and obedience, as a whole, his character is more strongly celebrated for his exceptional leadership. This is evidenced through the simple narrative descriptions such as the length of his life and comparisons with Moses' character, and his description as "the servant of the Lord."[5] Instead, it is contended that these early narratives in Judges reflect on the result of negligent religious training of one generation to the next. Looking back to 2:10, readers see the narrator describes the newer generation as one who does not know Yahweh nor His deeds of redemption for Israel. The

---

1. Campbell, *Joshua to Chronicles*, 67.
2. Ibid.
3. Rad, *Old Testament Theology*, 1:332.
4. Campbell, *Joshua to Chronicles*, 68.
5. Judg 2:8.

elders of Joshua's generation neglected to convey the importance of their religious mythos and ideals. The results are the accounts recorded in Judg 3:12—8:35. The Deuteronomist has selected the accounts that demonstrate this failure and its results in order to prepare future generations to take responsibility for religious education. In preparation for these narratives, the editor purposefully includes 2:11–19 as the explicit description of the result of this failure. Yairah Amit likewise agrees that 2:11–19 is a noticeable insertion from the Deuteronomist.[6] The lack of religious education results in apostasy. The people are imperfect in their obedience; even the leaders demonstrate moral digression as demonstrated later in Samson's character. The lack of spiritual leadership and religious education results in a downward slide of morality.

The elders have failed to communicate the works of Yahweh that they had witnessed firsthand. These visual and kinesthetic events clearly impacted their faith. This is evident in the clear repetition of Josh 24:31 and Judg 2:7, those "who had seen all the great work of the Lord" continued to serve Yahweh all of their days. However, those who lacked this experiential knowledge are depicted in the latter portion of Judges 2. They did not "know" Yahweh. The term "know" is translated from יָדַע (yada).[7] This generation did not "experience" (know) Yahweh.[8] Since they had not experienced Yahweh, they did not obey him and the result is the unfortunate apostasy and events that follow. Therefore, the Deuteronomist uses the accounts of 3:12—8:35 as a didactic tool to reinforce proper pedagogy.

The events in 3:12—8:35 demonstrate the sustained passivity of the nation and their apathy toward obeying Yahweh. The summary of 2:11–19 is fully portrayed in the ensuing collection. The phrase "Israel continued to do what was evil in the sight of the Lord" is repeated twice in 3:12 and 4:2. It is bracketed on both ends by the simpler statement, "Israel did evil in the sight of the Lord" in 3:7 and 6:1. Though the individual accounts reflect phases of time when the land is at rest following the deliverance of a judge, such as the forty years of rest following Othniel and eighty years of rest after Ehud, the opening inserted summary signifies sustained oppression. This is demonstrated in 2:15, "Wherever they went, the hand of the Lord was against them for evil, as the Lord had spoken and as the Lord had sworn to them, so that they were severely distressed." Furthermore, the cycles of apostasy, oppression, deliverance, and return to apostasy are also articulated

---

6. Amit, "Judges," 510.
7. Harris et al., *TWOT*, 848.
8. Ibid.

in the opening summary of chapter 2. Israel does evil,[9] Yahweh gives them over to their enemies,[10] Yahweh delivers them through a judge,[11] relapse[12] to apostasy.[13]

There are two peculiarities in the opening summary that further allude to its later insertion. The narrative sequence of 3:12—8:35 relates that God's deliverance is preceded by Israel's cry to Yahweh. This is found in 3:9, 15; 4:3, and 6:6. The later narratives in Judges express that deliverance follows after they confess their sin. Examples are found in 10:10, 15. This pattern continues into 1 Sam 7:6; 12:10 and 1 Kgs 8:47. These descriptions of confession and crying to Yahweh are not found within the opening summary.[14] This connects with the opening message to the sons of Israel in 2:1, "I will never break my covenant with you."

The chapters that follow the summary of 2:11–19 demonstrate a variation in the structure that subtly points to one of this book's theological frameworks. The description of the people crying out to God is scarcely presented in the text. The only story that plainly mentions repentance is the account of Jephthah in 10:10–15. However, the description within that pericope relates that it was the misery of the people, not the confession of sin.[15] It is also clear that Yahweh's response is neither immediate nor automatic, regardless of the sincerity of repentance. The marginalization of response to repentance and overall lack of repentance motif suggests that the interpretive key is found in 2:1. It is solely the graciousness of Yahweh that perpetuates the generations of Israel. Yahweh acts on their behalf despite their wickedness.[16]

However, Judg 2:1–5 presents its own anomaly. In his work on the double redaction theory, Richard Nelson offers a strong argument for the inconsistency of these verses. According to Judg 2:7–11, the unrestrained sin of the people does not begin until after Joshua's death. However, this does not harmonize with the statements of 2:1–5, where the people weep for their sins.[17] Nelson goes on to recognize that 2:1–5 does not adequately fit within the text. He reports that 2:1b–25a was added by one of the book's

---

9. Judg 2:11.
10. Judg 2:14.
11. Judg 2:16.
12. Judg 2:19.
13. Campbell, *Joshua to Chronicles*, 80.
14. Ibid., 82.
15. Judg 10:16.
16. Fretheim, *Deuteronomistic History*, 90.
17. Nelson, *Double Redaction*, 43.

successive editors to connect to the following 2:6 and provide an etiology for the idea of an incomplete conquest. It holds a secondary relationship to chapter 1 since the review of the conquest in Judges 1 does not point toward 2:1–5. This is evidenced by the chapter 1 refrain that sin is the cause of the failed conquest. Furthermore, the end of chapter 1 does not prepare the reader for an assembled people. The content of 2:1–5 is not mentioned in any of the proceeding chapters. However, 2:3 points forward to the events following these chapters. "Therefore, Judg 2:1–5 is not organically one with either Judges 1 or the following book of Judges but is, in fact, dependent on the content of both."[18] Nelson rightly concludes that 2:1–5 is the work of a later editor of the main Deuteronomistic History. He also rightly notes that this editor possesses a pessimistic view of the conquest and behavior of the people. This editor borrows the content of Judges 1 as an inclusion and background for 2:1–5.[19]

Judges 2:1–5 is strongly related with the Judg 6:7–10 account, as both passages share language borrowed from Exodus, thus posing the likelihood that 2:1–5 and 6:7–10 derive from the same author/editor. The introduction in 6:1–6, along with the interruption of 6:7–10, causes a rough editorial seam preceding the remaining Gideon narrative. This is not coherent with the expected smooth transitions of the DH.[20] This, along with the two phrases, "but you have not obeyed" and "the land which Yahweh swore to your fathers," suggest the work of a later editor. The phrase "you have not obeyed" occurs only five times.[21] It is used as an accusation that summarizes the totality of Israel's covenantal negligence.[22] The second phrase, "the land which Yahweh swore to your fathers," is a common phrase used in differing structures.

> The fuller expression includes the infinitive "to give" as a complement to the main verb. In the abbreviated version found in Judg 2:1, the verb "give" is understood, not expressed. In Deuteronomy proper both forms occur, the longer being more common; also in the Tetrateuch both appear, but the shorter form is more common. In the Deuteronomistic history, however, the expression is always in the long form. In contrast, secondary Deuteronomistic additions use the short form as well. Thus, Judg 2:1 shows an affinity to the Tetrateuch not characteristic of

---

18. Ibid., 44.
19. Ibid., 47.
20. Ibid., 48.
21. Judg 2:2, 6:10; 2 Kgs 17:14, 40; 21:9.
22. Nelson, *Double Redaction*, 51.

the historical and is actually closer to other secondary additions to the history: Deut 31:23 and Josh 21:43.[23]

Campbell likewise acknowledges the framing elements of 6:7–10 and the irregularity of its insertion within the Gideon narrative. Like Nelson, Campbell attributes these verses to a later editor.[24] Following this interruption, a patterned scene proceeds from Judg 6:11–24. As the Israelites experience oppression from the Midianites, the angel of the Lord appears to Gideon, though Gideon is oblivious to his identity. Gideon is commissioned as the next messenger. This pericope follows the stereotypical seven stages: meeting,[25] presentation of the mission,[26] refusal,[27] encouragement,[28] request for and giving of a sign,[29] acknowledgment and fear,[30] and further encouragement.[31] This familiar pattern of mission within biblical literature is used to indicate status as God's elect. A second example of this pattern is observable in the commission of Moses in Exod 3:1—4:17. Here in Judges, it is used to emphasize Gideon's commission by Yahweh.[32]

Verse 22 indicates the turning point for Gideon's acceptance. After he witnesses the visual sight of fire from the rock, Gideon confirms his recognition of Yahweh. The word translated to English as "saw" is from רָאָה (ra'ah). It is a common word for sight and suggests no other type of kinesthetic experience associated with the sight.[33] As a result of this affirmation, Gideon builds an altar that the DH records as existing "to this day" in Ophrah. This site is one of only five sites recorded as existing "to this day" from the Northern Kingdom of Israel.[34] Campbell, Nelson, and Geoghegan all concur that this passage originates with the main Deuteronomistic text. The established pattern of placing a tangible, visible memorial (or pedagogical tool) for those who did not experience the event is once again illustrated

23. Ibid., 51–52.
24. Campbell and O'Brien, *Unfolding DH*, 183.
25. Judg 6:11–13.
26. Ibid.
27. Judg 6:15.
28. Judg 6:16.
29. Judg 6:17–22.
30. Judg 6:23.
31. Amit, "Judges," 523.
32. Amit, *Reading Biblical Narratives*, 66.
33. Harris et al., *TWOT*, 2095.

34. The other sites from the Northern Kingdom include: Havvoth Jair (Deut 2:14; Judg 10:4), Geshur and Maacah (Josh 13:13), the destroyed temple of Baal at Samaria (2 Kgs 10:27), and Cabul (1 Kgs 9:13).

in the text. A latter editor draws additional attention to it by confirming its existence for his later audience.

Judges 11:29–40 offers a concerning episode for cultural observation. Though its religious significance is questionable, it nonetheless provides a tangible reminder of a significant event and thus will be fairly treated here. The context centers on Jephthah, who is displeased with his position among the Ammonites. He therefore offers a rash vow that he would offer to Yahweh anything that came from out of the doors of his house as a burnt offering when he returned in peace from the Ammonites. After his tremendous victory of the Ammonites, he returns home only see the tragic emergence of his only child from his home upon his return. He mourns his vow but willingly takes responsibility for his commitment. His daughter is also grieved. She takes her companions into the mountains to mourn for two months. It is interesting that she does not simply mourn for her impending death, but rather that she will die a virgin. The pericope offers an etiological conclusion that this is the reason for the virgins to annually commemorate this event with four days of elegies.

Commentators have mistakenly attempted to avert the death of Jephthah's daughter by concluding he had intended an animal sacrifice as the fulfillment of his vow. However, the designation of "whoever comes forth from the doors of my house"[35] certainly implies human origin. Other translations such as NASB and KJV translate this word as whatever or whatsoever. Though these are acceptable grammatical translations, they do not correctly convey the absurdity of Jephthah's vow. This act of intended devotion is not the means by which Yahweh chooses to be honored. Human life is considered sacred and should not be terminated for one's own advancement.[36] The narrator himself defers from explicitly depicting her death. Instead, the tragedy of this account centers on the virginity of Jephthah's daughter and the fact that there would be no further heirs from his lineage. His fulfillment of this vow will result in the loss of the family lineage, an utter failure from his cultural perspective. The tragedy that she had no children is interjected multiple times by the repetitive assertion of her virginity.

The object lesson of this account is the pathos of religious commitment. Jephthah had made a rash vow that resulted in victory but was immediately followed with severe tragedy, though it was his daughter, not himself, who paid the penalty. Facing a childless death, she grieves for her imminent fate. Despite her grief, she makes no attempt to avert the responsibility of her father's commitment to his vow. Despite their apparent limited knowledge

---

35. Judg 11:31 (RSV).
36. Cundall and Morris, *Judges and Ruth*, 147.

of Yahweh's full expectations, they are loyal to their religious obligations and they do recognize and fulfill the pledge Jepthah had offered.[37] Later audiences are reminded of this loyalty by the editor's claim that this account is the rationale for the annual commemoration elegy. It is a strong reminder for the sacredness of vows committed to Yahweh.[38]

The final five chapters in Judges are used to draw awareness to the disorder in society and call the readers' attention to the coming monarchy. This is supported by the four editorial refrains found at 17:6, 18:1, 19:1, and 21:25, "In those days there was no king of Israel." The bookends of this collection also include the phrase "every man did what was right in his own eyes." The narratives within this collection include the pagan idol of Micah and subsequent battle with Dan; the rape, murder, and slaughter of the Levite's concubine and subsequent battle with Gibeah; and the kidnapping and rape of women at Shiloh.

Poignant lessons are inferred from this collection as several items are emphasized. First, it is realized that nothing has changed during the period of the judges. Israel remains an unlearned nation in reflection of Yahweh's laws. Micah and his mother are described as serving Yahweh, yet the narrative reflects they are not obedient to his laws. Their molten image is a clear infraction of Exod 20:3. The Levite becomes Micah's hired hand and assumes the responsibility of his personal priest. Yet, nothing is indicated within the text that Micah's idol is not in accordance with Yahweh's laws. Danites later loot Micah's house and capture the Levite with an invitation for him to serve as priest for their tribe. He seemingly appreciates the additional notoriety he will receive from them and proceeds to steal the ephod, teraphim, and idol.[39] They then formulate a base-camp and name the location Mahaneh-dan, which is described by the editor as "existing to this day." This is also acceptably translated as "the camp of Dan."[40] The Danites go on to destroy the peaceful city of Laish and rename the location Dan. It is not until 18:30 that the Levite's identity is revealed as Moses' grandson, Jonathan, son of Gershom. Irony is deeply imbedded to demonstrate that, after only two generations, Moses' own family line is involved with the idolatrous priestly service. Amit points out the discrepancy of 18:31 and its anachronistic reference to Shiloh. He contends that this verse is likely an editorial addition to better connect to the following story. In addition, it is plausible that this verse was inserted to draw a parallel between the house of Micah

---

37. Cundall and Morris, *Judges and Ruth*, 149.
38. Num 30:2; Deut 23:21–23.
39. Judg 18:20.
40. Amit, "Judges," 548.

and house of God. This juxtaposition seems to draw attention to the illegitimate shrine at Dan and the centralized place of worship to Yahweh.[41] The editor draws attention to the account by validating the continued existence of the location, serving as a reminder and pedagogical feature.

The brutality of the culture continues in the narrative depicting the attack on a Levite's concubine. Like chapters 17 and 18, pagan ethos among the Levites is again demonstrated. In an attempt to avoid personal attack, the Levite offers his concubine to endure the savagery on his behalf. Not only this, but the narrative states that he forced her outside among the savages. He shows no emotion toward the incident until he finds her dead the following morning. He lifts the body of his concubine onto the donkey and later cuts her to pieces to use as a means to rally the tribes for war against Gibeah and ultimately Benjamin. It is suggested that the cutting of the concubine serves to foreshadow the cutting of the tribal allegiance following the intertribal war in chapter 20. Just as the concubine remains for four months in her father's home, the Benjaminites remain hidden for four months at the rock of Rimmon. The shifting of the narration between Israel acting as a single nation prior to the civil war[42] and the separation into their "own territories" demonstrates the decentralization intentionally represented in the final chapters of Judges that will contrast with the coming re-centralization under the Davidic monarchy.[43]

The final portion of this metanarrative[44] includes the attempt to retrieve wives for the surviving Benjaminites. They gather at Bethel, where they wail and weep. This is possibly a connection back to Judg 2:1–5. The Israelites attack Jabesh-gilead, killing all of the inhabitants except for the virgin daughters. When they learn these are not enough wives for the surviving Benjaminites, they attack at Shiloh to kidnap the virgins who go out to celebrate an annual festival.

The book concludes with the editor's reflection that the social immorality was due to a lack of monarchy. Israel's religious compromise and social savagery is evident through the final narratives concluding Judges. The Deuteronomist seeks to demonstrate Israel's obedience to the Torah is distorted, if not altogether neglected. The editors of the Deuteronomistic History have decisively reimagined the historical stories and formulated

---

41. Davis, "Structure, Repetition, Characterization."

42. See "the congregation assembled in one body before the LORD" (Judg 20:1); "all the people got up as one" (Judg 20:8); "So all the men of Israel gathered against the city, united as one" (Judg 20:11).

43. Davis, "Structure, Repetition, Characterization," 6.

44. Metanarrative is used here to refer to two or more short stories (narratives) that join to form a longer cohesive story.

the "data" according to the principles of Yahweh in harmony with his laws. Judges is designed to show the readers why Israel lost its land and became displaced in the sixth century.[45] The lack of religious training, mentioned in Judges 2, expresses the justification for moral degradation. Those who do not know Yahweh, those who have not been taught the religious ethos of their faith community, will neglect Yahweh's laws and as a consequence lose his favor. These accounts thus subtly remind the readers of the importance of religious instruction as well as include pedagogical features for re-learning and teaching this ethos.

SUMMARY

Along with its account of the effect of not teaching others the laws of Yahweh, Judges also includes several pedagogical features that focus readers' attention on how to teach the religious traditions of Israel. Similar to Joshua, Judges includes altars (visual), such as the altar erected by Gideon at Ophrah, and the explanation of a festival (kinesthetic), such as the festival of virgins that resulted after Jephthah's rash vow, that teach the pathos of religious commitment. Additionally, the names of religiously significant locations, such as Mahaneh-dan, are included so that later generations may inquire of its significance and also hear the account of its implication. A later editor emphasizes these pedagogical tools for active learning through his insertion of the phrase "and it stands to this day" so that his own audience may confirm their existence and substantiate the religious ethos taught through them.

---

45. Brueggemann, *Introduction to the OT*, 121.

Chapter 11

1–2 Samuel

As Judges shows the readers how Israel becomes displaced from their land, 1–2 Samuel begins the turning point back to the terms of the Mosaic Covenant. Originally a single text within the Hebrew Bible, the literary work of 1 and 2 Samuel constitute a third of the Former Prophets. It links the narratives between Joshua and 1–2 Kings, which respectively discuss the acquisition of land and its subsequent loss. Unlike the recorded continued demise of Israel throughout Judges, 1 Samuel begins to establish the upward momentum of social and religious development that peaks during the reign of King David. The hypothesis of the Deuteronomist editor and his revisions of the books of Samuel has continued to find favor. It is plausible that the individual stories arose from oral tradition and folklore of the Davidic Dynasty, designed to celebrate his impressive accomplishments.[1] Literary artisans later craft these accounts from the shared memory and historical imagination of tribal elders. The Deuteronomistic editor made use of existing documents, yet also freely added his own comments and content in the final compilation of 1–2 Samuel, as read in its present form. These sources were arranged to generate his perspective of the traditions that shaped the establishment of the monarchy.[2] Early evidence of the editor's revision occurs in 1 Samuel 2 with editorial remarks such as 2:18–21 and 2:26 that highlight the favor of Yahweh on Samuel.

Similar to stones recorded in Genesis 31 and Joshua 24, 1 Sam 6:18 records a stone that also acts as a "witness" to the Israelites. The context for its purpose is the loss and return of the Ark of the Covenant. The

---

1. Brueggemann, *Introduction to the OT*, 131.
2. Ibid., 132.

metanarrative (previously defined) begins in chapter 4 where the Israelite army camps at Ebenezer in preparation for their battle against the Philistines. First Samuel 4:3 recounts the loss of the ark as a scheme contrived by the elders, yet the departure of the Ark is narrated as Yahweh's will in Ps 78:59–62. Likewise, Campbell and O'Brien attribute the loss of the Ark to Yahweh and acknowledge it as part of the pre-Deuteronomistic History documents. First Samuel 5:1 also brings the readers' attention to Ebenezer in an explanation related to the movement of the Ark from the battle scene to their territory at Ashdod. Here, the story resumes with an account of the demise of the Philistine's deity, Dagon. In response, the Philistines seek to rid themselves of the burdensome Ark. The return of the Ark to Israelite possession is recorded in chapter 6. The cows halt in the field of Joshua in Bethshemesh. According to verse 14, a large stone was located in this field. Because of its accessibility, Joshua and the harvesters in the area used the rock as a improvised altar, where they sacrificed the cows that had pulled the cart. This same rock also served as a platform on which they placed the Ark of the Covenant. The lasting significance of this rock is recorded in 1 Sam 6:18b, "The large stone on which they set the ark of the Lord is a witness to this day in the field of Joshua the Beth-shemite." In its current form, the stone monument seemingly corresponds to the Israelite repossession of the Ark. However, Geoghegan argues that this memorial is the landmark for the villagers who had inappropriately viewed the Ark. Responding to this slaughter, they elect to send the Ark to a new location. This is recorded in chapter 7, as it comes to rest in the house of Abinadab at Kiriath-Jearim. Following its receipt, Samuel gathers "all Israel" at Mizpah where they repent for their sins before Yahweh. During the process of their offerings, the Philistines gather to attack Israel. However, the account is related that Yahweh confuses the Philistines, allowing the Israelites the victory. In response, Samuel takes a stone and erects it between Mizpah and Shen and names it, "Ebenezer."

Several items are related within this larger pericope that expands from 1 Sam 4:1b to 7:14. Here, in 4:3, the elders ask why the Lord defeated them. This question is not directly answered within the account. There is no direct rationale for their defeat recorded. However, the following narrative relates that Yahweh causes the demise of Dagon. Therefore, the narrative logic is that, if Yahweh was in control at Ashdod, then he was in control during the battle at Ebenezer.[3] The literary unit is then concluded with a victory against the Philistines following the repentance of the Israelites. This is memorialized at Ebenezer, meaning "stone of help." Scholars agree that these two re-

---

3. Campbell and O'Brien, *Unfolding DH*, 228.

cords of Ebenezer are likely different locations. The name is possibly used to merely mark the literary unit. It may also be used to connect Israel's defeat from the Philistines with their later victory, where past failure is reverted.

The memorial stone is erected at Ebenezer after Israelite victory over the Philistines. However, it is certainly likely that the narrative artisans ensured the connection with the previous defeat, thereby giving it the same identity. Both the defeat and the victory are attributed to Yahweh to vividly illustrate the importance of Israel's relationship with their God. Later generations may then verify the account through the visual observation of the remaining stone. The object lesson is that even an apostate people could find Yahweh again through faith and repentance. The visual reminder and location of tangible evidence is recorded at Ebenezer. Similarly, the micro-narrative account of the Ark at Bethshemesh can be further verified by the "witness" stone identified in Joshua's field. Also in the midst of the macro-narrative is the account of the gathering at Mizpah. Here, Samuel had called the Israelites together for repentance. He is recorded in 7:6 as judging the Israelites, which links the text back, again, to chapter 4 with Eli, who had judged forty years.[4] Here, Samuel is shown as Eli's successor and the final judge before the monarchy. Through these accounts, the editors have decommissioned the priestly family and cleared the way for Samuel while expounding the power of Israel's God.[5] Incorporated into these accounts are two landmarks available to authenticate their validity to later generations who may intensify their knowledge of Yahweh and the mythos of their faith community.

Later, in 1 Sam 12:17, a visual sign is given solely to the generation of Israelites who witnessed it. Rather than a permanent reminder for later generations, this sign confirmed the words of Samuel as he declared the rebellion and wickedness of his audience of Israelites. Within the context, the people have continually requested a human king to rule over them. The editors of 1 Samuel have taken strong efforts to demonstrate the negativity of this request. Campbell rightly states that the narratives are "unremittingly negative toward Israel's first king."[6] With the exception of a few verses, such as 1 Sam 14:47–48, the text is repeatedly negative toward Saul's reign as king. Even the request for a king is received negatively. As early as Judg 8:22–23, the Israelites are admonished for requesting a human ruler rather than accepting Yahweh as their ruler. They are reminded of the theocracy of Yahweh's kingship in 1 Sam 12:12. Verses 14 and 15 then evoke familiar

---

4. 1 Sam 4:18.
5. Campbell and O'Brien, *Unfolding DH*, 125.
6. Campbell, *Joshua to Chronicles*, 129.

phrases from Deut 10:12 and Josh 24:14, where they are instructed to fear the Lord and respond in obedience. Here in 1 Sam 12:14, they are told to "listen." This is translated from שָׁמַע (shama'), which means to hear intelligently and implies obedience to that which is heard.[7] Echoing the promises of Deuteronomy 28, Samuel tells them there will be blessings for obedience, but destruction for disobedience. In order to further solidify the validity of his statements, Samuel then tells his audience that he will request thunder and rain from Yahweh so that they will "see" and "know" that their request for a king is considered wickedness by Yahweh. The word translated here as "know" is the familiar word used throughout the Pentateuch in similar formulas, יָדַע (yada').[8] This word means to teach, literally by showing. This is reinforced within the context that they are preparing to gain knowledge through the visual sign they are set to receive. This familiar word is used repeatedly throughout the Pentateuch in texts such as Gen 18:21; 42:11; and Exod 3:7. It typically refers to learning through observing and experiencing through the senses, as demonstrated here in the acquisition of knowledge through sight. This is further validated with the second word, "see."[9] The demonstrated pedagogy, within this text, is the verbal instructions followed by a visual sign to assist those receiving the instruction with memory retention. It was not enough to merely hear Samuel rebuke their rebellion. The rationale for the visual pedagogical tool is to reinforce Samuel's words. This justification is plainly stated in 12:17.

It is complicated to identify Samuel's audience. At face value, 12:1 states simply that Samuel spoke to all of Israel. Used in connection with 11:15, it can be ascertained that they were possibly at Gilgal during this instruction. Similar assemblies have occurred, such as the gathering of "all Israel" at Mizpah earlier in 7:5. The acceptance that Samuel is the sole communicator to the entire nation at once is problematic. Yet no further information is furnished as to whether additional messengers were used to convey the information to those more distant from Samuel. It is also questionable whether every Israelite actually traveled to the sites of these assemblies, or just key leaders of the family clans. Nevertheless, the pedagogical account remains for the oral instructions to large audiences. As with the preceding texts discussed in the Pentateuch, it is likely that women and children were part of this audience. Therefore, in direct relationship to the above mentioned oral instructions and visual sign described in 1 Sam 12:17, they too would have witnessed the account. It is arguable that women and

---

7. Harris et al., *TWOT*, 2412, 2412a.
8. Ibid., 848.
9. Ibid., 2095.

children were not part of the oral instructions, that only male clan leaders were present; however, these individuals would have nonetheless experienced the thunderstorm and gained the ability to question the significance of the storm during harvest, thereby allowing the men to offer the insight they received from Samuel.

Further teaching occurs in 12:23 as Samuel explains that he will endeavor to instruct the Israelites. The word translated as "instruct" is from יָרָה (*yarah*). It is used in connection with the falling of rain or the shooting of an archer's arrow. In connection with instruction, it may reflect the direct distribution of knowledge as in pointing out truth or specifically addressing an issue.[10]

The Philistine army, and more specifically Goliath, is named as the audience of instruction in 1 Sam 17:46–47. Though they are not resident aliens, as have been a part of the previous focus in this book, the narrative maintains that a kinesthetic activity is designed in order to teach the Philistines the reality of Israel's God, Yahweh. In their dialogue with one another, Goliath taunts David by stating that he will give David's flesh to the birds of the sky and beasts of the field. David responds, that rather than dying by Goliath's hand, Yahweh will deliver Goliath to David in order for him to be beheaded. The storyteller then allows David to repeat Goliath's words by stating that he will give, not only Goliath's flesh, but the flesh of the entire Philistine army to the birds of the sky and beasts of the earth. The purpose of this victory is for all the people of the earth and specifically the Philistines to acknowledge the superiority of Yahweh. The word used for "know" in both verses 46 and 47 is again, יָדַע (*yada'*). Knowledge of Yahweh will be acquired through the visual demonstration of David's victory over Goliath.

The impact of this single victory remained explicit in the memories of Israelites for several generations. It is championed as one of David's greatest victories. David had entered the battle and implored Yahweh's title from Deut 20:1–5, the Lord of Hosts. Not only did he fight in the name of his God, but he gave Yahweh the credit for his victory so that all nations would come to understand the importance of his God. Nothing further is offered, within the biblical texts, for the outcome among the Philistines or other groups beyond Israel. The Philistines were likely chased from the territory. However, the focus of the narratives continues on the politics within Israel rather than the religious alterations of other nations. Nonetheless, the pedagogical aspect remains evident within this account. As with the demonstration noted in 1 Samuel 12, there is no lasting memorial mentioned in this narrative. However, the transmission of Israel's religious ideals, namely

---

10. Ibid., 910.

the superiority of Yahweh, is communicated through a visual experience that the Philistines could readily remember. The death of their most valiant warrior would no doubt encourage those who saw the battle to relay their experience to other non-eyewitnesses. The superiority of Israel's God would likely be conveyed through their various conversations.

Similar to the song of Moses recorded in Deut 31:19, David orders the Song of the Bow to be taught to the people of Judah so that they may remember deaths of Saul and Jonathon. Using familiar pedagogy, David ensures that the people learn and remember the significance of this historical event on Mt. Gilboa. Other recorded songs include the Song of Deborah and Barak in Judg 5:1 and the Song of Hannah's Thanksgiving, recorded in 1 Sam 2:1. Each of these recorded songs emphasize the importance of a historical event for Israel's culture. Unlike the previously recorded songs, David's Song of the Bow does not mention the name of his God, nor does it suggest that Yahweh's providence led to the deaths of Saul and Jonathon.[11] Instead, the emphasis appears to be on the historical value of the death of the first Israelite monarch. Beyond this historical record, nothing else is mentioned in the text as an essential object lesson for Israel, whereas Deborah's and Hannah's songs both highlight attributes and actions of Yahweh. For example, Hannah's song highlights the power of Yahweh to "intervene decisively in public affairs."[12] In each of these songs, as well as the Song of Moses, the pedagogical function is evident. The pneumonic device of poetry and song is an imperative part of the pedagogical tools essential for conveying significant historical and religious ideals.

Two additional locations are named in response to significant historical and religious events within 2 Samuel. These include Helkath-hazzurim and Perez-uzzah. The narrative documenting Helkath-hazzurim is located in chapter 2. The context includes a battle or tournament agreed upon by Joab and Abner. Each selected twelve contestants as representatives of their army. However all twenty-four received fatal wounds, settling nothing between the two armies. As a result, the location was named, Helkath-hazzurim, meaning field of rocks. Campbell claims that the connection between this combat and the following civil war is unclear.[13] However, this battle links the following events that lead to the full assertion of David's reign over Saul's territory. As stated in 2:17, the battle provoked by the initial contest ended in David's favor. This victory provokes the pursuit of Abner by Asahel, David's

---

11. Baldwin, *1–2 Samuel*, 183.
12. Brueggemann, *Introduction to the OT*, 133.
13. Campbell, *Joshua to Chronicles*, 147.

nephew. Upon Asahel's death by Abner, Asahel's brothers, Abishai and Joab chase Abner from the area and then sound the trumpet to close the battle.

The second location, Perez-uzzah, is recorded in 2 Samuel 6. Unlike Helkath-hazzurim, Perez-uzzah has strong religious affiliation. This popular story accounts for David's concern for bringing the Ark of the Covenant to Jerusalem. In their haste, they had not sought the appropriate provisions for transporting the Ark. During the journey, it begins to fall and Uzzah reaches to steady the religious relic. To his demise, regardless of his sound intentions, Uzzah has violated the religious law and is therefore struck dead by Yahweh. In his grief, David names the location Perez-uzzah. One of the textual editors later adds the statement "to this day" to ensure his modern audience associated the location with this account. Perez-uzzah means "[the Lord's] break out against Uzzah."[14] In his anger, David attributes Uzzah's death to Yahweh.

The initiative to transport the Ark to Jerusalem begins under David's command. Uzzah's death brings a temporary halt to its movement. Yet unlike the previous account of the Ark's long rest at the home of Abinadab, it remains with Obed-edom only a few short months. The blessings experienced by Obed-edom restore David's confidence. "The second stage of the journey is under YHWH's control. The signal is given by YHWH's blessing; without it, we are left to assume that David would have remained angry, afraid, and unwilling [to finish transporting the Ark]."[15] The location of Perez-uzzah offers two reminders. The first, like Meribah, it reminds later generations of absolute obedience to Yahweh's laws. Any deviation, no matter how trivial or innocent, still warrants correction. Second, this location marks the transition of Yahweh's election to transfer the ark, the symbol of his relationship with Israel, to Jerusalem.

Brueggemann, Campbell, and O'Brien rightly identify the lack of exilic editing and characteristic Deuteronomistic features within the narratives of 1 and 2 Samuel. However, though few, they are existent. The injected phrase "to this day" is found multiple times as is the focus of the Ark of the Covenant, an agreed theological focus of the Deuteronomist.[16] The Ark Narrative that extends from 1 Sam 4:1 through 1 Sam 7:1, and arguably picked up again in 2 Samuel 6, carries an ambiance similar to the Pentateuch. Previously in this book, it was argued that the editing of the final form of the Pentateuch carried Israel's ethos during two parallel emotive and theological journeys. As in Deuteronomy, Israel hopes for the land it is promised but

---

14. Baldwin, *1–2 Samuel*, 208.
15. Campbell, *Joshua to Chronicles*, 152.
16. Nelson, *Double Redaction*, 123–24.

does not possess, so in the final exilic editing Israel hopes for the land it is promised but does not possess. The pedagogical underpinnings within the Pentateuch's texts prepare the contemporary exilic audience for reentrance into this land and the reestablishment of the sacred ideals that are outlined in their religious laws. Likewise, Brueggemann points out a similar emotive parallel documented within the ark narratives of 1 and 2 Samuel:

> The key "character" is the ark of the covenant, a vehicle to signify the presence of YHWH in the narrative. The narrative as a whole has a dramatic movement from the *defeat of the ark* and then the inscrutable *reassertion of the ark* as YHWH is said to be headed home in glory. The narrative articulates at the same time (a) that the ark and YHWH who inhabits the ark will not rescue Israel in war because Israel (through the house of Eli) has been hopelessly corrupt, but (b) that YHWH's own reassertion of sovereign power and freedom cannot be resisted by the Philistines. The dramatic inversion from *defeat* to *reassertion* is perhaps in belated traditioning a pattern that pertains to Israel's own experience of *descent into exile* and anticipated *homecoming in splendor*.[17]

SUMMARY

While descriptions of pedagogy are sparse within 1 and 2 Samuel, they are present. The use of participatory learning through tangible locations and objects continues to draw on natural inquiry and active engagement from the learner. First and Second Samuel continues to reinforce the use of visual and tangible objects to perpetuate the didactic narratives included in these written accounts. Naysayers have the opportunity to attend the locations described and validate the authenticity of accounts they have heard. Similarly, apathetic and rebellious audiences are given immediate signs to capture their attention and support the validity of the instructions. They become immediate eyewitnesses to the splendor of Israel's God so that they too may become convinced of their need to worship and obey Yahweh and consequently teach this conviction to others.

---

17. Brueggemann, *Introduction to the OT*, 133.

Chapter 12

1–2 Kings

FIRST AND SECOND KINGS traces the course of corruption to captivity. Within these accounts are the experiences that result for those who receive the grace of God as well as the loss of protection for those who choose to turn and disobey. Imbedded in these stories is the experiential learning of the original characters as well as the ongoing religious artifacts used as tangible pedagogical tools for later generations. In both cases, active learning is recorded as the means for memorializing these accounts for future generations.

The purpose of the Deuteronomistic History is fundamentally supported by the suppositions and consistent reimagination of historical events that reflect theological ideals of Israel's claim of Yahweh as God. The Ark of the Covenant is discussed several times throughout the Deuteronomistic History in conjunction with the editorial inclusion, "until this day." The Levites are obligated to transport it in Deut 10:8; it is used in conjunction with the miraculous crossing of the Jordan River in Josh 4:7; the Levites bear the Ark as Joshua reads the law in Josh 8:30–35, the ramifications of improper handling of the Ark are recorded throughout 1–2 Samuel; and it is brought into Jerusalem to centralize religious worship to Yahweh in 2 Samuel 6.

The Ark's final appearance, in conjunction with the "until this day" annotation, occurs in 1 Kings 8. This pericope relates the Ark of Covenant coming to rest in its final habitation. Evidence that this narrative is among the earlier narratives incorporated in the Deuteronomistic History occurs in verse 8, where the poles are said to extend beyond the holy place before the inner sanctuary where they can be seen "to this day." Campbell and O'Brien note the priestly literary activity with the significance of the transfer of the ark into the newly built temple. They further point out the clarification of

Zion as the City of David in verse 1 as evidence for the blending of two major traditions.[1] Within the assembly, the editors note the elders, heads of tribes, leaders of households, Solomon, and finally the inconsequential people. This assembly of people is repeatedly reiterated throughout the chapter in both noun and verb form. The verb, from the root קָרָא (*qara'*), which means to call out or to recite,[2] is used in verses 1–2, describing Solomon's actions of assembling the people and announcing the beginning of this gathering. The noun is used in verse 14. After the cloud of Yahweh's glory fills the temple, Solomon turns to the assembly of people in order to bless them. Afterwards, he turns toward the altar to pray, in the presence of the assembly.[3] At the conclusion of his prayer, Solomon then turns back toward the assembly to bless them a second time.[4] The striking repetition of this word assists the reader in connecting it to the assembly of people for instruction described in Exod 12:3; 35:1; and Deut 4:10.

From within this assembly, the Levites seemingly emerge in order to transport the Ark to its final location within the newly constructed temple. As they do, a cloud fills the dwelling as a sign of Yahweh's acceptance of the Temple and presence among the people. Solomon's proceeding supplication focuses on the fulfillment of Yahweh's promises. Solomon makes seven requests for Yahweh to "hear" the people of Israel. Each of these is from שָׁמַע (*shama'*). Once, in verse 36, Solomon requests that Yahweh "teach" the Israelites how they are to behave. The word used here is from יָדָה (*yadah*). This word may have been selected in conjunction with its specific context and a play off of the drought and request for rain as a sign of forgiveness.[5]

The rationale for these seven requests is given in verses 60–61. Solomon asks Yahweh to hear and forgive the people for these seven offenses so that all the people of the earth will "know that the Lord is God." The word translated as "know" comes from יָדַע (*yada'*). The first six prayers request that Yahweh "hear in heaven" the prayers of the people. Each of these present something that is visibly observable including: condemn the wicked[6] return the people of Israel to their land,[7] send rain to show forgiveness,[8]

---

1. Campbell and O'Brien, *Unfolding DH*, 350.
2. Harris et al., *TWOT*, 2063.
3. 1 Kgs 8:22.
4. 1 Kgs 8:55.
5. Harris et al., *TWOT*, 910.
6. 1 Kgs 8:32.
7. 1 Kgs 8:34.
8. 1 Kgs 8:36.

relieve repentant sinners of famine,[9] bless foreigners who worship Israel's God, Yahweh,[10] and give victory in battle.[11] Also within these six requests, it is reiterated that the purpose for these visual signs of forgiveness is that others will fear the lord[12] and learn of Yahweh's great name.[13] The seventh prayer, or request, extends from 1 Kgs 8:46–53. This final request is distinct from the previous six because it adds additional description to the phrase "hear in heaven." Instead, it requests that Yahweh would "hear their prayers and supplication in heaven." This final request acknowledges that oppression from enemies is a result of Yahweh's action as punishment for sin. Therefore, Solomon requests that penitent believers be released from the control of their enemies. In addition, it associates this release from enemy control with the release from Egyptian bondage described in Exodus.

All seven requests are associated with a visual demonstration of Yahweh's providence and ability to intervene. This is likewise connected to the expected use of יָדַע (*yada'*) in verse 60. The principle rationale for Yahweh's actions is to allow this generation of believers to visibly experience and learn of the supremacy of their God. Likewise, the context also connects these acts to the religious tradition and long held story of the exodus from Egypt so that they are able to verify that the same God who delivered their ancestors from such an ominous enemy is also their current deliverer from the crisis or oppression they face. Furthermore, the religious ethos connected to this deliverance is the expectation of repentance from sin. As seen in several previous accounts, the national religious identity that sin brings punishment and repentance results in blessing are reinforced throughout all seven of these requests. Bound within this initial prayer and address to the people, during the commencement of worship in the newly constructed temple, is the re-teaching of this paramount religious truth.

Campbell and O'Brien point out the distinctive editorial pieces of chapter 8. In connection with 1 Kgs 8:1 they state, "The moment that the text begins here is a major highpoint of the Josianic DH. Fundamental to its understanding is the claim that, with the dedication of the temple, the dtr program outlined in Deut 12:10–12 is fulfilled."[14] The obtainment of land, the dwelling place of Yahweh and celebration of the people are all keys to the fulfillment of promise initiated in Deuteronomy 12. Campbell and O'Brien

---

9. 1 Kgs 8:39.
10. 1 Kgs 8:43.
11. 1 Kgs 8:45.
12. 1 Kgs 8:40.
13. 1 Kgs 8:42.
14. Campbell and O'Brien, *Unfolding DH*, 349.

skillfully argue the text signals and text-history of 1 Kings 8 to demonstrate the various additions and approximate periods of the various texts before they were edited into the current final form. Elements such as vocabulary, key phrases, and thematic emphasis support their conclusion. Campbell, and O'Brien affirm the later addition of Solomon's prayer in 1 Kgs 8:27–53. With the exception of verses 28–29a, Campbell and O'Brien attribute this to a later editor who contributed to the text following the original DH. Nelson, on the other hand, somewhat waivers in his discussion on this text. He adds that the reference to Yahweh shifts from second to third person. Nelson also notes that the text does not decisively demonstrate whether the Temple is still standing based on Solomon's words in his recorded prayer, and alludes that this could be a later addition. He mentions that some verses such as 26 and 28 are likely later, but the overall content coincides with the focus of an independent people, still in their own land rather than those of exile.[15] However, he plainly asserts that verses 44–51 are an obvious addition by the exilic editor.[16] Like Nelson, Campbell and O'Brien note the striking absence of the Temple references in Solomon's prayer. They note the phrase "toward this place" in verse 29 as a vague reference that what is no longer in the Temple.[17] The NASB translates "place" as "house," which seemingly carries more of a connection to the Temple. The word used is הַמָּקוֹם (*maw-kome'*), which does leave the location open to something beyond the Temple. Though "house" is not an inappropriate translation, the semantic range allows for far more ambiguity.[18]

Campbell and O'Brien's assertion that Solomon's prayer shifts the focus to the people and communicates a later insertion are correct. They go on to state that the seven requests within the overall structure of the prayer are framed by verses 29b–30 and verses 52–53 as an introduction and conclusion. They also note:

> There are five signals that point to the collection of seven prayers as a later expansion of the Dtr's prayer for the dedication of the temple. (i) The literary seam identified above—vv. 29b–30—that introduces the collection. (ii) The literary seam of 52–53 that concludes the collection and links it to the surrounding context. V. 52 provides a link to the immediate context (cf. v. 54) by echoing the language of vv. 29–30 and by reintroducing the king as one in need of prayer; he is not mentioned in any of the seven

---

15. Ibid., 70.
16. Nelson, *Double Redaction*, 72.
17. Campbell and O'Brien, *Unfolding DH*, 354.
18. Harris et al., *TWOT*, 1999h.

prayers. V. 53 provides a link to the larger context by recalling the promises to Moses (cf. v. 56). (iii) All the prayers address situations that affect the people, not the king. The prayer for the individual in vv. 31–32 is hardly a reference to the king. (iv) The majority of the prayers are preoccupied with the forgiveness of sin (cf. vv. 34, 36, 39, 46–50). The verb "to forgive," *sa*[set macron over a]*laḥ*, occurs elsewhere in Deuteronomy—2 Kings in passages that are later than the Josianic DH; Deut 29:20 (Heb 29:19), and 2 Kgs 5:18; 24:4 . . . The occurrence in Deut 29:20 is heading in the reverse direction to the tenor of these prayers; they are unlikely to be from the dtr revision (national focus). (v) The prayers presume divine approval of the temple which, in the text, is not granted until 9:3. Cross attributed 8:25b, 46–53 to his Dtr2. Nelson attributed 8:44–51 to his Dtr2.[19]

It is further asserted that Campbell and O'Brien are correct with their admittance that the late addition of these verses does not necessarily mean a late composition. It is plausible that verses 44–45 are pre-exilic since they speak of a military campaign with no mention of defeat. However, these verses should be read in conjunction with the overall context. The language, content, and setting of 46–51 are "clearly exilic."[20] It is clear that the events rooted in Solomon's own time continued to develop with enough force that the exilic editor brings additional emphasis for his present audience. This chapter enhances the narrative attributed to the Temple yet also acknowledges the religious restraints of the exiled people and allows accessibility to Yahweh, apart from the Temple. "The development of chapter 8 shows the way in which the 'historian' characteristically reformulates texts in order to make them pertinent to and authoritative for the generation of the exile."[21]

As a whole, the pedagogy articulated in 1 Kgs 8:12–61 continues to affirm the legitimacy of visual and tangible means of reinforcing oral stories and instructions that relate the religious ethos and cultural heritage of the Israelites. The later addition of this pericope is certainly conceivable and supported by multiple scholars. It is therefore attested that these seven requests/prayers that comprise Solomon's overall prayer and address to the people is written in such a way to reinforce the pedagogical ideals of the final editors of the Deuteronomistic History. Overlaid with the essential religious truth of obedience and repentance toward Yahweh are the primary modes by which religious education occurs: visual and kinesthetic techniques. Israelites, as well as converted foreigners, would have a variety of means by which

19. Campbell and O'Brien, *Unfolding DH*, 356.
20. Ibid., 356.
21. Brueggemann, *Introduction to the OT*, 150.

they could either visually see, or tangibly experience the validity of the truth proclaimed by their fellow faith adherents. Deliverance from enemies, relief from famine and drought, blessing, and condemnation of the wicked are witnessed firsthand, by the current audience, so they would come to "know," יָדַע (*yada'*), the supremacy of Yahweh and His expectation of obedience to His laws. The validity of the existence of their God is affirmed through His actions that they are able to witness for themselves. Furthermore, this pericope juxtaposes the deliverance from the Egyptians with the deliverance that the modern audience would experience, thus allowing the modern audience to embrace the validity of the didactic accounts they no doubt heard from the storytellers among their ancestors. Religious ethos and firsthand experience are again intertwined to formulate pedagogy.

Following the dedicatory sacrifices at the new Temple, Yahweh responds to Solomon. Within this response, Yahweh affirms his consecration of the Temple. As long as Israel maintains obedience to Yahweh's laws, His blessing will remain on the people. However, he warns that if they become negligent to His laws and statutes, the Temple will be destroyed and Israel will become a mockery to passersby.

The abrupt change from singular to plural verbs in verses 6–9 as well as the shift from Solomon to the people signal a later addition for these verses.[22] Campbell and O'Brien are correct in their hesitation to affix a firm date to this addition. The language of destruction is not enough evidence to support an exilic period for its composition. However, there is enough evidence to support its revision from the main Deuteronomistic History document. The insertion of 1 Kgs 9:6–9 offers tangible evidence for the consequences of disobedience. Though the date of composition is arguable, the addition of these verses allows the later audiences to learn from the "heap of ruins." Even the dwelling place of Yahweh is subject to his providence. There is nothing too grand or sacred that it is beyond loss when disobedience occurs. Yahweh expects obedience to His laws and any disassociation from this truth results in regrettable consequences for all to see and touch. This reality is likely fresh within the memories of the exilic community. As the final revisions of the Pentateuch and Deuteronomistic History come together, the editors include aspects pertinent for the exiled people upon their return home to reinforce the continuing religious expectations.

The apparent editor's use of "until this day" is clearly present by its use in 2 Kgs 2:22. Here, the Deuteronomist's concern for prophecy is demonstrated as he highlights its fulfillment. Within the narrative, Joshua's curse

---

22. Campbell and O'Brien, *Unfolding DH*, 360.

on Jericho is referenced.[23] The salt used to clarify the water was not enough to clean the entire water supply. Therefore, the cleansing of the water is illustrated as a miraculous event by Yahweh, through Elisha. Joshua's curse is thus lifted, making Jericho habitable. This account could be considered an etiological explanation for the origin of fresh water. The tangible fresh water required explanation, which the Deuteronomist supplied. A closer analysis of the causal connection in verse 22 reveals variations in form and content of the account. וַיְרַפֵּא (from רָפָא, *rapha'*)[24] is aorist, thus Elisha's action of throwing salt serves as an introduction to the main point, which focuses on Yahweh's word.[25] Childs brings attention to this as he addresses the plausibility of this story stemming from an etiological tradition. However, he correctly identifies the reshaping of the account to be used in conjunction with a series of narratives that use the phrase "according to the word" as a refrain. First Kings 17:16; 2 Kgs 2:21; 4:44; 5:14; and 7:6 are used collectively as a theological pattern to highlight the effect of Yahweh's word through these miraculous accounts.[26] Therefore, the use of "until this day" in verse 22 is clearly a secondary addition to an earlier recorded story. This narrative explanation supports the case of a tangible object, in this case water, that preceded the necessity of narrative to join it to a theological reality. A later editor finds value in the tangibly evident drinking water and draws the readers' attention to its pedagogical function for teaching a theological reality through the insertion of the later phrase, "until this day."

SUMMARY

The texts of 1–2 Kings incorporates signs as experiential learning for the original audience, seemingly reverting to the pattern recorded in Exodus. However, unlike Exodus, 1–2 Kings also utilizes the editorial phrase "until this day" as a means of contemporizing the story and maintaining a tangible peg article tool for the ongoing active learning for later generations. Therefore, the associated pattern of a visible reference preceding oral account is again established in the text. The prominence of active learning and student engagement is again highlighted by later editors for the ongoing religious training of future generations.

---

23. Josh 6:24; and 1 Kgs 16:34.
24. Harris et al., *TWOT*, 2196.
25. Childs, "Study of the Formula," 288.
26. Ibid., 289.

Chapter 13

Part Three Summary

THE EDITORIAL ACTIVITY OF the Deuteronomistic History is uncontested among biblical scholars; what is disputed is the extent and timeframe for which the narratives were reshaped.[1] Though they do not agree on which texts were edited during the exilic period, many scholars do agree on an exilic editor who finalized these documents into their present form.

Increasingly, critical interpreters are cautious of the historical reliability of the accounts within 1–2 Kings. At face value, these two books assume to address the rise and fall of the monarchy of the Northern Kingdom of Israel and Southern Kingdom of Judah. The alleged sources of Prophetic Record, royal archives, and folklore obscure the accuracy of these accounts. Nevertheless, the "historian(s)" endeavor to piece together the various stories to account for the sources and collected memory. An overly complicated dissection of sources is unnecessary for this writing. For the purpose of this study, the overall unity of the Deuteronomistic History is factored along with the clear signs of editing that are the natural result of the transmitters who shaped the sources for the reimagination of cultural and religious identity and religious restoration.

It is readily identified that the purpose is not a historical report but rather the theological significance that is associated with these accounts. The various editors are merely being true to the traditions passed on to them. Alongside these theological themes is the pedagogy associated with the means for perpetuating their memory.

The Deuteronomistic editors did not indiscriminately propagate any truth but rather selectively used accounts that could be made consistent

---

1. Knoppers, *Reconsidering Israel*, 292.

with the teachings of Deuteronomy.² This is illustrated through the DH's presentation of Joshua with Josiah's reforms in mind.

> Joshua is to obey Deuteronomy's law of the king by meditating on the book of the law day and night (Deut 17:18–19; Josh 1:7–8). Josiah fulfills the law of the king by reading and obeying the book of the law (2 Kgs 22:16; 23:2, 24–25).³

Content was reworked so that it aligned with the final editor's theological reality and intellectual pursuit of Yahwistic faith. He further ensured the inclusion of pedagogical tools and schema to ensure the religious ethos of his culture was preserved through the correct teaching of these accounts. This chapter relates the narratives that include pedagogical descriptions or examples of how religious ethos should be or were used.

The pedagogical paradigm presented in the Deuteronomistic History is the use of memorials and cleverly named locations that mark where major religious events occurred. These locations then serve as visual and tangible reminders, not only for those who originally witnessed them, but for later generations as well. This is confirmed by the repeated phrase, "until this day," inserted by a later editor. Rather than relying solely on memory and oral instructions, the paradigm repeatedly integrated within the Deuteronomistic history is the incorporation of visual cues to reinforce the validity retold accounts. In addition to storytelling, visual instructional methods are used in the Deuteronomistic History as a means for religious education. This pedagogy is repeatedly highlighted by a later editor who reworked the text to draw attention to the need for religious instruction. This is supported by the insertion of Judg 2:11–19, or emphasizing an existing pedagogical feature through the inclusion of his phrase, "until this day."

The paradigm for incorporating tangible and visual pedagogical features is illustrated in both the final forms of the Pentateuch and Deuteronomistic History. However, it is Wisdom Literature that is often used for illustrating the pedagogical features of the Hebrew Bible. For this reason, the following chapter will survey the Wisdom corpus for examples of pedagogy and compare its emphasis with that of the Pentateuch and Deuteronomistic History.

---

2. Ibid., 292.
3. Nelson, "Double Redaction," 325.

Part Four

Conclusion

THE OBJECTIVE OF THIS study is to investigate whether or not the specific means of educating adults, foreigners, and children were purposefully included or highlighted within the final forms of the Pentateuch and Deuteronomistic History. This has entailed a survey of these narratives for underlying pedagogical principles behind the human behaviors recorded in the various accounts. In conclusion of the research presented, it can be argued that the final forms of the Pentateuch and Deuteronomistic History do contain examples of active learning pedagogy that are repeatedly used.

A group who refuses to educate successive generations is a people who will perish without heritage. The major characteristic of the Hebrew Bible is its active communication that passes to successive readers. Within this text is the preservation of guidance necessary to secure the religious faith traditions into the heritage of the faith community. In addition to these ideals, the writers and editors take necessary precautions to retain and teach their idealized form of religious instruction. Not only is the ethos of the writers included but the means of education (pedagogy) is also purposefully preserved.

EXPLORATION OF THE RESEARCH QUESTIONS

The research presented throughout this writing thoroughly explores the research questions established in the introduction. In order to explore the research questions, chapter 1 introduced the concept of active learning while chapter 2 of this book concentrated on the literary interpretive approach used within an inductive or deductive study of the Bible. Since one focus of this book sought to verify whether or not editors purposefully include or highlight pedagogical features, chapter 2 also demonstrated why a literary approach to the Hebrew Bible is more conducive to this study to adequately demonstrate recorded pedagogy than a historical approach would allow. The second focus of chapter 2 was a discussion of the role of editors in relation to the Pentateuch and Deuteronomistic History.

In support of the two focuses for chapter 2, the chapter began with a discussion of the literary approach as well as a brief review of advocates and opponents of these areas. Since advancing the continuing debate in these areas was not the objective, this study relies on the scholarship and dates of Walter Brueggemann, Antony Campbell, Mark O'Brien, and Richard Nelson for their research throughout the later chapters of this book. Although there is some variation in their respective arguments, they are all consistent with the final form of the biblical texts discussed in this book taking place in the sixth century BC. While this study does use their research, the focus remains on the editorial activity related to pedagogical features rather than pinpointing specific dates for this activity.

The existence of editorial activity within the Pentateuch and Deuteronomistic History is uncontested among biblical scholars. Furthermore, the appropriation of borrowed material and contextualization of earlier material causes interpreters to inquire as to how the faith communities identified narrative accounts that preserved their understanding of their God, Yahweh. As the stories are retold, minor modifications are used to add clarity to the accounts for the younger generations. Through the inclusion of specific details the writers highlight elements within the narratives that help preserve the validity of the story, such as geographical features or rationale for annual sacred festivals. When necessary, later editors bring additional attention to these pedagogical features. Along with their theology, the writers and editors preserved their teaching techniques as the primary means for preserving their religious and cultural identity. This important feature of literary criticism was then used in subsequent chapters where the purposeful inclusion of instructions and examples of pedagogy was defended.

Part 2 built on the role of editors established in chapter 2 as it proceeded to demonstrate that informal instructional methods can be observed within the final form of the Pentateuch. As the characters identify the strengths and weaknesses of their cultural identity and religious beliefs, they incorporate them into their teaching praxis. Part 2 also seeks to defend that the editors of the Pentateuch purposefully gathered the narratives in such a way that they demonstrate a particular means for teaching religious ethos. Stories with didactic properties are utilized and knowledge was gained from the impressions these stories leave for the hearers. The means by which the characters teach others to remember cultural and religious obligations becomes part of an amassed collection that strategically imparts not only knowledge, but the method of teaching. The repetitious theme of learning through experiential learning, "make them known," from יָדַע (*yada'*), occurs in Deut 4:9, depicting learning through kinesthetic experience. Part 2 further documented and supported that the adult community, described within the Pentateuch, had witnessed or experienced the results of Yahweh's actions. Additionally, they had received verbal instructions from Moses. Within Deuteronomy, as the characters prepare for entrance into the land promised to them, they are held responsible for remembering their experiences and instructions from Moses in order to pass this information on to their children. The word used in this context is יָדַע. They are also directed to respond to questions with a condensed account of principle factors for their faith as illustrated in Deut 6:21–24. The expected outcome for teaching children was found in Deut 31:13. Children are to observe the actions of their faith community and witness the resulting blessing. They then also hear the accounts that produced the faith in their elders so that they would likewise morally revere Yahweh and become obedient to his laws as well as perpetuate the cycle of instruction.

In addition to documenting the examples of pedagogy, part 2 also addressed and documented evidence of editorial revisions that arguably highlight pedagogical features. One example of this came from Genesis 17. Here, Abram has received a theophany and is told that he and his descendants will participate in a covenant with Yahweh. Those who adhere to this covenant are to be circumcised as a sign and means of remembering the importance of this covenant. Here, oral instruction is joined with action as a means of active learning as well as a future visual reminder. Furthermore, future descendants are taught the rationale for their cultural custom for circumcision and its religious significance. As discussed within chapter 4, Genesis 17 is a later insertion of P material while Genesis 16 reflects vocabulary consistent with J. Within the chapter 17 text, Abraham's fruitfulness is assimilated with Adam's fruitfulness in Gen 1:28. Thus, he is purposefully presented within the trajectory of promise as the text situates him as an assurance of the fundamental relationship between Yahweh and his chosen people through the statement in Gen 17:8, "I will be their God." The significance of Genesis 17 is that it closely connects Abraham's promise to be the "father of many" with the cultural custom of circumcision. As a later addition to the text, editors have made the conscious effort to connect the pedagogical feature of circumcision with its religious significance within their culture.

A second example of textual revision pertaining to a pedagogical feature was located in Exod 10:1–2. This passage does not include a visual or kinesthetic pedagogical feature. However, the editorial arrangement to place this text with Exod 9:16 connects it with the visual presentation of the plagues to increase the impact and reinforce the expected pedagogical pattern of active learning. The adult faith community is clearly commanded to instruct their children so that they will identify the supremacy of Yahweh in Exod 10:2. This forms an addendum to 9:16 and is used to indicate that the primary purpose for the plagues is to enable both the Egyptian and Israelite communities to recognize the supremacy of Yahweh. Though Exod 10:1–2 does not include its own pedagogical feature, when observed in the context of 9:16, the plagues become the active learning experience underpinning the audible instructions. Furthermore, the ongoing Passover festival that is attributed to the plagues becomes the ongoing pedagogical tool that addresses and reinforces the memory of this event. As it was expounded on within chapter 5, literary critics differ on the original source material for Exod 10:2. However, there is consensus that it did not originally follow 9:16 and is evidence of editorial activity. Here again, a text is revised in order to highlight the significance of a pedagogical feature and its association with religious mythos. This, along with the other examples presented are in chapter 5, continues to form the basis for the conclusion that the editors do purposefully bring the readers' attention to pedagogical features.

Likewise, part 3 accounted for the editorial inclusion of the repeated phrase "until this day" as evidence of intent to draw attention to visual and kinesthetic features within the texts of the Deuteronomistic History. In addition to this editorial activity, part 3 also documented the continuation of the pattern established in part 2 for active learning through visual and kinesthetic pedagogical features. One of the pedagogical features used within the Deuteronomistic History is the stacking of stones as memorials and monuments. A prominent example of this technique for active learning engagement is located in Joshua 4. Here, the Israelites are commanded to select one stone for each of the twelve tribes from the bottom of the Jordan River as they finish their miraculous crossing into the land of Canaan. The purpose of the stacked stones is recorded in Josh 4:7; they are a sign, or reminder, of Yahweh's action in the lives of the Israelites. This pile of stones is meant to reassure this generation of faith adherents as well as future generations of their past encounters with Yahweh and their religious ethos of his involvement with his covenant people. The dual miraculous crossings of waters, after they escape Egypt and as they enter into the Promised Land, also confirms for them that the same God who delivered them from Egypt is with them as they begin their conquest of Canaan. They further memorialize this event through the stacking of stones as a pedagogical tool for active learning. It offers both a visual and kinesthetic teaching tool for

PART FOUR: CONCLUSION 171

future generations to inquire of its significance and hear the testimony of the account. A later editor then revises the story with the addition of verse 9, "and they are there to this day," for future readers and hearers of the account to recognize the continued importance of this pedagogical feature. Furthermore, it highlights the significance of the event and recorded pedagogy within the account.

The literary composition of Joshua 1–9 focuses on events within the Israelite camp in preparation for the events that will be described involving non-Israelites in later chapters. Joshua 7 intentionally juxtaposes the victories at Jericho and Ai to demonstrate the contrast between the consequences of obedience and disobedience to Yahweh. Likewise, both a pile of stones on Achan's grave and the naming of the location, Achor ("troubled") signifies the importance of the event and the intention to use these as pedagogical tools to remember and later teach this significance to others.

A third example of active learning is recorded in Judg 11:29–40 with an explanation for the annual four days of elegies from virgins. Here, the text centers on Jephthah who is displeased with his position among the Ammonites and offers a rash vow in an effort to earn favor and support from Yahweh. Much to Jephthah's dismay, he recognizes the absurdity of his vow when it ends in the death of his daughter. Nevertheless, he honors the commitment to Yahweh and his daughter mourns, not her death, but that she will die a virgin and childless. Later audiences are reminded of the penalty for rash vows and the law's caution against them,[1] as the writer lays claim that this incident is the rationale for the annual virgins' lament.

As observed earlier in Joshua, the use of memorials and monuments as pedagogical tools extends throughout the Deuteronomistic History and is observed again in 1 Sam 6:18. Here, the stone on which the Ark of the Covenant was set upon its return to the Israelites is recorded as a "witness" to the significance of this event. A second memorial pertaining to the Ark of the Covenant is recorded in 2 Samuel 6. Here, David concerns himself with bringing the Ark into Jerusalem. The fatal mistake of Uzzah results in David's lament and his naming of the location, Perez-uzzah, meaning, "[the Lord's] break out against Uzzah."[2] Later, an editor highlights the important pedagogical feature of this location and its significance to the religious pathos of this event by inserting the statement "to this day," and thus ensuring his modern audience correctly associates the name of the location with the testimony of the account.

---

1. Num 30:2; Deut 23:21–23.
2. Baldwin, *1–2 Samuel*, 208.

Evidence was provided in chapter 4 of this book that identified the use of monuments, locations, and altars as visual and kinesthetic pedagogical tools for teaching others the religious importance for specific locations. Like the Pentateuch, the Deuteronomistic History also continues the use of festivals for kinesthetic learning as found in Judg 11:29–40. The editorial activity throughout each of the examples presented in this chapter demonstrates a conscious effort from later editors to emphasize the pedagogical features throughout the Deuteronomistic History for their continued use by later faith adherents.

The original research questions guiding the research are answered and supported. In addition to storytelling, the Pentateuch and Deuteronomistic History incorporate examples of visual imagery and kinesthetic events in the religious education of faith adherents. These two learning styles are sub-theories under the larger conceptual framework of active learning, which accounts for learning through role play, behavior observation, and dialogue.[3] Examples of these include, but are not limited to: rock monuments (visual), priestly attire (visual), religious festivals (kinesthetic), and symbolic actions such as circumcision (kinesthetic). It was also established and supported that later editors of the Hebrew Bible have revised this literature in such a way to purposefully emphasize some of the key pedagogical features. Examples of this include the insertion of phrases such as Exod 20:1, Josh 8:30–35, and the repeated phrase, "until this day."

Previously published literature related to pedagogy of the Hebrew Bible has remained centered on the didactic use of oral and written narratives and formal education systems. Within the parameters of formal education, writers such as James Crenshaw, Henry Marrou, and Christopher Rollston have focused on support for the existence of schools. The topic of pedagogy is not the direct focus of these texts. Several writers address the didactic properties of the Hebrew Bible. Writers such as Yairah Amit attend to the moral value of the Hebrew Bible as it intrinsically seeks to instill theological perspective. However, the fundamental question of how faith adherents were taught is largely unaddressed. Presently, Walter Brueggemann has published the only study distinctly related to the Pedagogy of the Hebrew Bible. However, as described in chapter 1, his work is a combination of brief biblical examples that are then addressed in the context of modern Christian education. His main objective is the role of Christian education, which obscures his systematic approach of the biblical texts. Because of this, he leaves several key texts related to pedagogy superficially addressed or ignored. Throughout the progress of this research, no additional sources

---

3. Farrell, "Active Learning."

directly related to pedagogy in the Hebrew Bible were located or mentioned by other sources used.

Ongoing studies related to learning theory and active learning remain a central focus within the discipline of education. A secondary survey of literature related to this topic was conducted upon the completion to this writing to determine whether newer studies alter the conceptual framework established by Howard Gardner and Neil Fleming, discussed in chapter 1. While multiple studies are available within the last two years, they do not advance the original research and conclusions set forth by Gardner and Fleming. Instead, recent studies focus on the application of the active learning theory such as the study by Richa Thaman that examines active learning in Respiratory Physiology[4] or Alade and Ogbo's study on chemistry students' learning styles preferences.[5] In addition to the application of this original theoretical framework, other publications, such as that from John Cuthell,[6] merely restate the original conclusions of Fleming and Gardner without contributing new information that advances the original research. Finally, there are a few scholars, such as Jill Farrell, who offer relevant articles that continue to describe and define the original concept. However, once again, there are no new research findings that alter or advance the conclusions originally established by Gardner and Fleming.

ASSESSMENT OF THIS RESEARCH METHODOLOGY

In response to the content of this research, it is concluded that there is substantial evidence to support that the editors of the Pentateuch and Deuteronomistic History purposefully draw the readers' attention to the paradigm of teaching through visual and kinesthetic experiences. The original research questions sufficiently guided the selection of the content used within this study. Given the scarcity of sources and contribution of scholars on pedagogy within the Hebrew Bible, this research sought to address the lack of published research pertaining to methodology of religious education described within the Pentateuch and Deuteronomistic History. The methodology for research includes the deductive study of biblical texts. Two criteria were used for selecting the texts for this study. First, passages that describe or provide examples of pedagogy were reviewed. Passages containing specific descriptions of pedagogy were selected for further examination. Second, passages discussed by Campbell and Friedman because of their editorial

---

4. Thaman et al., "Promoting Active Learning," 27–34.
5. Alade and Ogbo, "Comparative Study."
6. Cuthell, "Towards a Theory."

activity were surveyed. Those that corresponded with passages selected in criteria one were investigated further to determine whether the pedagogical feature was a purposed inclusion or emphasis made by the later editor(s).

Following the selection of biblical texts, these examples of pedagogy were compared with Fleming's VARK Learning Styles to determine whether a pattern of methodology existed. It became evident, early in this study, that visual and kinesthetic illustrations are created as means for active learning to support the oral stories and instructions for religious education. After this comparison with Fleming's Learning Styles, the previously published material from scholars such as Robert Alter, Antony Campbell, Richard Friedman, Richard Nelson, and Mark O'Brien were then used to document and summarize the role of editors in given passages. Specific dates of editors are beyond the scope of this research but the synthesis of other scholarly work in redaction criticism offered sufficient support toward the discussion for the role of biblical editors in texts related to pedagogy. These texts were then cross referenced with biblical theologians such as Walter Brueggemann, Brevard Childs, Katherine Dell, and Gordan Wenham for the purpose of assessing their additional instructional and theological insight. When determined relevant, their conclusions were included.

This methodology efficiently generated a survey of several contributing scholars on each passage selected. It reinforced the initial conclusions regarding the pedagogical features and evidence of editorial inclusions and adapted well with the various collections between the Pentateuch and Deuteronomistic History. This methodology also continued to validate that the particular focus of pedagogy and connection with learning styles is unaddressed by contributing scholars in biblical literature.

POSSIBILITIES FOR FUTURE STUDY

A strong pedagogical emphasis within the Hebrew Bible does seem to extend beyond the texts studied in this book. Wisdom Literature readily reveals similar themes of active learning theory. Since the Wisdom corpus is often the primary literature studied when examining teaching and learning, the instruction in the Writings with a comparison between that and the Pentateuch and Deuteronomistic History will be examined in a future study. Gerald Sheppard has already exposed the concept of Wisdom Literature used as "a theological category associated with an understanding of canon which formed a perspective from which to interpret Torah . . ."[7] Within the Wisdom corpus, writers utilize nature as a pedagogical tool

---

7. Shepperd, *Wisdom as Hermeneutical Construct*, 13.

to teach religious ethos. One example explored is Yahweh's providential control of nature as illustrated in Job 38–41 where the writer illustrates this ethos through the object lessons of sun, sea, ox, and steed. Fundamental truths related to humanity are vicariously taught to Job and later to readers of this account through the observations of these four elements from nature.

Psalms, on the other hand, bears a striking resemblance to the pedagogical features observed in the Pentateuch and Deuteronomist History. However, like Wisdom Literature, it supports the use of the observation of nature and humanity that is more similar to Wisdom Literature instead of monuments as observed in the DH. This too will be part of a follow up study on the pedagogy of the Hebrew Bible.

Prophetic imagery is well identified and documented. Nearly every prophetic text links the message content with some type of imagery. It is plausible that this is a purposed paradigm of religious education that is extended into this literature genre. It would be interesting to determine whether any of the included imagery is the product of an editorial insertion that expanded the emphasis of an oral address. Nevertheless, it is doubtful that the nude ministry of Isaiah would have concluded without inquiry from passersby and the opportunity for narrative response and religious teaching from the prophet regarding the shame of the nation due to it religious apathy.[8] The phrase "to this day" seldom occurs in prophetic literature. When it is included in a text, it is used in connection with actions of the people rather than a validation of the continued existence of a location or monument.

The use of imagery within religious education is fairly dominant within the Gospels. Examples include Jesus' instruction to not worry in connection to the imagery of a clothed field used in Luke 12:28 and the popular illustration of the faith of a mustard seed recorded in all three synoptic Gospels. Additional research may conclude that the writers of the Gospels purposefully include the pedagogy of visual imagery and kinesthetic opportunities, gleaned from the Hebrew Bible, within their descriptions of Jesus' teachings as his own pedagogical means of religious education.

It would also be interesting to assimilate the research of this book into an impact case study within a current church setting. The implications for active learning theory for religious education is astonishing. Integrating varying teaching styles to accommodate different learning preferences, particularly for adult learners, is largely ignored in religious education. "It is possible that the act of validating students' strengths, interests, and preferences is an important first step that helps build the students' self-confidence

---

8. Isa 20:3.

and enables them to take control over their own learning."[9] Using active learning as a framework for curriculum development and developing teaching skills that balance the diverse learning strengths of students, both child and adult, results in more diverse experiential learning activities which in turn increase student participation and content retention.[10] As supported in both the Pentateuch and Deuteronomistic History, the primary means for religious instruction is active learning. Oral instructions are purposefully connected to an active learning experience in order to deepen their impact. Furthermore, significant encounters with Yahweh are memorialized through either a special name attributed to the location or religious symbolism used as a means for ensuring the ongoing memory of the event. In other words, the testimony itself is intentionally associated with something that can be personally "experienced" by others.

While there is room for additional research in the genres not selected for this book, the use of the Pentateuch and Deuteronomistic History adequately supports the purposed inclusion of pedagogy in religious education. The writers and editors of these genres sought to record not only their religious ethos for future generations, but they also include the means for this religious education to ensure these later generations would have the ability to experience Yahweh through their observations similarly to the earlier generations who experienced the original accounts first hand. Through experiential learning, learners come to know (יָדַע, yada') their God. For these writers, knowledge is not the accumulation of facts, but the ability to see and feel the effects of the actions of their invisible God. Memorials, festivals, and attire all become the means of creating these experiences for active learning so that the learners not only acquire knowledge, but they accept the ethos of the elder generation and begin to practice the culture taught. Not only this, but through these actions, they themselves become another means of other faith adherents witnessing the blessings and curses extended to those who either obey or disobey Yahweh.

CONTRIBUTION TO BIBLICAL RESEARCH

The importance of this study is the verification that, though the Pentateuch and Deuteronomistic History do not overtly describe how to train other faith adherents, pedagogy was observed through the descriptions of religious events and various narrative accounts of when instruction was to occur. Previously published research addresses the literary composition,

---

9. Jarvis and Parker, *Human Learning*, 56.
10. Ibid.

editorial activity, theological content, and narrated mythos. Additionally, the argument toward the development of formal education sites was already addressed. However, this book is the foremost research directly related to the presumption that the writers and editors purposefully included and emphasized examples of pedagogy for religious instruction. Additionally, these pedagogical features align with the current VARK conceptual framework of Neil Fleming. As Yahweh's faith adherents observed and identified weaknesses in their religious identity, writers incorporated modifications to their teaching praxis in order to instruct future generations. Pivotal actions, religious experiences, and Yahweh's self-disclosures are documented by various means of visual and kinesthetic objects including festivals, monuments, and named locations. These are then used in the religious training whereby parents and elders use the questioning from others as an opportunity to relate pieces of the amassed account of Yahweh's interaction with humanity and the religious ethos of the faith community.

The clearest example of this paradigm is located in Exod 12:24–26, where parents are instructed to prepare for questions from their children when they observe the Passover. Parents are to respond with a testimony of their deliverance from Exodus and the sovereignty of Yahweh. While this was the clearest example, several others exist including those found in Deut 6:20 and Psalm 78. A subsidiary to this paradigm was the call to remember visual or kinesthetic events experienced. Observers of the event are repeatedly called to "remember" (זָכַר, *zakhar*),[11] as demonstrated in Deut 16:3 and Num 15:39. Additionally, attention is also drawn to the effect of neglecting to teach proceeding generations, such as the inclusion of Judg 2:1–5.

In conclusion of the research from parts 2 and 3, one of the primary pedagogical tools utilized in the Pentateuch is religious ceremony; examples include Passover and Feast of Booths. Children observed the religious symbolism incorporated into these festivals and the regalia of the priests. As a result of these visual aids of attire, and kinesthetic environments of festivals, children would question their parents who were charged with the responsibility to educate their children. Instead of households, adult faith adherents were primarily educated in the context of an assembly. However, these assemblies were also often held in the context of a festival in order to connect the audible instructions with the kinesthetic environment of the festival. In addition to commemorating Yahweh's actions through festivals, some festivals were established as a ceremony for remembering the sacredness of vows. These can be observed in texts such as Num 30:2 and Deut 23:21–23.

---

11. Harris et al., *TWOT*, 551.

According to the Deuteronomist, apostasy is the direct result of the lack of religious education. Therefore, accounts depicting this cause and effect are selected in order to prepare future generations to take responsibility for religious education. Texts such as Judg 2:11–19 are purposefully inserted to explicitly draw attention to the failure that results from religious ignorance. Here, the narrator clearly establishes that the newer generation described in Judges does not know Yahweh or his redemptive actions. The religious mythos is seemingly not taught to the successive generation by those who had experienced them. In preparation of the narratives included in Judges, a later editor has decisively endeavored to include this description to ensure readers make the clear connection between the loss of blessing and neglecting to teach Yahweh's covenantal expectations along with the experiences of the religious elders. Through this we see not only the editor's emphasis of pedagogy for religious instruction, but also his warning of the consequences for neglecting to pass on the religious ethos and mythos of the community.

Illustrating pedagogy, the example of Josh 8:30–35 included a kinesthetic event, followed by a tangible memorial, and concludes with the verbal instruction of a leader to the assembly of people. An altar is built and sacrifices are offered, in accordance with the Mosaic Law. Following this, the narrative closes with the description of Joshua inscribing the words of the law upon the stone and then audibly reading them. Here, within chapter 8, the audience first sees the visual demonstration of covenant through the erection of the altar and sacrifices before they audibly hear the instructions of this covenant. It is closely assimilated with the victory at Ai in order for the participants to associate divine blessing with obedience. The Deuteronomistic History provides several examples of memorials uses as tangible locations for present and future learning of the characters. Additionally, locations were suitably named to provoke inquiry into the epistemology of the name. Bochim, in Judges 15, is an example of this pedagogical feature. Similar to the stone memorials, this location of "weeping" commemorates the result of failed obedience to Yahweh.

While visual and tangible items and locations are used to initiate curiosity, pneumonic devices, such as songs, are also used to convey significant historical and religious ideals. Both the Pentateuch and Deuteronomistic History include this feature. Examples of preserved songs include the Song of Moses,[12] Song of Deborah,[13] Song of the Bow,[14] and Hannah's Thanks-

---

12. Deut 31:9.
13. Judg 5:1.
14. 2 Sam 1:17–27.

giving.[15] The Song of the Bow is highlighted with the specific instructions for parents to teach the song to their children in order to remember the horrific ordeal of the deaths of Saul and Jonathon. The songs are a deviation of other patterns of pedagogy included in the Hebrew Bible. Whereas other oral instructions include some type of visual or tangible object associated with the instruction, these are noticeably absent when songs are used as the means for transferring and retaining knowledge.

The discussion regarding the timing of the editorial phases of the Pentateuch and Deuteronomistic History remain ongoing, though the acceptance of the editing itself is largely uncontested. Texts such as 1 Kgs 8:12–61 highlight later editors' affirmation of the legitimacy of visual and tangible means of reinforcing oral religious instruction and offers support of the intentional inclusion of pedagogical ideals. Additionally, the later insertion of the reoccurring phrase "until this day" supports the later editors' intention to draw attention to pedagogical elements, places, and memorials within the existing text in order to focus the readers' attention to a feature with pedagogical function and the necessity to retain its theological significance.

The authors and editors of the Pentateuch and Deuteronomistic History purposefully record and emphasize their pedagogy for instruction in order to ensure the ongoing religious education that included visual and kinesthetic educational tools alongside the oral story narrative. Beyond the inherent didactic quality of the Hebrew Bible, pedagogy is recorded and continuously reiterated to connect the oral narrative to tangible festivals, locations, and memorials. Story is not told for the sake of telling story. Instead, the pattern presented is learners first observe an event, location, or object and inquire of its significance thereby engaging the teacher to then retell the story behind the religious significance of the artifact in question. The clearest example of this pattern is the discussion of the Passover in Exodus 14.

The nation is also required to remember personally observed accounts of Yahweh's activity in their history. The pattern presented here often includes, "remember" (זָכַר, zakhar), "know" (יָדַע, yada'), and then a call to action such as keeping Yahweh's commandments as presented in Deut 8:2. Each of these calls to remember includes the implication of teaching others so that they do not forget. For later generations who did not personally observe the event, a festival or monument memorializes Yahweh's activity as a pedagogical tool for kinesthetic teaching as demonstrated through the feast of unleavened bread in Deut 16:3 and the stone monument described in Joshua 4.

---

15. 1 Sam 2:1.

The inclusion of these pedagogical features can then be compared with modern studies relating to learning theories, specifically the conceptual framework of active learning as presented through Neil Fleming's VARK Learning Theory. When these are compared, it becomes observable that the foremost teaching paradigm used within the Pentateuch and Deuteronomistic History is active learning through visual and kinesthetic features that are combined with oral teaching/story. The learners are meant to experience the concept as well as hear it. Lenore Borzak defines experiential learning as a, "direct encounter with the phenomena being studied rather than merely thinking about the encounter, or only considering the possibility of doing something about it."[16] Though it is over thirty years old, Borzak's definition of experiential learning continues in popularity and support by more recent scholars such as David Kolb.[17] This conceptual framework of active/experiential learning through sight and touch is transferrable to the examples illustrated within the Pentateuch and Deuteronomistic History. Here, it is observed that the authors and editors of this literature intentionally included and emphasized the pedagogical tools that later generations were to use.

In order to truly know Yahweh, one had to experience him. While he could not be seen, the affects of his involvement with Israel could be seen. For later generations who could not experience these accounts first hand, monuments, locations, symbolism in attire, and liturgy were purposefully grafted in to the mythos of this literature so that later audiences could verify the authenticity of the account. The story allows the audience to experience the pathos while the object associated with the story helps them to relate the ethos with the mythos. When combined, later faith adherents gain the ability to experience for themselves what earlier generations portray through their stories and descriptions. Knowledge is created through action and social interaction. Memory (oral story) is combined with visual, tangible, and kinesthetic experiences, thus implementing all four aspects of Fleming's VARK learning theory.

There are seldom examples of isolated verbal instruction without the distinct connection to active learning, specifically, visual or kinesthetic practice. In order to know Yahweh, the learner must experience him. Therefore, the writers and editors of the Pentateuch and Deuteronomistic History take great care to ensure pedagogy is recorded to retain the means for this continued experience and the persistence of orthodox religious instruction.

---

16. Borzak, *Field Study*, 9.
17. Kolb, "David A. Kolb on Experiential Learning."

Bibliography

Aalders, Gerhard Charles. *Genesis*. Bible Student's Commentary 1. Translated by William Heynen. Grand Rapids: Zondervan, 1981.

Alade, Oluwatomi M., and Angela C. Ogbo. "A Comparative Study of Chemistry Students' Learning Styles Preferences in Selected Public and Private Schools in Lagos Metropolis." *IOSR* 4 (Jan 2014) 45–53. Accessed February 12, 2014. http://www.iosrjournals.org/iosr-jrme/papers/Vol-4%20Issue-1/Version-1/J04114553.pdf.

Albright, William F. *Archeology of Palestine*. Rev. ed. Baltimore, MD: Penguin, 1960.

Alter, Robert. *Art of Biblical Narrative*. 2nd ed. New York: Basic, 2011.

———. *Art of Biblical Poetry*. New York: Basic, 1985.

———. *The David Story*. New York: W. W. Norton, 1999.

———. *The Five Books of Moses*. New York: W. W. Norton, 2004.

———. *The Wisdom Books: Job, Proverbs, and Ecclesiastes; A Translation with Commentary*. New York: W. W. Norton, 2010.

———. *The World of Biblical Literature*. London: Society for Promoting Christian Knowledge, 1992.

Alter, Robert, and Frank Kermode, eds. *The Literary Guide to the Bible*. Cambridge: Belknap, 1987.

Amit, Yairah. "Judges." In *The Jewish Study Bible*. Edited by Adele Berlin and Marc Zvi Brettler, 508–57. New York: Oxford, 2004.

———. *Reading Biblical Narratives: Literary Criticism and the Hebrew Bible*. Translated by Yael Loten. Minneapolis: Fortress, 2001.

Armstrong, Thomas. "Multiple Intelligences in the Classroom." 3rd ed. Accessed November 30, 2011. http://www.ascd.org/publications/books/109007/chapters/MI-Theory-and-Its-Critics.aspx.

Baldwin, Joyce. *1–2 Samuel*. Downers Grove, IL: IVP Academic, 2008.

Barr, James. *History and Ideology in the Old Testament: Biblical Studies at the End of a Millennium*. New York: Oxford University Press, 2000.

Berlin, Adele, and Marc Zvi Brettler, eds. *The Jewish Study Bible*. New York: Oxford, 2004.

Birch, Bruce C., et al. *A Theological Introduction to the Old Testament*. Nashville: Abingdon, 1999.

Bonwell, Charles, and Jim Eison. *Active Learning: Creating Excitement in the Classroom*. Washington, DC: Jossey-Bass, 1991.

Borzak, Lenore. *Field Study: A Source Book for Experiential Learning*. Beverly Hills, CA: Sage, 1981.

Bray, Gerald. *Biblical Interpretation: Past and Present*. Downers Grove, IL: InterVarsity, 1996.

Bright, John. *A History of Israel*. 2nd ed. London: Westminster, 1972.

Bromiley, Geoffrey, ed. "Education." *International Standard Bible Encyclopedia*. Seattle, WA: Biblesoft Electronic Database, 2006.

Bruce, F. F., et al. *The Origin of the Bible*. Edited by Philip Comfort. Wheaton, IL: Tyndale, 1992.

Brueggemann, Walter. *The Creative Word: Canon as a Model for Biblical Education*. Philadelphia: Fortress, 1982.

———. *Genesis*. Atlanta: John Knox, 2010.

———. *An Introduction to the Old Testament: The Canon and Christian Imagination*. Louisville, KY: Westminster John Knox, 2003.

———. "Passion and Perspective: Two Dimensions of Education in the Bible." *Theology Today* 42 (1985) 172–80. Accessed October 1, 2012. http://web.ebscohost.com/ehost/pdfviewer/pdfviewer?sid=a94b2fe9-1a5e-442e-825e-975b5b912f6d%40sessionmgr4&vid=7&hid=15.

Campbell, Antony. *Joshua to Chronicles*. Louisville, KY: Westminster John Knox, 2004.

Campbell, Antony, and Mark O'Brien. *Sources of the Pentateuch*. Minneapolis: Augsburg Fortress, 1993.

———. *Unfolding Deuteronomistic History: Origins, Upgrades, Present Text*. Minneapolis: Fortress, 2000.

Childs, Brevard. *Introduction to the Old Testament as Scripture*. Philadelphia: Fortress, 1979.

———. *Memory and Tradition in Israel*. London: SCM, 1962.

———. "A Study of the Formula 'Until This Day.'" *Journal of Biblical Literature* 82 (Spring 1963) 279–92.

Compayré, Gabriel. *The History of Pedagogy*. Translated by W. H. Payne. Boston: D. C. Heath, 1885.

Craigie, Peter C. *The Book of Deuteronomy*. Grand Rapids: W. B. Eerdmans, 1976.

Crenshaw, James L. "Education in Ancient Israel." *Journal of Biblical Literature* 104 (Dec 1985) 601–15.

———. *Education in Ancient Israel: Across the Deadening Silence*. New York: Doubleday, 1998.

Cross, Frank Moore. "The Themes of the Book of Kings and the Structure of the Deuteronomistic History." In *Canaanite Myth and Hebrew Epic: Essays in the History of the Religion of Israel*, 274–89. Cambridge: Harvard Univ. Press, 1973.

Cundall, Arthur, and Leon Morris. *Judges and Ruth: An Introduction and Commentary*. London: Tyndale, 1968.

Cuthell, John. "Towards a Theory of Visual Learning." Accessed February 12, 2014. http://www.mirandanet.ac.uk/vl_blog/wp-content/uploads/2010/02/Towards-a-Theory-of-Visual-Learning1.pdf.

Davis, Amanda. "Structure, Repetition, and the Characterization of Levites in Judges 17–21." *Glossolalia*. Accessed May 17, 2012. http://glossolalia.sites.yale.edu/node/50/attachment.

Dever, William. *What Did the Biblical Writers Know, and When Did They Know It? What Archaeology Can Tell Us about the Reality of Ancient Israel.* Grand Rapids: W. B. Eerdmans, 2001.

Dobson, John. "A Comparison between Learning Style Preferences and Sex, Status, and Course Performance." *Advances in Physiology Education* 34 (Dec 2010) 197–204.

Enns, Paul. *The Moody Handbook of Theology: Revised and Expanded.* Chicago: Moody, 2008.

Estes, Daniel. *Hear My Son: Teaching and Learning in Proverbs 1–9.* Edited by D. A. Carson. Downers Grove, IL: InterVarsity, 2003.

Farrell, Jill Beloff. "Active Learning: Theories and Research." *The Lookstein Center for Jewish Education* 7 (Summer 2009). Accessed October 7, 2013. http://www.lookstein.org/online_journal.php?id=260.

Fleming, Neil, and David Baume. "Learning Styles Again: VARKing up the Right Tree!" *Educational Developments* 7 (Nov 2006) 4–6. Accessed April 18, 2012. http://www.vark-learn.com/documents/educational%20developments.pdf.

Fishman, Tayla. *Becoming the People of the Talmud: Oral Torah as Written Tradition in Medieval Jewish Cultures.* Jewish Culture and Contexts. Philadelphia: University of Pennsylvania Press, 2011.

Fokkelman, Jan. *Reading Biblical Narrative: A Practical Guide.* Translated by Ineke Smit. Leiderdorp, NLD: Deo, 1999.

Fretheim, Terence. *Deuteronomistic History.* Nashville: Abingdon, 1989.

Friedman, Richard. *The Bible with Sources Revealed.* New York: HarperCollins, 2005.

Furnham, Adrian. *The Psychology of Behaviour at Work: The Individual In The Organization.* Hove, SXE: Psychology, 2005.

Gardner, Howard. *Frames of Mind: The Theory of Multiple Intelligences.* New York: Basic, 1993.

———. *Intelligence Reframed: Multiple Intelligences for the 21st Century.* New York: Basic, 1999.

———. "Multiple Intelligences: The First Thirty Years." 2011. Accessed April 24, 2014. http://multipleintelligencesoasis.org/wp-content/uploads/2013/06/intro-frames-10-23-10.pdf.

Geoghegan, Jeffery. "'Until This Day' and the PreExilic Redaction of the Deuteronomistic History." *Journal of Biblical Literature* 122 (2003) 201–27.

Gerhardsson, Birger. *Memory and Manuscript with Tradition and Transmission in Early Christianity.* Translated by Eric Sharpe. Grand Rapids: W. B. Eerdmans, 1998.

Gese, Hartmut. "Wisdom Literature in the Persian Period." In *The Cambridge History of Judaism*, vol. 1, *The Persian Period*, edited by W. D. Davies and Louis Finkelstein, 189–218. Cambridge: Cambridge University Press, 1984.

Giles, Emily, et al. "Multiple Intelligences and Learning Styles." Accessed April 18, 2012. http://projects.coe.uga.edu/epltt/index.php?title=Multiple_Intelligences_and_Learning_Styles.

Gladwell, Malcolm. *The Tipping Point: How Little Things can Make a Big Difference.* New York: Back Bay, 2002.

Good, Carter V., ed. *Dictionary of Education.* New York: McGraw-Hill, 1945.

Gunn, D. M. "Narrative Patterns and Oral Tradition in Judges and Samuel." *Vetus Testamentum* 24 (July 1974) 286–317.

Gunn, David, and Danna Fewell. *Narrative in the Hebrew Bible.* Oxford: Oxford University Press, 1993.

Haley, Alex. *US News World Report*, 1992. Quoted in Stephen Schaefer, *Building Great Working Relationships at Work and at Home*. St. Paul, MN: No Limits, 2005.

Hamilton, Mark, ed. *The Transforming Word*. Abilene, TX: Abilene Christian University Press, 2009.

Hamilton, Victor. *Handbook on the Pentateuch*. 2nd ed. Grand Rapids: Baker Academic, 2005.

Harris, R. Laird, et al., eds. *Theological Word Book of the Old Testament*. Chicago: Moody, 1980. Biblesoft Electronic Database.

Havinghurst, Robert. *Human Development and Education*. New York: Longmans, Green, 1952.

Hess, Richard. *Joshua: An Introduction and Commentary*. Leicester, ENG: InterVarsity, 1996.

Howe, Michael. *Principles of Abilities and Human Learning*. Hove, SXE: Psychology, 1998.

Isbell, Charles. *The Function of Exodus Motifs in Biblical Narratives: Theological Didactic Drama*. Studies in the Bible and Early Christianity. New York: Edwin Mellen, 2002.

Jaffee, Martin. "How Much 'Orality' in Oral Torah? New Perspectives on the Composition and Transmission of Early Rabbinic Tradition." *Shofar: An Interdisciplinary Journal of Jewish Studies* 10 (Winter 1992) 53–72.

———. "A Rabbinic Ontology of the Written and Spoken Word: On Discipleship, Transformative Knowledge, and the Living Texts of Oral Torah." *Journal of the American Academy of Religion* 65 (Autumn 1997) 525-49. Accessed July 20, 2012. http://www.jstor.org/discover/10.2307/1465650?uid=3739256&uid=2&uid=4&sid=21101098172741.

———. *Torah in the Mouth: Writing and Oral Tradition in Palestinian Judaism 200 BCE—400 CE*. Oxford: Oxford University Press, 2001.

Jarvis, Peter, and Stella Parker, eds. *Human Learning: A Holistic Approach*. New York: Routledge, 2005.

K12 Academics. "Kinesthetic learning." 2004. Accessed November 30, 2011. http://www.k12academics.com/pedagogy/kinesthetic-learning.

Kellenberger, Edgar. Review of *A Plague of Texts? A Text-Critical Study of the So-Called 'Plagues Narrative' in Exodus 7:14—11:10*, by Bénédicte Lemmelijn. *The Journal of Hebrew Scriptures* 10 (2010). Accessed January 16, 2012. https://ejournals.library.ualberta.ca/index.php/jhs/article/view/11336/8668.

Knoppers, Gary. *Reconsidering Israel and Judah: Recent Studies on the Deuteronomistic History*. Edited by Gary Knoppers and J. G. McConville. Winona Lake, IN: Eisenbrauns, 2000.

Knowles, Malcolm. *The Modern Practice of Adult Education: From Pedagogy to Andragogy*. Englewood Cliffs, NJ: Cambridge, 1980.

Knowles, Malcolm, et al. *The Adult Learner: The Definitive Classic in Adult Education and Resource Development*. Amsterdam: Butterworth-Heinemann, 2005.

Kolb, David. "David A. Kolb on Experiential Learning." 2010. Accessed February 12, 2014. http://infed.org/mobi/david-a-kolb-on-experiential-learning.

Kuenen, Abraham. *Historisch-kritische Einleitung in die Bücher des Alten Testaments*. Leipzig, DEU: Otto Schulze, 1982.

LaSor, William. *Old Testament Survey: The Message, Form, and Background of the Old Testament*. 2nd ed. Grand Rapids: W. B. Eerdmans, 1996.

Lemmelijn, Bénédicte. *A Plague of Texts? A Text-critical Study of the So-called 'Plagues Narrative' in Exodus 7:14—11:10*. Leiden, NLD: Brill, 2009.

Levine, Christoph. *The Old Testament: A Brief Introduction*. Translated by Margaret Kohl. Princeton, NJ: Princeton University Press, 2005.

Lowe, Stephen. "You are My Witnesses: A Biblical Theology of Christian Education." Evangelical Theological Society Regional Meeting, Grand Rapids Baptist Seminary, March 20–21, 1998.

Machinist, Peter. "Ecclesiastes." In *The Jewish Study Bible*. Edited by Adele Berlin and Marc Zvi Brettler, 1603–22. New York: Oxford, 2004.

Marguerat, Daniel, and Yvan Bourquin. *How to Read Bible Stories: An Introduction to Narrative Criticism*. Translated by John Bowden. London: SCM, 1999.

Marrou, Henry I. *A History of Education in Antiquity* (1956). Edited by Barbara Fowler and Warren Moon. Translated George Lamb. Madison, WI: University of Wisconsin Press, 1982.

McClintock, John, and James Strong. *McClintock and Strong Encyclopedia*. Seattle, WA: Biblesoft Electronic Database, 2006.

McConville, J. G. *Apollos Old Testament Commentary: Deuteronomy*. Edited by David Baker and Gordon Wenham. Downers Grove, IL: InterVarsity, 2002.

McDonald, Lee Martin. *The Biblical Canon: Its Origin, Transmission, and Authority*. Peabody: Hendrickson, 2008.

Meyers, Carol. "Joshua." In *The Jewish Study Bible*, edited by Adele Berlin and Marc Zvi Brettler, 462–507. New York: Oxford, 2004.

Miller, Frederic, et al., eds., *Dating the Bible: Higher Criticism, Textual Criticism, Biblical Manuscript, Torah, Documentary Hypothesis, The Bible and History, Synoptic Problem, Markan Priority*. Lexington: Alphascript, 2010.

Mortimore, Peter, ed. *Understanding Pedagogy and its Impact on Learning*. London: SAGE, 1999.

Murphy, Roland E. *The Tree of Life: An Exploration of Biblical Wisdom*. 3rd ed. Grand Rapids: W. B. Eerdmans, 1990.

Nelson, Richard. *Double Redaction of the Deuteronomistic History*. Sheffield: JSOT, 1981.

———. "The Double Redaction of the Deuteronomistic History: A Case Still Compelling." *JSOT* 29 (2005) 319–37.

Niditch, Susan. *Judges: A Commentary*. Louisville, KY: Westminster John Knox, 2008.

Noth, Martin. *A History of Pentateuchal History*. Translated by Bernhard Andersen. Atlanta, GA: Scholars, 1981.

Olson, Dennis. *Deuteronomy and the Death of Moses: A Theological Reading*. Minneapolis: Fortress, 1994.

Osborne, Grant. *The Hermeneutical Spiral: A Comprehensive Introduction to Biblical Interpretation*. Downers Grove, IL: InterVarsity, 1991.

Pashler, Harold, et al. "Learning Styles Concepts and Evidence." *Psychological Science in the Public Interest* 9 (2009) 105–19.

Pazmiño, Robert. *Foundational Issues in Christian Education*. 2nd ed. Grand Rapids: Baker, 1997.

Pemberton, Glenn. "The Rhetoric of the Father in Proverbs 1–9." *JSOT* 30 (2005) 63–82.

Petric, Paulian-Timotei. "The Reader(s) and the Bible(s) 'Reader Versus Community' in Reader-Response Criticism and Biblical Interpretation." *Sacra Scripta* 10 (2012) 54–68.

Rad, Gerhard von. *Old Testament Theology*. 2 vols. Translated by D. M. G. Stalker. New York: HarperCollins, 1961.

———. *Wisdom in Israel*. Nashville: Abingdon, 1972.

Rendtorff, Rolf. *The Problem of the Process of Transmission in the Pentateuch*. JSOTSS 89. Translated by J. J. Scullion. Sheffield: JSOT, 1990.

Richter, Sandra. *The Epic of Eden: A Christian Entry into the Old Testament*. Downers Grove, IL: IVP Academic, 2008.

Ridderbos, Jan. *Deuteronomy*. Translated by Ed M. Van der Mass. Grand Rapids: Zondervan, 1984.

Rollston, Christopher. "Scribal Education in Ancient Israel: The Old Hebrew Epigraphic Evidence." *Bulletin of the American Schools of Oriental Research* 344 (Nov 2006) 47–74. Accessed October 1, 2012. http://www.jstor.org/stable/25066977.

Routledge, Robin. *Old Testament Theology: A Thematic Approach*. Downers Grove, IL: InterVarsity, 2008.

Seters, John Van. *Prologue to History: The Yahwist as Historian in Genesis*. Louisville, KY: Westminster John Knox, 1992.

Shepherd, Gerald. *Wisdom as a Hermeneutical Construct: A Study in the Sapientializing of the Old Testament*. Berlin: Walter de Gruyter, 1980.

Slavin, Robert. *Educational Psychology*. Upper Saddle River, NJ: Prentice Hall, 2009.

Sonnet, J. P. *The Book within the Book: Writing in Deuteronomy*. Biblical Interpretation Series 14. Leiden, NLD: Brill, 1997.

Steinberg, Naomi. *The World of the Child in the Hebrew Bible*. Sheffield, SYK: Sheffield Phoenix, 2013.

Strong, James. *Biblesoft's New Exhaustive Strong's Numbers and Concordance with Greek and Hebrew Dictionary*. Seattle, WA: Biblesoft, 2006.

Student, Gil. "On the Authorship of the Torah." *Torat Emet* (2001). Accessed April 12, 2010. http://www.aishdas.org/toratemet/en_torah.html.

Thaman, Richa, et al. "Promoting Active Learning in Respiratory Physiology: Positive Student Perception and Improved Outcomes." *NJPPP* 3 (2013) 27–34.

Tigay, Jeffery. "Exodus." In *The Jewish Study Bible*, edited by Adele Berlin and Marc Zvi Brettler, 102–202. New York: Oxford University Press, 2004.

Vanhoozer, Kevin. *Is There a Meaning in This Text? The Bible, the Reader, and the Morality of Literary Knowledge*. Grand Rapids: Zondervan, 2006.

Vanhoozer, Kevin, et al., eds. *Theological Interpretation of the Old Testament: A Book-by-Book Survey*. Grand Rapids: Baker Academic, 2005.

Weiser, Artur. *The Old Testament: Its Formation and Development*. Translated by Dorethea M. Barton. New York: Association, 1961.

Wenham, Gordan. *Exploring the Old Testament*. Vol. 1, *A Guide to the Pentateuch*. Downers Grove, IL: InterVarsity, 2003.

———. "Pentateuchal Studies Today." *Themelios* 22 (Oct 1996) 3–13.

Whybray, R. Norman. *The Making of the Pentateuch: A Methodological Study*. JSOTSS 53. Sheffield, SYK: JSOT, 1987.

———. *Proverbs*. Grand Rapids: W. B. Eerdmans, 1994.

Wright, C. H. *God's People in God's Land: Family, Land, and Property in the Old Testament*. Grand Rapids: W. B. Eerdmans, 1990.

www.ingramcontent.com/pod-product-compliance
Lightning Source LLC
Chambersburg PA
CBHW062041220426
43662CB00010B/1595